HISTORY AND STRUCTURE OF FRENCH

T. B. W. REID

HISTORY AND STRUCTURE OF FRENCH

Essays in the Honour of Professor T. B. W. Reid

EDITED BY
F. J. Barnett, A. D. Crow,
C. A. Robson, W. Rothwell,
S. Ullmann

OXFORD
BASIL BLACKWELL
1972

0 631 14000 X

C

Text set in 11/12 pt. Monotype Bembo, printed by
letterpress, and bound in Great Britain at The Pitman
Press, Bath

Contents

Thomas Bertram Wallace Reid

M.A. (Oxon.), M.A., L.L.B. (Dublin), M.A. (Manchester), L. ès L. (Montpellier), Officier d'Académie.

T. B. W. Reid's scholarly life has been lived almost entirely in three of the great Universities of the English-speaking world—Dublin, Manchester and Oxford. He went up in 1919 from Armagh Royal School to Trinity College, Dublin, where the professor of the Romance Languages was T. B. Rudmose-Brown; the Department produced also such diversely distinguished graduates as Samuel Beckett and Dr. Conor Cruse O'Brien. Reid followed a *cursus honorum* which embraced a wide range of studies and included virtually all the major awards which his University could give—Hutchinson Stewart Literary Scholar, First Senior Moderator in Modern Literature, Prizeman in Old French and Provençal, Irish, and Law. As a student he was once lectured to by a young Dubliner called Enid Starkie—a circumstance he vividly recalled in a graceful speech of tribute on behalf of the Oxford Faculty on the occasion of Dr. Starkie's retirement in 1965.

Dublin was followed by Montpellier, home of Millardet and the *Revue des langues romanes*, where Reid was *lecteur d'anglais* as well as taking the *licence;* Montpellier by three years as a schoolmaster, at Frome County School, an interval which, suggests an interesting contrast with the more confident assumptions of more recent generations of young scholars. One may connect with this experience the qualities which Reid was later so signally to display as a lecturer—thorough digestion and control of the material to be deployed, and a perspicuous clarity of exposition.

From 1929 to 1958 his life and work were closely bound up with the University of Manchester, arguably during this period the most impressive centre of scholarship and study in the field of Modern Languages in the United Kingdom. Assistant Lecturer in 1929, Lecturer in 1935, he was elected in 1945 to Chair of Romance Philology, taking up the distinguished succession of John Orr (who allegedly cast him as Rectus in the dialogue on Homonymics), and of Mildred Pope. Here he influenced a large number of philological and medieval scholars now widely scattered through the University world; and here he produced important articles on various aspects of the French historical grammar which has always been central to his scholarly interests— articles characteristic of their author's linguistic perspicacity and encyclopaedic knowledge of texts. From this period too date the editions for which the *grand public* of students knows him best; the *Fabliaux*, and the *Yvain* whose meaty economy of comment, whether or not imposed by wartime stringency, has won the gratitude of successive generations of students of Chrétien. While fully engaged in the work and administration of his Department, and responding without stint to the many calls made upon Romance Philology by related subjects. Reid also played an important part in the general affairs of the great civic University; as Dean of the Faculty of Arts in 1950 and 1951; most notably as pro-Vice Chancellor in 1957–8, bearing a heavy administrative weight and taking a leading role in a vigorous and innovating period.

In 1958, Reid succeeded to the Chair of the Romance Languages at Oxford, and the Professorial Fellowship at Trinity, held since 1930 by the considerable figure of Alfred Ewert. In his second Trinity College, Reid was a valued and much-liked member of Governing Body and Common Room, who willingly undertook his share of the committee chores endemic to collegiate life. He also made a point of getting to know personally the undergraduates of the College studying in his field. At University level, the transition from a professorial-departmental to a tutorial-collegiate university was effected with skill and speed, and the interesting ambiguities of an Oxford Arts professorship effortlessly comprehended. Reid immersed himself in the work of the Oxford Faculty, supervising numerous graduate students and taking a central part in lecturing on the large volume of philological and medieval study which Oxford demands of its under-graduates. Lecturing stimulated research, as research illuminated teaching, and from these years emerged studies on Beroul's *Tristran* and the text of the *Jeu de Saint Nicolas*, the latter in particular a model of textual criticism, conservative in principle, ingenious and learned in execution, convincing in effect. He retired from the Chair in 1968.

He has been over the years a Council Member (or officer, or Pre-sident) of nearly all the principal bodies connected with French studies, with Philology, with Medieval Studies, in this country; and in a different professional context, has been President of the Oxford branch of the A.U.T. For 1965 and 1966 he was Chairman of his

Faculty Board—the most onerous task which a Faculty can lay on one of its members. Since 1962—and happily still—he has been President of the Anglo-Norman Text Society; with characteristic modesty he was only with difficulty induced to join his name, as editor of Vol. II of the *Romance of Horn*, to that of the late Miss Pope, whose *Nachlass* he completed and comprehensively revised.

Reid stands firmly in the central tradition of Romance Philology— a title he is perfectly happy to retain for his subject—seeking always to refer linguistic description to germane and extensive empirical data, asserting a continuing validity for the diachronic study of language, and turning a sceptical or sardonic eye on some of the loftier formulations of linguistics. In debate, as everywhere, he has displayed the combination of courtly manners with trenchant expression which is a traditional *cachet* of his native island. Above these debates, and informing all his work, have been the central intellectual and academic virtues, conspicuously displayed—great learning, never ostentatious or gratuitous, but immediately and generously available to students and colleagues; generosity combined with severity, which took the harshness from criticism of a student's work and left a salutary stimulus; and the eloquent conviction that the subject which he professed was a worthy and equal member of the community of humane studies— in the closing words of his Oxford inaugural lecture "a social science that is human and humane."

Tim Reid's friends and colleagues, to mark their appreciation of forty years' scholarly life, and to wish him long and active years of retirement, offer him this collection of studies, in friendship and esteem, on his seventieth birthday.

D. M. STEWART
Fellow of Wadham College, Oxford

The Development of the Old French Possessives of Singular Person Reference

F. J. BARNETT

Trinity College, Oxford

The broad lines of the development of Latin *mĕus, -a, -um, tŭus, -a, -um, sŭus, -a, -um* into Old French are fairly well understood: the Old French tonic series, *miens, mien, mien, miens, meie, meies, tuens*, etc., *toue*, etc., *suens*, etc., *soue*, etc., shows diphthongization of tonic vowels, loss of atonic final vowels other than [a], which weakens to [ę], and remodelling of the nominative singular and nominative and accusative plural on the accusative singular in the masculines; the atonic series, *mes, mon, mi, mes, ma, mes, tes, ton*, etc., *ta*, etc., *ses, son*, etc., *sa*, etc., continues by regular process of sound charge reduced forms, *mus, mum, mi, mos, ma, mas, tus*, etc., whose existence in Late Spoken Latin is vouched for by Virgilius Maro Grammaticus (fl. 600 A.D.).[1]

[1] Cf. M. Manitius, *Geschichte der lateinischen Literatur des Mittelalters*, Munich, 1911, pp. 119–27, and F. J. E. Raby, *A History of Secular Latin Poetry in the Middle Ages*, 2nd ed., Oxford, 1957, Vol. I, pp. 153–7; the latter places our author a little earlier, referring to him (p. 153) as '. . . the curious and enigmatic figure of Virgilius Maro, the grammarian, who belongs, perhaps, to Toulouse and to the latter part of the sixth century'.

The passage relating to the possessives, which may be consulted in *Virgilii Maronis Grammatici Opera*, ed. J. Huemer, Leipzig, 1886, *Epitomae*, VI p. 47, reads as follows: 'sunt et alia pronomina, quae in latinitate ussitate non habentur et tamen indubie recipiuntur genere masculino ut *mus*, genitiuus *mi*, datiuus *mo*, accusatiuus *mum*, uocatiuus *mi*, ablatiuus *mo* et pluraliter *mi morum mis mos o mi a mis*, feminino *ma mae mae mam o ma a ma*, pluraliter *mae marum mis mas mae a mis*, neutrum *mum*, pro quo in ussu habetur *meus*, sic erit et *tus* pro *tuus*'.

Sporadic earlier attestations of reduced forms are quoted by F. Sommer (*Handbuch der lateinischen Laut- und Formenlehre*, Heidelberg, 1948, §§ 266–8), C. H. Grandgent (*An Introduction to Vulgar Latin*, New York, 1962, p. 388) and E. Bourciez (*Éléments de linguistique romane*, 5th ed., Paris, 1967, § 102(c)). It is not safe to conclude that the examples quoted from Archaic Latin were direct forerunners of the Late Spoken Latin forms because of the long interval of time separating the former from the latter, but the examples quoted from inscriptions,

There are, however, several aspects of the development which remain obscure, and it is these that I propose to discuss and attempt to elucidate in this article. It will, of course, be necessary to take into account the general Romance situation in relation to some of the points discussed, but I shall not attempt to deal systematically with the evolution of the possessives in any language other than French.

The first point concerns the treatment of the tonic vowels in the feminine of the first person and the masculine of the second and third person possessives of the tonic series. In these instances, the Old French forms present the diphthongs *ei* (*meie*, etc.) and *ue* (*tuen, suen*, etc.), which imply development from Late Spoken Latin [ẹ] and [ọ], respectively, instead of from [ę] and [ǫ], the Late Spoken Latin vowels which normally correspond to Classical Latin *ĕ* and *ŭ*, as found in *mĕa*, etc., and *tŭum, sŭum*, etc. On the other hand, the masculine forms of the first person (*mien*, etc.) and the feminines of the second and third (*toue, soue*, etc.) present no problem since they show the regular diphthongizations—[ę] (< *ĕ*) > [ie], [ǫ] (< *ŭ*) > [ou].

Various explanations of these anomalies have been put forward, but none is wholly satisfactory. For example, Louis Kukenheim suggests in a recent book[2] that *mĕa* may have given way to *mēa* by a lengthening of the tonic vowel perhaps due to 'un besoin de l'expressivité, vu le caractère tonique du possessif', or again that the lengthening might be by analogy with the long *ē* of the personal pronoun *mē*, or yet again—although he thinks this less 'vraisemblable'—that the [ę] of **męa* may have closed to [ẹ] under the influence of a putative closing of the vowel in **męi* caused by the presence of final -*i*. The obvious objection to all these suggestions is: why should the factors mentioned have affected *mĕa* (or **męa*) but not *mĕus, mĕum*, etc.? Again, with regard to his explanation of *tŭŭs* > **tǫọs* > **tọọs*—'dissimilation provoquée par le caractère affectif du pronom'—we are given no reason why 'affectivity' should be thought to have induced dissimilation.

Other theories are based more systematically on an alleged special treatment of vowels in hiatus. Thus, Miss M. K. Pope (*From Latin to Modern French*, Manchester University Press, 1934, §. 131) states the following principle (in support of which she cites the authority of

---

together with the widespread occurrence of reduced forms in Romance, do indicate that the process of reduction began long before the time of Virgilius Maro Grammaticus.

[2] *Grammaire historique de la langue française, Les Parties du discours*, Leiden, 1967; all the suggestions mentioned appear on p. 49.

Meyer-Lübke)[3]: 'in Late Latin . . . the tonic vowel . . . was differentiated if juxtaposed to a final flexional vowel that was homophonous or almost homophonous: L.L. *tǫụs, *tǫụm < *tọụs, *tọụm . . . *męa < *mẹa . . . *dịẹs < *dịẹs. . . .' In one sense, of course, this statement is unexceptionable: *tǫụm, etc., and *męa, etc., are the necessary forerunners of the corresponding Old French forms, and, as compared with *tọụm and *mẹa, etc., they certainly show a greater degree of differentiation of the tonic from the flexional vowels. In another sense, however, the statement is not illuminating. The fact that differentiation did not already occur in Classical Latin *tuus, tuum, tuos, suus*, etc., shows that the juxtaposition of 'homophonous or almost homophonous' vowels does not, in itself, suffice to induce differentiation. There must, therefore, have been factors operating in Late (Spoken) Latin, but not in Classical Latin, which precipitated the change, and upon the nature of these factors Pope throws no light. One of the tasks which I have set myself in this article is, accordingly, to attempt to identify these factors, which must, presumably, be sought in structural differences between Classical and Late Spoken Latin. Before leaving Pope's theory, however, we may note that the 'homophonous or almost homophonous' description is in any case less obviously applicable to *męa, etc., than to the *tǫụs, etc., forms.

Another type of hiatus-vowel theory is that held by H. Lausberg (*Lingüística románica*, I, Madrid, 1965, p. 187, and II, ibid., 1966, p. 873), who does not speak of dissimilation but of 'algunas perturbaciones y tendencias niveladoras'. The only French forms directly concerned are those that developed from *męa, etc., not those from the *tǫos, etc. forms, which Lausberg appears to regard as the result of adjustments made to the second and third person forms to reproduce a feminine-closed-vowel/masculine-open-vowel opposition originally established in the first person possessives (*męa (or *mia*)/*mẹum, etc.). (On this latter point Lausberg's approach has something in common with my own, as will be seen below, although our views by no means coincide.)

As far as the *męa forms are concerned, the possibility does have to be considered that Northern Gallo-Romance participated in a general Romance development, since these forms are frequently postulated as the common ancestors of the *mia* forms attested, at the medieval or the

---

[3] Cf. W. Meyer-Lübke, *Einführung in das Studium der romanischen Sprachwissenschaft*, 3rd ed., Heidelberg, 1920, § 128.

modern stage or both, in most of the Romance languages.[4] In support
of this postulation it can be argued that the -*ęa* sequence appears to
have developed to -*ia* over a large part of Romania, as, for example, in
the imperfect indicatives in -*ia* ($< -(i)\bar{e}(b)a(\ )$), and such widely diffused
forms as *via* and *sia*( ) (present subjunctive of the verb 'to be') ($< v\breve{\imath}a$,
**s\breve{\imath}a*( ), supposedly through an intermediate *vęa, *sęa( ) stage). Un-
fortunately, as pointed out by several scholars, e.g. Meyer-Lübke,
Bourciez and García de Diego,[5] it is, in general, difficult to establish
with certainty that there was a special treatment of vowels in hiatus
because of the narrow range of the forms concerned and the impos-
sibility in most cases, of ruling out the influence of related forms. Thus,
the -*ia* imperfects might be the result not of an -*ęa* > -*ia* sound change,
but of an extension of the Latin fourth-conjugation -*i(b)a*( ) terminations
to verbs of the second and third conjugations; the *via* forms might
have resulted from the adoption of a *vīa variant in some areas of
Romania under the influence of *vīta*;[6] and the *sia*( ) forms might be
explained by the influence of *fīa*( ), etc.[7] As to the *mia* forms themselves,

---

[4] *Mia* forms are found in Italian, Sardinian (as well as *mea*), Engadinish,
Surselvan, Old Provençal, Old Catalan (as well as *meva*), Spanish and Old
Portuguese; *mio* forms are found in Italian, Surselvan (*miu*), and Spanish. These
lists are not necessarily exhaustive.

[5] Cf. Meyer-Lübke, op. cit., §. 128 (apparently with special reference to 'labial'
vowels in hiatus); 'Die geringe Zahl der Beispiele und der Umstand, dass es sich
fast durchweg um Formen handelt, die analogischen Umgestaltungen unter-
worfen sein können, macht allerdings eine genaue Beurteilung fast unmöglich';
Bourciez, op. cit., §. 102(b) (with specific reference to the possessives): 'Par leur
nature même, ces divers mots étaient très exposés à réagir les uns sur les autres';
Vicente García de Diego, *Gramática histórica española*, Madrid, 1951, §. 59: 'La
actividad de la analogía en los pronombres hace peligrosas las explicaciones
puramente fonéticas'. García de Diego has the alleged *męa forms specifically in
mind, and earlier in the section quoted he expresses his doubts about their existence: 'La oposición entre *mieo* y *mía* en lo antiguo ha hecho pensar que el femenino
tendría distinto vocalismo que el masculino, admitiéndose que en latín *mea*
tendría *e* cerrada por disimilación de *e* ante *a*, aunque esta cerrazón no bastaba y
había que admitir un latín *mia'.

[6] For examples of the common *via vitae*, *via vivendi* collocations see C. T.
Lewis and C. Short, *A Latin Dictionary*, Oxford, 1955, s.v. *via*.

[7] Although eventually destined to disappear as an independent verb, *fieri*,
probably in a 'regularized' form, must have continued to have considerable
currency for some time in Late Spoken Latin, as its survival suppletively as part
of the verb 'to be' in Rumanian shows. As far as a possible influence on *sia* is
concerned, it is interesting that the present subjunctive is among the forms which
have survived in Rumanian—(*să*) *fie*.

they might be the result of a remodelling on the, originally masculine, vocative *mi*, the use of which was extended to the feminine in Late Spoken Latin, and which may itself have survived marginally as an independent feminine form in one or two of the Romance languages.[8] The wider distribution of *mia* than *mio* forms in the Romance languages does, indeed, suggest that, in some languages at least, the *mi*-base was originally restricted to the feminines and was only subsequently extended in certain cases to the masculines,[9] but this fact is, of course, compatible both with the **męa > *męa > mia* hypothesis and with that based on direct remodelling of the feminine forms on vocative *mi*.

There is, therefore, some doubt whether **męa* forms were current throughout Romania in Late Spoken Latin, and it may be that, where the evidence of later forms points to their certain occurrence, e.g. in Northern Gallo-Romance and in Rheto-Romance (cf. Bourciez, op. cit., §§. 512(d) and 527(b)), they were the result of factors peculiar to the languages concerned. If, however, they were of general occurrence, it is more likely that they resulted from a levelling process (Lausberg) than from dissimilation (Meyer-Lübke and Pope). As

---

[8] Cf. F. Sommer, op. cit., §. 271, Anm. 1, who quotes *mi soror* (Apuleius); and cf. Bourciez, op. cit., §. 102(a): 'dans l'usage vulgaire cette forme fut étendue aux noms féminins (*Mater mi!* Jul.-Val. 157, 31; *mi domna!*)'. According to Grandgent (op. cit., §. 387), *mi domina* was common; he gives references to H. Goelzer, *Étude lexicographique et grammaticale de la latinité de saint Jérôme*, Paris, 1884, p. 282, and to A. Dubois, *La Latinité d'Ennodius*, Paris, 1903, pp. 261-2.

For the preservation of vocative *mi* in Old Provençal *midons*, followed by *sidons*—used, incidentally, with feminine reference (cf. W. D. Elcock, *The Romance Languages*, London, 1960, p. 83)—see O. Schultz-Gora, *Altprovenzalisches Elementarbuch*, Heidelberg, 4th ed., 1924, §. 118. *Mi* also appears as a feminine possessive adjective in Old Spanish side by side with *mie* at a time when the shortened *mi, tu, su* forms had not yet come into general use, but whether it continues vocative *mi* or is the result of a reduction of *mie* (<*mia*) in proclitic position is difficult to determine. García de Diego (loc. cit.) appears to favour the former hypothesis: 'La forma *mia* sin intermedio de un supuesto romance **mea*' (to judge by the context he presumably means **męa*) 'es posible que se haya formado sobre *mi*'.

[9] The wider distribution of forms in *mi*- in the feminine is indicated in footnote 4 above. As far as their occurrence in the masculine in some languages is concerned, we have to reckon with the possibility of independent developments from Latin. Thus, some authorities (e.g. M. A. Pei, *The Italian Language*, New York, 1941, §§. 49 and 123, and García de Diego, op. cit., §. 59) regard the *mio* forms of Italian and Spanish as regular developments of the -*ęo* sequence, pointing to apparently similar developments of *deo* and *e(g)o* to *dio* (*dios*) and *io* (*yo*).

remarked above, there is no obvious reason why the -ęa sequence should have undergone dissimilation since the 'gap' between [ę], presumably a mid-front vowel and [ɑ], presumably a low-back vowel is not an uncomfortably narrow one from either the articulatory or the acoustic point of view. On the other hand, given that the -ęa forms discussed above—*vęa, *sęa, imperfects in -ęa, etc.—did occur commonly throughout a large part of Romania, the -ęa sequence, which seems to have confined to the feminine first person possessives, may well have been eliminated by levelling on the commoner sequence.

Apart from the possible case of the *męa forms, it is not necessary to suppose that the development of the Old French forms was determined by factors operating universally throughout Romania,[10] although

[10] Some scholars, e.g. Antonio Badía Margarit (Gramática histórica catalana, Barcelona, 1951, §. 129) and Pierre Bec (Manuel pratique de philologie romane, I, Paris, 1970, p. 46), regard the formation of mia, etc., as part of a more general process by which not only mĕ- but also tŭ- and sŭ- were closed in hiatus with -a to mę-(>mi-) and tų-, sų-. No such closing occurs in the second and third person forms in French, and, consequently, these theories can hardly be quoted in support of a phonetic origin of Northern Gallo-Romance *męa, except to the extent that they might be taken to lend colour to the view that special treatments of vowels in hiatus occurred widely throughout Romania. But it is not in any case necessary to suppose that the tua and sua forms—tu- and su- occur more commonly in the feminines and may be presumed to have been originated in that gender in most cases—are of phonetic origin. For the striking fact about their distribution is that, while less widespread than the mia forms, they never occur except where mia is also found. This distribution suggests that they are secondary formations introduced, in some regions, to generalize an early opposition between feminine forms with close vowels and masculine forms with open vowels, of which masculine me-/feminine mi were the first members, the series being continued with to-/tu-, so-/su-. If that was so, the opposition was subsequently obscured by the generalization, in various languages, of mi-, tu- and su- stems in both genders, or by the adoption of te-, se- forms in the masculine, or again by the generalization of -i- or -e- throughout the stems of both genders and all three persons.

Because of the succinctness of expression necessitated by the multitude of facts included in his invaluable manual, it is not clear whether Lausberg (op. cit., §. 187) takes a similar view of the origin of the tu-, su- forms in general, but he does appear to regard the Provençal forms at least as due to an extension of the close-vowel/open-vowel opposition between masculines and feminines originating in the first person possessives.

It should be noted that the tu- and su- forms of Sardinian may simply continue the Classical Latin stems since ŭ regularly develops as u in that language. The Italian tuoi, suoi forms suggest the possibility that not only they but also tuo and suo developed by regular sound change from tǫ-, sǫ- forms, in which case the gender-linked vocalic opposition may have taken the form mę-/mi-, tǫ-/tu-, sǫ-/su- in some parts at least of Italy.

some of the French developments have parallels or analogues in at least some other regions. The determining factor in the development of the French tonic series was, I believe, the creation, in the Late Spoken Latin of Gaul, of a matching atonic series, the two series being complete in both genders, both numbers and in two cases (nominative and oblique), and structurally opposed to one another, the opposition being realized in various ways at the morpho-phonemic level but basically as a disyllabic/monosyllabic opposition.[11] The development of the atonic series will be discussed separately below; here I am con-

[11] There are at least traces of reduced atonic forms in most of the Romance languages. The series is most complete in Old French, being attested in all three persons, both numbers, both genders and in the nominative and oblique cases. In Old Provençal it is almost complete, but tonic forms are there used suppletively in the masculine nominative plural of the three persons (cf. Schultz-Gora, op. cit., §. 117). In accordance with their general structure, only one case at most is represented in the other languages, with the possible exception of Rheto-Romance. The series is otherwise complete in Old Catalan (cf. F. de B. Moll, *Gramática histórica catalana*, Madrid, 1952, §. 273), and, possibly, in Old and dialectal Italian (cf. Bourciez, op. cit., §. 433, and G. Rohlfs, *Historische Grammatik der italienischen Sprache und ihrer Mundarten*, II, Berne, 1949, §. 430). It is fragmentary in Rheto-Romance, where, according to Bourciez (op. cit , § 527(b)), *mes, tes, ses* masculine nominative forms and *ma, ta,* (?*sa*), *mes, tes,* (?*ses*) feminines are found; *to, so* forms are also said to occur in Friulan. In Rumanian, including the South-Danubian varieties, only *tu, su, ta, sa* are found (cf. *Istoria limbii romăne*, published by a collective of the Academy of the Socialist Republic of Rumania, II, Bucharest, 1969, pp. 246–7). In Old Spanish only *to, tos, so, sos* are attested (cf. Lausberg, op. cit., §. 754), and in Old Portuguese only *ma, ta, sa* (cf. P. Bec, op. cit., p. 347).

It lies outside the scope of this article to enter into a detailed discussion of the relations of these forms to the tonic forms in the Romance languages other than French, but two points are of particular relevance to an assessment of the French situation: the first is the incompleteness of the atonic series in all the other languages except Catalan and, possibly, Old and dialectal Italian; the second is the tendency for their use to be restricted to certain contexts, the commonest being with nouns of relationship (cf. Lausberg, op. cit., §. 755: 'Es característico . . . el empleo con nombres de parentesco'). These facts make it unlikely that any systematic and general opposition of the tonic and atonic forms, such as underlies the development of the French possessive system, ever existed in the majority of the other languages. Moreover, the remodelling of the Classical Latin forms by such analogical developments as the introduction of **teus* and **seus* forms based on *meus* and the creation of *mia*, and consequently *tua* and *sua* forms, which may in some cases have influenced the masculines, had the consequence that only in the development of French did any such system of oppositions as may have existed—e.g. possibly in the case of Provençal—determine the evolution of tonic forms continuing those of Classical Latin.

cerned with the fact that, once it came into existence, the tonic vowels of the tonic series acquired a new and more important function. In Classical Latin their role had been a subordinate and redundant one: ĕ had served as a first-person marker merely in reinforcement of *m-*, the primary marker, in opposition to ŭ, the marker of the second and third persons conjointly, the specific markers of the second and third persons being *t-* and *s-* respectively. In the Late Spoken Latin of Northern Gallo-Romania, however, their primary role became that of assuring the disyllabic character of the tonic series in opposition to the monosyllabic atonic series. Thus, at the earlier stage, the occasional articulation in rapid speech of *tuus, tuum, suus, suum*, etc., as *tus, tum*, etc., would have been, initially, an accident of *parole*, and *tus*, etc., and *tuus*, etc., could co-exist as contextual, or even free, variants without this duality constituting a modification of *langue*. Once, however, in Late Spoken Latin, the monosyllabic atonic series, **tos, ta*, etc., had been formalized, it became a matter of structural concern to preserve the disyllabic character of the tonic series against such accidents of articulation, with the result that the forms in which the difference between the tonic and contact final vowels was minimal, i.e. the nominative and accusative singular and the accusative plural of the second and third person masculine possessives, were modified by dissimilation, through opening, of the tonic vowel [ọ] to [ǫ]—**tóos > *tọos, *tóom > *tọom, *tóos > *tọos, *sóos > *sọos*, etc.

The result, as far as Proto-French is concerned, was the creation of a more stable dual system, the first stage of which was probably somewhat as follows:

Tonic, disyllabic series

*mẹos	*mẹi	*mẹa (or *mẹa)	*mẹas (or *mẹas)
*mẹom	*mẹos	*mẹa (or *mẹa)	*mẹas (or *mẹas)
*tọos	*tọi	*tọa	*tọas
*tọom	*tọos	*tọa	*tọas
*sọos	*sọi	*sọa	*sọas
*sọom	*sọos	*sọa	*sọas

Atonic, monosyllabic series

*mọs	mi	ma	*mas
*mọm	*mọs	*ma	mas
*tọs	*ti	*ta	*tas
*tọm	*tọs	*ta	*tas
*sọs	*si	*sa	*sas
*sọm	*sọs	*sa	*sas

There then occurred internal adjustments making for a greater measure of symmetry by regularizing the masculine-open-tonic-vowel/ feminine-close-tonic-vowel opposition evident in *tǫos/tǫa, etc., so that *tǫi and *sǫi gave way to *tǫi and *sǫi. As far as the feminines of the first person are concerned, whether we regard the *mǫo-(*mǫi)/*mǫa- opposition as already realized or effected only at this stage obviously depends on whether or not we accept that the Late Spoken Latin of Gaul participated in a general Romance closing of *mǫa to *mǫa on the lines discussed above.

The system as presented above calls for one further comment, viz. on the retention of -m (> -n) in the masculine accusative singulars as contrasted with its fall in the feminines. Given the early formation of monosyllabic unstressed forms, which I discuss below, the preservation of -m in the atonic masculines presents no problem since such preservation is generally accepted as regular in monosyllabic forms. As far as the atonic feminines are concerned, the strong tendency to eliminate case flexion in that gender, which operated earliest in forms belonging to the first declension, would account for the loss of -m in mam, which brought it into line with tonic accusative *mea. As to the tonic masculines: once given symmetry of flexional pattern between the tonic and atonic feminines, the masculines of the two sets would naturally tend to develop a parallel symmetry, and this could be achieved either by dropping -m in the atonics or by restoring -m in the tonic series. The Old Provençal forms (cf. Schultz-Gora, op. cit., §. 117) may indicate a tendency towards a solution on the former lines—mo, to, so matching mieu, tieu, sieu—but the occurrence of mon, ton, son as alternative atonic forms makes this uncertain in view of the optional use of 'separable' final -n in many Provençal forms. In the north it was the second solution that prevailed, *mom, *tom, *som being matched by *meom, *toom, *soom. It is, of course, the case that this solution resulted in a divergence of the flexional pattern of masculine possessives from that of the masculine nominals, in which the accusative singular subsequently comes, in the vast majority of words, to coincide with the nominative plural as basic forms with zero flexion, to which in the nominative singular and accusative plural flexional -s is added. This divergence between the possessive and nominal patterns was, as we shall see below, the probable cause of an eventual remodelling of the masculine tonic possessives on the accusative singular, which brought miens, mien, mien, miens, etc., into line again with murs, mur, mur, murs and bons, bon, bon, bons, when the link between tonic and atonic possessives had weakened and the tonic series had been attracted into the orbit of the nominals.

At this point we may turn to a consideration of the development of the atonic forms, *mus, mum, mi, mos, ma, tus*, etc., which, as we have seen, came, in the Spoken Latin of Gaul, to form a complete set structurally opposed to the tonic forms. As regards the details of the process of reduction, there are two main types of explanation current. The first supposes that the only forms to the reduction of which phonetic factors contributed were those containing the *-uu-* and *-uo-* sequences, the reduction in these cases being seen as favoured by the affinity of the vowels in hiatus, possibly as part of a general reduction of these sequences in atonic position, as exemplified by *mortuum* > **mortu, quattuor* > **quattor*, etc. (cf. Lausberg, op. cit., §§. 251 and 344), and that, where other monosyllabic forms were introduced—*mus, ma, ta*, etc.—it was by direct analogy with *tus, tum, tos*, etc. The other type of explanation postulates a preliminary shift of accent to the final syllable in proclitic usage—*méa* > **meà* > **mẹà* > *ma*, etc.—a shift which, in Pierre Fouché's view (*Phonétique historique du français*, II, Paris, 1958, pp. 168–9), preceded the reduction of even the homophonous-vowel forms—**tuùm pátrem*, etc., being preliminary to **tum pátre*, etc.

Neither of these theories is inherently implausible, and all that can safely be said by way of comment on them is that, from the phonetic point of view, it is not necessary to postulate a shift of accent preliminary to reduction in the case of the homophonous-vowel forms, but that the reduction of the non-homophonous-vowel forms is unlikely to have occurred without such a shift, unless they were exposed to the analogical influence of previously reduced *tus*, etc., forms. Beyond this it is hazardous to go, but the fragmentary nature of the reduced system as attested in several Romance languages[12]

---

[12] Cf. footnote 11 above. Lausberg (op. cit., §. 754) regards the fact that the only reduced forms attested in Old Spanish—*to, tos, so, sos*—are of homophonous-vowel origin as an indication that the process of reduction began with the latter. The Old Spanish evidence certainly points in that direction, and the fact that in Rumanian only *tu, su, ta, sa* are attested can be interpreted as supporting evidence if we regard the feminines as secondary to the masculines in that language; but in the case of Old Portuguese, where only *ma, ta, sa* are found, we should then have to assume that **to, *so* forms had earlier existed, had given rise to analogical feminines, and had then fallen before the earliest attestations of the language. This situation, together with the fragmentary nature of the system as attested in Rheto-Romance, serves as a reminder that in no case can we be certain that the attested forms coincide with those originally introduced. It is for this reason that I have avoided reaching a firm conclusion on this question.

suggests that a universal shift of accent did not occur since this would, presumably, have disposed all forms equally to reduction. One is inclined, therefore to conclude that the homophonous-vowel forms were probably reduced without preliminary shift of accent, and to leave open the question whether the reduction of the other forms, where it occurred, was due to analogy or to a shift of accent or to a combination of both factors.

Whatever the details of the process, however, we should not lose sight of the basic factor predisposing to reduction, viz. the merely subordinate and redundant role of the stem vowels in the Classical Latin forms, to which attention was drawn above when discussing their new function in the tonic series of Late Spoken Latin. For it was this factor that made it possible for unstressed *meus* to be reduced to *mus*, *tuus* to *tus*, *mea* to *ma*, etc., without loss of identity, and, indeed, with a gain in the symmetry and economy of the system. The situation would, of course, have been different if stem *e* and *u* had been perceivable as forming a unit with the person-marking consonants, but *me-*, *tu-* and *su-* bear no consistent relationship to other first, second and third person pronominal forms since the *mě-/mē* relationship is not parallel to *tǔ-/tē* and *sǔ-/sē*, and the *tǔ-/tū* relationship is also isolated. These structural considerations, taken together with considerations of comparative phonetic predisposition to contraction, make it probable that the reduction of at least the *tuus*, *suus* forms occurred before the introduction in some regions of analogical *teus, *seus forms in the second and third persons of the tonic series, which, by extending the *mě-/mē* relationship to *tě-/tē* and *sě-/sē*, do enable the stem vowels to be seen as forming a unit with the initial consonants.

Another obscure point in the development of the Old French possessives concerns the factors which led to the replacement of *mieos, *miei, *mieos, *tuoos, *tuoi, etc., the presumed etymological forms of the nominative singular and nominative and accusative plural of the tonic masculines, by *miens*, *mien*, *miens*, *tuens*, *tuen*, etc., i.e. forms based on the etymological accusative singulars *mien*, *tuen*, *suen*.

The main factor probably was a loss of structural symmetry between the tonic and atonic series resulting from the fall of atonic final vowels in the masculines of the former, which weakened the cohesion of the dual system and exposed the tonic forms to analogical influence by the nominals, with which they had functional affinities. But, before we examine the structural consequences, the fall of the atonic finals itself calls for a comment since their position in hiatus with the tonic vowels might have been expected to result in their retention through the formation of triphthongs similar to those found in Old Provençal and Engadinish *mieu(s)*, etc., and parallel to such forms as *dieu(s)* in Old French.[13]

The fall of the atonic finals in Francien is probably to be seen as a consequence of the retention in that dialect of etymological forms of the second and third person possessives—**tuoos, *tuoon, *suoos, *suoon* —which do not lend themselves to the creation of triphthongs, in preference to the creation of analogical forms based on the first person —**tieus, *sieus,* etc.—similar to those of Old Provençal and Engadinish, which, by reason of the contrast between stem and flexional vowels, are readily capable of forming triphthongs. Given their phonetic composition, **tuoon,* etc., must almost inevitably have been contracted to **tuon,* etc., a contraction strongly favoured by the coexistence of such forms as **nuof* (< *novum*) and **buon* (< *bonum*); and once this had occurred, **mieon,* etc., were presumably contracted in their turn to *mien,* etc., the process again being favoured by the analogy of such forms as *bien* and *rien.* It is, however, possible that an independent phonetic factor was involved in the reduction of the first person forms if, as Pope thinks (op. cit., §. 855(b)), *Breona* > *Brienne* is a parallel development.

It will be seen that these reductions result in the creation of monosyllabic forms, **mies, mien, *tuos, *tuon,* etc., and thereby destroy the disyllabic/monosyllabic opposition between the tonic and atonic series which, as we have seen, was an essential feature of the dual possessive system as originally formed in Late Spoken Latin. It is, therefore, important to note that, at this later stage, the distinction of

[13] Triphthongized forms do seem to have had some currency in northern French dialects, as the attestation of such forms as *miue* (<*mieue,* formed analogically on a lost **mieus*) shows (cf. Pope, op. cit., §. 858; and Schwan-Behrens, tr. O. Bloch, *Grammaire de l'ancien français,* 3rd ed., Leipzig, 1923, Pts. 1 and 2, §. 326).

As in so many other cases, the evidence of the *Strasbourg Oaths* is difficult to interpret. The *meos* and *meon* forms in that text point to late retention of the atonic vowels, but whether this evidence is considered relevant to Francien developments depends on the view taken of the dialect represented in the *Oaths* and upon the degree to which the graphies are thought to be archaizing or etymologizing. We are unfortunate in having no example in the text of tonic forms of the masculine second and third person possessives. The *Eulalia,* however, does provide an example of *suon* (l. 15).

tonic from atonic forms was in no case still dependent on the preservation of this opposition. For, whereas at the earlier stage, *tǫos, etc., could be kept distinct from tǫs, etc., only by preserving the disyllabic character of the former, the diphthongized *tuos, etc., forms were in no danger of confusion with their atonic analogues—tos, etc.—thanks to the distinctive vocalic composition of the two series.

Nevertheless, the fall of the atonic finals did make it impossible for the two series to continue to be perceived as forming a symmetrically structured system, as will be clear from the following analytical table, which presents the possessive system as it probably was before and after this change came about:

The system before the fall of final vowels

m-(i)e-os	m-(i)e-i	m-ø-os	m-ø-i
m-(i)e-on	m-(i)e-os	m-ø-on	m-ø-os
t-(u)o-os	t-(u)o-i	t-ø-os	t-ø-i
s-(u)o-os, etc.			
m-e(i)-a	m-e(i)-as	m-ø-a	m-ø-as, etc.
t-o(u)-a	t-o(u)-as	t-ø-a	t-ø-as, etc.
t-(u)o-os	t-(u)o-i	t-ø-os	t-ø-i
s-(u)o-os, etc.			

The system after the fall of final vowels

m-ie-s	m-ie-i	m-o-s	m-ø-i
m-ie-n	m-ie-s	m-o-n	m-o-s
t-uo-s	t-uo-i	t-o-s	t-ø-i
t-uo-n	t-uo-s	t-o-n	t-o-s
s-uo-s, etc.			
m-ei-a	m-ei-as	m-ø-a	m-ø-as, etc.
t-ou-a	t-ou-as	t-ø-a	t-ø-as, etc.
s-ou-a, etc.			

It will be seen that, whereas in the older system it is possible to present identity of flexion——*os*, *-on*, *-i*, *-os*, *-a*, *-as*——in combination with symmetrical opposition of the tonic to the atonic forms, the vocalic nucleus of the former, realized as *-(i)e-*, *-(u)o-*, *-e(i)-* and *-o(u)-*, being consistently opposed to a zero nucleus in the latter, in the new system identity of flexion can be presented only by admitting an asymmetrical distribution of the zero nucleus in the atonics. It is, therefore, improbable that the atonic series was perceived as structured in the way represented in the second part of the table; it is much more likely to have been perceived as composed uniformly of initial consonant plus syllabic flexion——*m-os*, *m-on*, *m-i*, *m-os*, *t-os*, etc., *m-a*, etc., *t-a*, etc. But a parallel analysis of the tonic series——*m-ies*, *m-ien*, *m-iei*, *m-ies*, *t-uos*, etc., *m-eia*, etc., *t-oua*, etc.——is hardly credible since it implies the recognition of an implausibly complicated series of flexional oppositions between the two sets: *-ies/-os*, *-uos/-os*, *-ien/-on*, *-uon/-on*, *-iei/-i*, *-uoi/-i*, *-eia(s)/-a(s)*, *-oua(s)/-a(s)*.

The consequence probably was that the two series were perceived as of quite different structure: the atonic series as *m-os*, *m-on*, *m-a*, *t-a*, and so on; the tonic series as *mie-s*, *mie-n*, *mei-a*, *tou-a*, and so on. Thus weakened by loss of structural symmetry the possessive system was no longer sufficiently cohesive to resist the forces tending to draw its two components further apart. The decisive disruptive influence proved to be that exerted by the nominal (noun-adjective) system upon the tonic series, probably in virtue of functional affinities arising from the pronominal and predicative uses of the latter. The upshot was that, while the atonic series continued to be accepted as an aberrant flexional type assimilated to the group of noun-qualifiers tied to the pre-nominal position——*li*, *lo*, *li*, *los*, *cist*, *cest*, *cist*, *cez*, *cil*, etc.——the tonic series was remodelled on the commonest nominal pattern, viz. basic form in the accusative singular and nominative plural, basic form plus *-s* in the nominative singular and and accusative plural. Thus it came about that the **mies*, *mien*, **miei*, **mies*, **tuos*, **tuon*, **tuoi*, **tuos*, **suos*, etc., pattern gave way to *miens*, *mien*, *mien*, *miens*, **tuons*, **tuon*, **tuon*, **tuons*, **suons*, etc. The reason for the choice of the accusative singulars *mien*, **tuon*, *suon* as the basic forms is not far to seek: they alone end in a consonant other than flexion *-s*, and they alone are coincident with nominal basic forms such as *bien* and *buon*. The operation of analogy in the remodelling process can be represented by such proportions as

bien:*biens*::*mien*:*miens*
buon:*buons*::*tuon*:*tuons*.

It was, presumably, by a similar process that forms based on the accusative singular were generalized in the case of the monosyllabic noun *rien(s)* (< *res, rem, res, res*).

It will be noted that the feminine forms, **meia* (> *meie*), **meias* (> *meies*), **toua* (*toue*), **touas* (> *toues*), **soua* (> *soue*), etc., which at the **meia*, etc., stage, are parallel in flexion both to the atonic feminine possessives and the feminine nominals, and, at the *meie*, etc., stage, continue to be parallel to the feminine nominals, underwent no corresponding process of remodelling. Indeed, the influence of the tonic feminines may have made itself felt, at the *meie* stage, as a further factor drawing the masculines into the nominal orbit.

At a later stage (thirteenth century), the process of assimilation to adjectival flexion was carried a step further when *moie, teue* (or *toie*), etc., began to give way progressively to *mienne, tienne*, etc., i.e. to forms bearing the same relation to *mien, tien*, etc., as *bone* to *bon*, etc. This process can be seen as part of the wider contemporary one by which basic-form-in-final-consonant/basic-form-plus-*e* was coming to be accepted as the predominant masculine/feminine opposition in the adjectival system—cf. *fort/forte*, etc., beside *bon/bone*, etc.

All these developments reflect a progressive assimilation of the tonic possessives to the nominal system. On the other hand, the progressive replacement, from the later twelfth century, of *tuen, suen*, etc., by forms modelled on the first singular *mien*—giving *tien, sien*, etc.—which prepared the way for the introduction of the analogical feminines *mienne, tienne, sienne*, etc., mentioned above, represented an internal adjustment of the tonic set in the interests of the economy of the system, as is shown by L. M. Skrelina in a recent article.[14] In this case too the feminines may have influenced the development of the masculines since the introduction of *toie, soie*, etc., in line with *moie*, etc., as alternatives to *teue, seue*, etc., preceded the replacement of *tuen, suen*, etc., by *tien, sien*, etc. The preference in the feminines for the first person nucleus (*m*)*oi-* over that of the second and third person, (*t*)*eu-*, (*s*)*eu-*, in spite of the fact that the latter was shared by the possessives of two persons, was presumably due in part to the support the *moi-, toi-, soi-* stems enjoyed in the tonic personal pronoun forms *moi, toi, soi*, but evidence of a predominance of the first person forms in the creation of a uniform series of possessives in the masculine—sometimes with

---

[14] 'De l'économie de certains changements grammaticaux en ancien français', *La Linguistique*, 1968, pp. 61–78.

extension to the feminine—is in any case provided by several other Romance languages, as we have seen.

To sum up: the Old French possessive system of singular person reference developed on lines which have some features in common with other Romance languages, but, in a number of important ways, it stands apart from the rest. In particular, it appears to have continued for several centuries, without disruptive analogical changes, the Late Spoken Latin dual system of tonic and atonic forms, which seems to have been more completely realized in Northern Gallo-Romance than elsewhere. Thus, there is no evidence from Francien of early remodelling of the second and third person masculine tonic forms on those of the first person to produce forms of the *teus, *seus type, in contrast with Rumanian,[15] Engadinish, Provençal, Catalan and Portuguese; no raising of e to i, or remodelling on vocative mi, in the first person tonic feminines, in contrast with Italian, Sardinian (alternative form), Engadinish, Surselvan, Provençal, Old Catalan, Spanish and Portuguese; and no corresponding raising of [ǫ] (or [ų]) to [ų] in the second and third person tonic feminines, in contrast with Italian, Sardinian (possibly), Provençal (alternative form), Old Catalan, Spanish and Portuguese. Instead, the tonic series continues the Classical Latin forms, the only changes not in conformity with 'sound laws' of general application being a reinforcement of the tonic-disyllabic/atonic-monosyllabic opposition by dissimilatory opening of [ǫ] to [ǫ] in the homophonous-vowel masculines, followed by a systematization of a secondary masculine-open-vowel/feminine-close-vowel opposition within the tonic series. The first important break in continuity of development from Late Spoken Latin follows upon the loss of atonic final vowels in the masculine forms of the tonic series, which impairs the overall symmetry of the possessive system. The consequent weakening of the link between tonics and atonics, together with the increasingly distinct syntactical functions of the two series, results in the tonic series being drawn into the orbit of the nominals, and in a generalization of masculine forms based on the accusative singular, perceived as a consonantal stem with zero flexion. The penultimate development in Old French is an internal adjustment, which takes the form of a generalization of the central vocalic complex -oi- in the feminines, -ie- in the masculines, derived in both cases from the first person

[15] This is the current view of the origins of tău and său among Rumanian scholars (cf. A. Rosetti, Istoria limbii române de la origini pînă în secolul al XVII-lea, Bucharest, 1968, p. 112).

possessives, resulting in a marked gain in the economy of the system. The final stage is the unification of the tonic system by the assimilation of the feminines to the masculines on the model of the adjectives— *mien, mienne, tien, tienne,* etc., corresponding to *bon, bone* and *fort, forte.* The introduction of these new forms, which is in part due to the growing tendency to specialize the tonic possessives in pronominal function, provides, in its turn, the basis for a continuation of the process of specialization in the Middle French period, the division between the functions of the tonic and atonic series being virtually absolute by the beginning of Modern French.

In this article I have sought to bring out only what seemed to be the most important factors that determined the course of development of the French possessives, and I have concentrated discussion on points which have been comparatively neglected hitherto. There were undoubtedly other factors, which would have to be included in a complete account, e.g. the use of the definite article with the tonic possessives, which must have emphasized their affinity with the nominals and favoured their eventual specialization in pronominal usage.

The development of the Old French possessives is a striking example of the way in which well-defined linguistic systems tend to evolve in the direction of greater internal coherence and economy, and, accordingly, to undergo modifications which cannot be accounted for by phonological factors alone. At the same time, it illustrates their accessibility to influence by other systems with which they come, in the course of their evolution, to acquire functional and formal affinities. From the point of view of method, therefore, it is a particularly clear case of the necessity to take structural factors into account when attempting to solve problems in historical linguistics.

Truth and Falsehood in the *Tristran* of Béroul

BRIAN BLAKEY

Professor and Chairman, Department of Romance Languages,
McMaster University

If a resurrected Tristran and Iseut were once more to stand before us charged with perjury, it seems they would have no lack of prosecutors. As one modern critic would have it, the pair are guilty of 'shameless deceit and untruthfulness', because 'they lie and commit perjury without turning a hair'.[1] Another critic, while tacitly admitting their offence, pleads in mitigation a 'sympathie béroulienne', a 'zèle partial et vindicatif' on the poet's part that overlays and disguises the lovers' falseness.[2] This latter plea may attract our sympathy, for it is consonant with the medieval belief that truth cannot exist without God, a belief that underpinned the system of ordeals and trials by combat; consequently, we are asked to believe, because God preserves the lovers throughout their tribulations, they are innocent *ipso facto* and must be considered exempt from the accepted social and judicial rules of their age. Yet it is difficult to reconcile such a convenient and sweeping exoneration with the general abhorrence of perjury so prevalent in those same Middle Ages, witness Alain Chartier in *La ballade de Fougères*:

> A Dieu et aux gens detestable
> Est menterie et trahison,
> Pour ce n'est point mis à la table
> Des preux l'image de Jason,
> Qui pour emporter la toison
> De Colcos se veult parjurer.[3]

---

[1] J. Crosland, *Medieval French literature*, Oxford, 1956, pp. 102–3.

[2] P. Le Gentil, 'La légende de Tristan vue par Béroul et Thomas', *Romance Philology*, VII (1953–4), p. 112.

[3] Cited by J. Huizinga, *The Waning of the Middle Ages*, New York, 1954, pp. 87–8.

In the absence of contrary proof, one is led to believe that for a medieval aristocrat the alleged 'shameless deceit and untruthfulness' could not but result in dishonour and disgrace. There is no reason to suppose that the public for which Béroul was writing would have accepted or even understood that the supposed deceit and treachery of the lovers could be justified in any sense by the evident sympathy of the author, however convenient it may be for us moderns to have recourse to a facile explanation of this kind. Still less convincing is Pierre Le Gentil's argument that, irrespective of right or wrong, the very violence of the lovers' suffering aroused compassion: 'Est-ce que la passion lorsqu'elle se déchaîne n'est pas capable des pires excès? Est-ce qu'elle ne trouve pas dans sa violence même une excuse et une justification? Du moins, dominée qu'elle est par une sorte de fatalité, ne doit-elle pas bénéficier de beaucoup d'indulgence et de pitié?'[4]; this interpretation is a curious anachronism, unjustifiable in the medieval context. For if the lovers are guilty as charged, then by implication Béroul is portraying God as the supporter and abettor of a blatant untruth, which would constitute a denial of the religious and judicial systems of his day and a subversion of the feudal society that was largely sustained by those very concepts of faith and law. Is Béroul then a cynic and subversive, however implausible that may seem, or does he rather employ a system of truth and falsehood with which we are unfamiliar and which in consequence we misunderstand?

In the assessment of Béroul's handling of truth and falsehood in his *Tristran*, critical attention has tended, understandably, to focus on the spectacular ambiguous oath sworn by Iseut at Mal Pas. Pierre Jonin alone appears to have taken into account other oaths employed in the text, but he considers only those of Iseut and examines them only to assess the author's religiosity.[5] Yet the *Tristran* contains a series of oaths, of which Iseut's sensational *deraisne* is but one example, and it would appear to be a fault of method to concentrate on the solitary case without examining the entire series of oaths present in what remains to us of Béroul's version, for we are aware of the extreme importance accorded to the sworn word in medieval society; for instance, the chronicles abound in examples, both of the solemn oath

[4] In 'L'épisode du Morois et la signification du *Tristan* de Béroul', *Studia philologica et litteraria in honorem L. Spitzer*, Bern, 1958, p. 272.

[5] P. Jonin, *Les personnages féminins dans les romans français de Tristan au XIIe siècle* (Publications des Annales de la Faculté des Lettres, Aix-en-Provence, nouv. sér. n° 22), Gap, 1958, pp. 339 ff.

sworn on relics and witnessed by high dignitaries, and of the less formal oath, sworn spontaneously at moments of intense emotion.

A few examples drawn from the chronicles indicate the social and judicial rôle of the oath and also illustrate its mechanisms:

I. The Black Prince, incensed at the faithlessness of Jean du Cros, Bishop of Limoges, who had helped negotiate the handing over of that city to the French, 'swore on the soul of his father—an oath which he never broke—that he would attend to no other business until he had won the city back and had made the traitors pay dearly for their disloyalty'. When the English army arrived before Limoges, the Prince 'swore that he would not leave until he had it at his mercy'. After the city was stormed, three thousand of the besieged were put to the sword; the bishop was seized and brought before the Prince, who 'looked at him very grimly. The kindest word he could find to say was that, by God and St. George, he would have his head cut off'. Later, the Duke of Lancaster requested his brother to deliver the prisoner to him, after which, through the intercession of the bishop's friends, Pope Urban V asked the Duke to hand over his prisoner 'in such persuasive and amicable terms that the Duke felt unable to refuse'.[6]

II. Jean de Joinville, annoyed by a quarrelsome knight in his retinue, ordered the offender to leave, saying to him 'for, so God help me, you shall never again be one of my men'. The errant knight appealed for help to Gilles le Brun, Constable of France, who interceded on his behalf, but Joinville claimed that he could take the knight back into his quarters only if the legate were to release him from his oath. Accordingly, the Constable and the knight went to the legate and told him what had happened. The legate replied that he could not release Joinville from his oath, because it was a reasonable one since the knight well merited this punishment. The incident is narrated not to illustrate the dangers of quarrelsome behaviour, but so that the reader 'may refrain from taking any oath without

---

[6] Froissart, *Chronicles.* . . . Translated and edited by G. Brereton, Baltimore, 1968, pp. 175–80. The Black Prince's oaths varied in frangibility, to judge by Froissart's parenthesis; one is reminded of Louis XI, who sent specially to Angers for the cross of St. Laud to take an oath upon, for he distinguished between oaths taken on one relic and on another (cited by J. Huizinga, op. cit., p. 187).

reasonable justification. For, as the wise man says, "Whoever swears too lightly, just as lightly he breaks his oath".'[7]

III. Elsewhere, Joinville relates how he advised King Louis to ask the Templars for a loan of 30,000 *livres* needed to ransom the King's brother, the Count of Poitiers. Étienne d'Otricourt, Commander of the Temple, refused the King's request, claiming that 'all the money placed in our charge is left with us on condition of our swearing never to hand it over except to those who entrusted it to us'. After a bitter exchange between Joinville and the Commander, the issue was resolved by the Marshal of the Temple, Renaud de Vichiers, who agreed with the Commander that 'we could not advance any of this money without breaking our oath', but went on to observe that the King could always seize the money, if he saw fit to do so. Joinville was ordered to effect the seizure; the Marshal said that he would accompany him 'and be a witness of the violence I [Joinville] should do him'. When they reached the treasure, which was kept in the hold of a galley, the Treasurer of the Temple, unaware of the real situation and seeing Joinville weak with illness, refused to deliver up the keys. Joinville took an axe to break open the door, whereupon the Marshal intervened, saying 'Since you evidently intend to use force against us, we will let you have the keys.'[8]

IV. The *Estoire d'Eracles* relates how the son of Saladin, having requested permission to cross the land of Count Raymond of Tripoli, was authorised to do so, on condition that he went and returned between sunrise and sunset and that he took nothing, either in any town or any house. The outward journey passed without incident, Count Raymond having instructed his people to lie low; however, on the return journey, the strong Saracen party was attacked in open country by a much inferior force of Crusaders led by the Master of the Temple. Of the one hundred and forty attackers, only four escaped; many of the inhabitants of Nazareth, believing the Saracens routed, went out of the city in search of plunder and were in their turn captured by the Saracens, who then re-crossed the river before night fell. The chronicler observes that Saladin's son 'kept his promise to the Count of Tripoli well, for

---

[7] Joinville, in Joinville et Villehardouin, *Chronicles of the Crusades*. Translated . . . by M. R. B. Shaw, Baltimore, 1963, p. 307.

[8] Joinville, op. cit., pp. 258-9.

they [the Saracens] did no damage either in castle or town or house, except to those whom they found in the fields'.[9]

In these four examples we may see in operation most of the elements usual in the oath situation. In the first two, the swearers consider themselves bound by their words, even though the oath was employed informally and in anger, and although Joinville, especially, clearly regrets his hastiness; we may surmise that the Black Prince, too, having regained his calm, realized the political expediency of sparing the bishop. If the swearer considers himself bound by his oath but wishes to avoid fulfilment of its conditions, either he may ask for the oath to be dissolved by the Church, or he may have recourse to the stratagem whereby responsibility is transferred to another, as when the Black Prince releases his prisoner to the Duke of Lancaster and thereby loses the power to fulfil his oath. In the third and fourth examples, from Joinville and the *Estoire d'Eracles*, both examples of more deliberate and legalistic oaths, we see the importance attached to exact conformance with the formal provisions: the Marshal of the Temple adheres strictly to his oath by refusing to lend the money, but sees no wrong in suggesting a way to circumvent the difficulty, if this will assist the king, although he is at the same time careful to safeguard his own honour and reputation by a token claim of submission to *force majeure*; the Saracen prince adheres unswervingly to the literal word of his engagement towards Raymond of Tripoli and thereby escapes any censure by the Christian chronicler. (Indeed, blame in the matter is reserved for a Crusader, Reynald de Châtillon, who by his breaking of a sworn truce has irritated the Saracens and who shortly afterwards pays for his faithlessness at the hands of Saladin himself.[10]) The insistence on formal observance of the oath is characteristic; the same insistence on formal correctness extended to the initial swearing of the oath, for we know that a slip of the tongue while swearing nullified the oath, except in the case of foreigners, whose faulty command of the language exempted them from this otherwise accepted convention.[11] To complete this sketch of the oath-mechanism, it is perhaps necessary to state an obvious fact: in the absence of his sworn word, medieval man often did not scruple to manipulate the truth, if we are to judge by the chroniclers' accounts of intrigue, disloyalty and treacherousness.

[9] *Estoire d'Eracles*, cited by R. Pernoud, *The Crusades*. . . . Translated by E. McLeod, New York, 1964, pp. 159–61.

[10] Ibid., p. 169.

[11] See J. Huizinga, op. cit., p. 233.

When one approaches the *Tristran* with these ideas in mind, it is
evident that Iseut, in swearing the ambiguous oath at Mal Pas: 'Q'entre
mes cuises n'entra home, Fors le ladre qui fist soi some [Tristran in
disguise], Qui me porta outre les guez, Et li rois Marc mes esposez'
(ll. 4205–08),[12] escapes being struck down by a vengeful God, not
because God is indulgent of a blatant lie, but because her oath is true
in form. Iseut is clearly aware of this distinction, since she stipulates in
advance that the form of the oath shall be hers to choose: 'Escondit
mais ne lor ferai, Fors un que je deviserai' (ll. 3233–4). Had she been
forced into using an unambiguous form of words, she could not have
sworn for fear of divine retribution. In this way, Iseut herself gives us a
further demonstration, if that were necessary, of the mechanism of the
oath, wherein the form of words is vital to the oath's acceptance, for
God would not be willing to countenance a lie. The form of the oath
satisfies the world of men, because they are misled by it; because it is
not untrue, it is acceptable to God, who acts as supreme and all-knowing
arbiter.[13]

Having thus defined the underlying machinery of the oath by
examination of the four examples drawn from chroniclers and of the
most striking case in Béroul's text, we may test against it those instances in the poem where God is invoked by the lovers as guarantor
of their veracity. By invocation of God is to be understood a statement
with which God's name is associated; although it has been claimed[14]
that locutions of the type *si m'aït Dex* and *par Deu omnipotent* 'n'ont
plus qu'un sens exclamatif', it is far from proven that in such cases 'les
mérites de Dieu sont évoqués sans raison et n'ont aucun rapport avec le
contexte'. Especially would it seem hazardous to argue from the usage
in *Aucassin et Nicolette*, a work noted for its irreligious flavour, that in
any other text the same formulas must therefore be considered so
many empty phrases; until a particular case is proven, we must assume
that these formulas retained much of their original significance for
author and public, the more so in a serious work such as the *Tristran*,
which is perhaps lacking in doctrinal expertise but is nonetheless

[12] Quotations are taken from A. Ewert's edition, *The romance of Tristran by
Béroul*, 2 vols., Oxford, 1958–70.

[13] It is difficult to share Helaine Newstead's view that 'the validity of Isolt's
oath is tested not by an ordeal, as in Thomas, but by the judgement of King
Arthur' ('The equivocal oath in the Tristan legend', *Mélanges offerts à Rita
Lejeune*, 2 vols., Gembloux, 1969, p. 1083); Arthur's function is not to judge the
oath but to defend the right, once God's acceptance of the *deraisne* is manifest.

[14] By P. Jonin, op. cit., pp. 340–43.

permeated with the more spontaneous religiosity so typical of its age. After all, in the following century even, did not a citizen of Paris have his lips and nose seared for a simple blasphemy, on the orders of Louis IX, who was wont to say: 'I would willingly allow myself to be branded with a hot iron on condition that all wicked oaths were banished from my realm'?[15] As we have already seen in considering Iseut's comportment in the ambiguous oath episode, the queen is at great pains to avoid blasphemy: why should this be, if the sin means nothing to her or to the contemporary reader? Therefore we must accept, at least as a working hypothesis, that blasphemy is unthinkable for the lovers and that each statement containing an invocation of God represents the truth as Tristran and Iseut see it.

In the opening lines of the Béroul fragment, Iseut calls God's vengeance upon herself if she is guilty of untruth in her claim never to have loved any other than the one who took her maidenhead: 'Mais Dex plevis ma loiauté, Qui sor mon cors mete flaele, S'onques fors cil qui m'ot pucele Out m'amistié nul jor!' (ll. 22–5). This is essentially the same oath that she later swears solemnly at Mal Pas, with a slight variation in the terms. If the one is acceptable to God, then so is the other. In the course of her first encounter with the hermit Ogrin, Iseut is completely truthful: 'Sire, por Deu omnipotent, Il ne m'aime pas, ne je lui, Fors par un herbé dont je bui, Et il en but . . .' (ll. 1412–15), thus she need not hesitate in calling upon God to vouch for the truth of her statement. When Tristran assures Mark: 'Ainz nu pensames, Dex le set' (l. 561), this is again the literal truth, for God knows indeed that the lovers' fault was never intended. A last example of swearing in God's name is Iseut's affirmation to Tristran: 'Ne je, par Deu omni-potent, N'ai corage de drüerie Qui tort a nule vilanie' (ll. 32–4). The exact wording of this informal oath is highly significant, in that the queen qualifies her denial of *drüerie* by the restrictive *qui tort a nule vilanie*, thus relying on God to differentiate—as Heavenly Judge—between *drüerie*, of which she is guilty in the eyes of men, and *drüerie qui tort a nule vilanie*, of which she considers herself innocent.

Thus, of five cases where the lovers call upon God to guarantee the truth of their statements, only one represents an oath where form and intent coincide, that of Iseut to Ogrin at their first meeting; the four others depend on a legalistic interpretation of the form of words, as in the third and fourth chronicle examples. Yet it is true to say that, whenever God's name is invoked, Béroul never allows his two principal

[15] Joinville, ed. cit., p. 336.

characters to use a demonstrable untruth, so avoiding blasphemy on his part and on theirs. If such a system must be categorized either as cynicism or as a naïvely subtle conception of justice,[16] one cannot but endorse the latter view. On the initial charge of perjury, it would appear that Tristran and Iseut are not guilty, if judged in accordance with the morality of their age; it is paradoxical that certain modern critics should have arrived at the opposite verdict by applying a medieval doctrine—'Le fait juge l'homme'—which does not fit the case. There remains the additional count of lying. As we remarked earlier, lying and perjury were sharply distinguished in the Middle Ages, much as they are in our modern courts of law; perjury was and is a serious and punishable offence, whereas lying was in medieval times a more venial fault, so far as we can ascertain. If Tristran and Iseut shrink from perjury, do they feel the same constraint in the avoidance of all falsehood?

Having seen that Iseut was not guilty of perjury when she swore her innocence of *drüerie qui tort a nule vilanie*, we must accept that Tristran is not lying either when he claims: 'C'onques nul jor, n'en fait n'en dit, N'oi o vos point de drüerie Qui li tornast a vilanie' (ll. 2228-30). There is no invocation of God at this point—understandably, since he is addressing Iseut, whom he has no need to convince—but the form of words is identical to that earlier used solemnly by the queen.[17] In view of this confirmation, it is difficult to share the shocked concern of Pierre Le Gentil, who asks, in the later of his two articles on the *Tristran*: 'N'offre-t-il pas une fois de plus, avec une confondante audace, de soutenir par les armes qu'entre Iseut et lui il n'y a jamais eu "druerie tournant à vilenie"?'[18] Why should Tristran not reaffirm what God has already accepted from Iseut as a true account of their condition? Again, two other apparent lies are formally true: '. . . Que nos amors jostent ensemble, Sire, vos n'en avez talent' (ll. 30-31), says Iseut to Tristran, who in turn affirms: 'Onques n'oi talent de tel rage' (l. 253); these statements are almost an echo of Tristran's earlier explanation: 'Ainz nu pensames, Dex le set', which is guaranteed by God, as we have already seen. That neither of the lovers had a will to commit

---

[16] A phrase ('conception naïvement subtile de la justice') used by J. Bédier in his *Roman de Tristan par Thomas* (SATF), Paris, 1905, tom. II, p. 184.

[17] King Arthur employs a similar qualification when he indicates the intended scope of Iseut's disclaimer: 'Qu'el onques n'ot amor conmune A ton nevo, ne deus ne une, Que l'en tornast a vilanie, N'amor ne prist par puterie' (ll. 4163-6) and again: 'Que Tristran n'ot vers vos amor De puteé ne de folor' (ll. 4193-4).

[18] 'L'épisode du Morois', p. 272.

adultery is undeniably true, and the same can be said of Tristran's claim in his letter to Mark: 'Qu'onques amor nen out vers moi, Ne je vers lui, par nul desroi' (ll. 2573–4), since their error was unwitting. In the course of Iseut's second encounter with Ogrin, she asserts: 'De la comune de mon cors Et je du suen somes tuit fors' (ll. 2329–30), a claim that one is compelled to accept as truthful, despite the speculations of M. Le Gentil to the contrary,[19] for there is nothing in Béroul's text to suggest a continuance of physical love-making after this point in the narrative.

We are left with four cases where the lovers appear to lie unequivocally. Iseut tells Tristran, in the hearing of Mark: 'Sire, molt t'ai por lui amé, Et j'en ai tot perdu son gré' (ll. 79–80). It is untrue that Iseut has loved Tristran for Mark's sake; the only mitigating factor is that in this early scene Mark is spying on the lovers, who therefore have little compunction in misleading him. It would have been tempting to see irony in Iseut's remark, with a play on the words *por lui*—'in place of him'—but Iseut is here repeating an argument she has just used: 'Por ce qu'eres du parenté Vos avoie je en cherté' (ll. 71–2), which admits of no such interpretation. The three remaining instances of lying are all on Tristran's side: firstly when he tricks his captors at the chapel by escaping after he has promised to return to them: 'Et quant je Dé proié avrai, A vos eisinc lors revendrai' (ll. 937–8), which would seem condonable as a *ruse de guerre*, especially as Tristran considers himself unjustly and harshly treated and has not given his parole; on two other occasions he apparently denies his adultery: 'Ainz me lairoie par le col Pendre a un arbre q'en ma vie O vos preïse drüerie' (ll. 128–30), and again: 'C'onques o lié n'oi drüerie, Ne ele o moi, jor de ma vie' (ll. 2857–8), unless we are to suppose that Tristran uses the word *drüerie* to denote that *amor de puteé* of which he considers himself innocent, an explanation which is perhaps not impossible when one remembers the care taken elsewhere by Béroul's protagonists in their choice of words.

Where is the 'shameless deceit and untruthfulness'? Five times we have heard the lovers invoke God to guarantee the truth of their utterances, which are indeed true in form; we had seen earlier, in the historical examples, how adherence to the formal wording of an oath was held to be honourable and above reproach. Four times the lovers employ the same formulas that elsewhere are guaranteed by God, so that we cannot doubt their veracity. On only four occasions do

[19] Ibid., p. 273.

Tristran and Iseut make statements which are not obviously true in
form or intent: the hero employs a *ruse de guerre*, the heroine misleads
a spy, both actions we can condone; in the light of this evidence of
Béroul's scrupulous concern for the lovers' reputation, how can we be
sure that Tristran's use of *drüerie* is a departure from the truth?

Contrast with this careful handling of the lovers' affirmations Béroul's
consistent portrayal of King Mark as a liar and oath-breaker, either
directly, as when the king misleads his barons as to his motive for
leaving court, claiming he has a rendezvous with a *pucele* whereas he
is in fact going with the forester to seek out the lovers in Morrois
(ll. 1931–7), and again on his return: 'Li rois lor ment, pas n'i connut
Ou il ala ne que il quist Ne de faisance que il fist' (ll. 2060–62); or
indirectly, as when he consistently fails to accomplish what he has
sworn or said that he will do:

> Par ire a juré saint Thomas
> Ne laira n'en face justise
> Et qu'en ce fu ne soit la mise.   (ll. 1126–8)

> Et dist mex veut estre penduz
> Qu'il ne prenge de ceus venjance
> Que li ont fait tel avilance.   (ll. 1954–6)

> Iriez s'en torne, sovent dit
> Q'or veut morir s'il nes ocit.   (ll. 1985–6)

Mark does none of these things. Even his three *felons* say of him: 'Ja
n'i tendra ne fei ne veu' (l. 3094). All this in studied opposition, as
we have seen, to the poet's painstaking preservation of the lovers'
credibility.[20]

After this analysis and comparison of cases drawn from the chronicles
and from Béroul's text, is it necessary to state that Béroul is neither
cynical nor more naïve than his contemporaries? He is adhering to a
system of truth, or rather truthfulness, patently different from our own,
a system in which one was not bound to be truthful, unless one had

---

[20] A. Ewert's mistranslation of: 'Tant ait plus [mis, beau] sire Ogrin, Vostre
merci, el parchemin, Que je ne m'os en lui fïer' (ll. 2411–3) as 'However much is
put in the letter . . . I dare not trust him' (ed. cit., vol. II, p. 204) would make
Tristran sound unduly suspicious of Mark's good faith; the true sense of these
words is surely 'Let there be added to the letter . . . that I dare not trust him',
i.e. until Mark has replied to Tristran's letter and agreed to the terms proposed.

sworn to be so. Perjury was universally abhorred, because it involved a denial of God, which was the ultimate blasphemy; private lying was socially admissible, especially if the individual felt in any way constrained to lie. The combination of these two factors, the individual's tendency to lie and the general abhorrence of perjury, conferred upon the oath a peculiar importance in medieval society, both as a formal judicial procedure and also as a spontaneous indication of personal veracity. For us it is perhaps easier to accept the ritual that often surrounded the swearing of an oath than it is to understand the rigorous formalism with which its provisions were undoubtedly interpreted; nevertheless, it is essential to our understanding of medieval life and letters that we do not under-estimate the almost magical power of the sworn word, cornerstone of the political, social and judicial systems of an age.

Some Hitherto Unknown Fragments of the
Prophécies de Merlin

FANNI BOGDANOW

Lecturer in French, University of Manchester

When Geoffrey of Monmouth decided to place a series of prophecies in the mouth of Merlin he began a tradition which was to be very fruitful throughout the Middle Ages.[1] Numerous writers were to use Merlin as a mouthpiece, often for political purposes. Between 1272 and 1279 a Venetian, writing in French and referring to himself by the pseudonym 'Maistre Richart d'Irlande' composed a long series of prophecies attributed to Merlin and now known as the *Prophécies de Merlin*. Merlin's pronouncements here refer mainly to the political events which occurred in Italy and the Holy Land in the 12th and 13th centuries, but the author, in order to liven up the work, interwove it with a considerable amount of material copied or adapted from the Arthurian prose romances. Of the extant thirteen manuscripts of the *Prophécies de Merlin* listed by Lucy Allen Paton in her edition of the prophetic material,[2] four (B.N. fr. 350; Brit. Mus. Harley 1629, Add. 25434; and the MS. formerly at Maggs Bros. Ltd., and now in Dr. Bodmer's Library, Geneva) have preserved the bulk of the Arthurian incidents. The rest, as Lucy Allen Paton has shown, have deliberately omitted most of the Arthurian sections. It is not without interest to note, therefore, that in the State Archives of Modena have been preserved fragments from four different hitherto unknown manuscripts

[1] See R. H. Taylor, *The Political Prophecy in England* (Columbia Univ. Studies in English), New York, 1911; Paul Zumthor, *Merlin le Prophète*, Lausanne, 1943, pp. 49–114.—I should like to thank here Dr. F. Whitehead for valuable advice in the preparation of this article.

[2] *Les Prophécies de Merlin*, edited from MS. 593 in the Bibliothèque Municipale of Rennes by Lucy Allen Paton, 2 vols. (Modern Language Association of America), New York, London, 1926. The Arthurian material has been summarized, but not published, by L. A. Paton.

of the *Prophécies de Merlin* all of which contain some of the Arthurian material. One of these fragments I published some years ago in *Romance Philology* XVI (1963).[3] In the following pages, written as a tribute to Professor T. B. W. Reid, I propose to publish Modena III.

Modena III consists of a double parchment folio (326 × 240 mm). The top has been cut away in both folios. There are two columns to each page, with 54 lines per column on f. 1r, 49 on f. 1v, 59 on f. 2r and 49 on f. 2v. There are coloured initials, and on f. 1v is a large illuminated initial. The writing, though small, is quite legible. The narrative contained in these two folios is not consecutive, but belongs to different sections of the *Prophécies de Merlin*.

Folio 1r and f. 1v col. 1 (fragment A) has preserved a portion of one of Perceval's adventures, his combat with the Chevalier de la Tour on behalf of the Maiden of the Pavilion. Perceval in the course of his adventures comes to a Tower whose lord keeps a lady captive in a pavilion because she refuses to marry him. The damsel who is bound 'a fil de fer' begs Perceval to free her, and the next morning Perceval and the lord of the Tower engage in a combat. Modena III, f. 1a begins with this battle.[4] After vanquishing the knight Perceval continues on his journey until he comes to a stone on which is inscribed one of Merlin's prophecies. At the damsel's request Perceval returns to the tower and the following morning knights the lady's squire.

Three of the manuscripts of the 'Arthurian' group of *Prophécies de Merlin* MSS. contain the whole of the Modena narrative: B.N. fr. 350, ff. 413c–414a; Bodmer, f. 94a ff.[5] and Modena II.[6] Of the others,

---

[3] The rest I shall publish later.

[4] The passage immediately preceding the opening of our fragment is as follows in MS. B.N. fr. 350, f. 313d: 'Que vous diroie ge? Il se partent li uns de l'autre pour prendre place, et puis s'entrevienent li uns contre l'autre au ferir des esperons, mez tex fu l'aventure au joindre des glaives que li chevalier de la tour brisa son glaive. Mes Percheval fiert lui si durement que il l'abat a la terre lui et le cheval tout en .i. mont. Et puis hurte avant pour parfurnir son poindre, et descent et voit que li chevalier estoit ja relevés et avoit geté son escu devant son vis et s'espee ostee du fuerre et venoit encontre lui l'espee levee encontre mont. Lors prent Percheval son escu par les enarmes et le gete devant son vis'.

[5] Paton, vol. I, pp. 387–8 épisode 7c, summarises the incident. The episode is lacking in Brit. Mus. Add. 25434, which has a lacuna after f. 94d extending from Paton, vol. I, p. 383 n. 2—p. 390 n. 2, and in Brit. Mus. Harley, 1629, which has after f. 66d a lacuna extending from Paton vol. I, pp. 333–88, n. 3.

[6] Modena II consists of 16 parchment folios, dating from the late 13th or beginning of the 14th century. It contains several sections of the *Prophécies de Merlin* which I shall publish elsewhere.

Rennes MS. 593 and the 1498 printed edition of the *Prophécies de Merlin* have preserved Merlin's prophecy inscribed on the stone.[7]

Whereas Modena II, B.N. fr. 350 and the Bodmer MS. follow up Perceval's exploits with Morgain's adventures,[8] Modena III (f. 1c–d) passes on to the beginning of Golistan's adventures as he goes in search of Segurant le Brun, an incident related at an earlier point in the other 'Arthurian' manuscripts of the *Prophécies de Merlin* (B.N. fr. 350, ff. 399d–400a; Brit. Mus. Add. 25434, ff. 72b–c; Harley 1629, ff. 42b–c; Bodmer MS., f. 65c–d).[9]

Modena III, f. 2 (fragment B) relates how Sagremor, after recovering from his illness, reproaches Arthur for his neglect of his duties. Daguenet, to whom Arthur has entrusted his kingdom, makes preparations to meet the Saxons who are marching on Winchester. On the way to Winchester, Gauvain lays siege to the castle at Dover which Meleagant has seized from Arthur. On Meleagant's suggestion, he and Gauvain engage in a single combat. As agreed, Meleagant hands the castle over to Gauvain after each has unhorsed the other. This narrative corresponds to B.N. fr. 350, ff. 415c–416c and Bodmer MS., f. 98b–100a. Brit. Mus. Harley MS. 1629, f. 68c–d has only preserved the equivalent of Modena III, § 12 lines 1–32.[10]

As the Bodmer MS. is not available at present, and as the other extant manuscripts of the 'Arthurian' group do not all include the

[7] The Rennes version has been published by Paton, vol. I, p. 260, Chapter CCXXI. This corresponds to our text, § 4, l. 54 to § 6, l. 82. The 1498 printed edition (*Le premie* (sic) *second volume de Merlin: Les prophéties de Merlin*. Antoine Verard, Paris, 1498, 3 vols.) has the prophecy in vol. III, f. 35c–d. The other MSS. belonging to the Rennes group do not contain the prophecy: Berne, Stadtbib. MS. 388, f. 93c omits the equivalent of Paton, I, Chapters CCXXI–CCXXIII; B.N. fr. 15211 breaks off after Paton, Chapter CCXX; B.N. fr. 98 omits the content of Chapters CCIX–CCXXIII; Arsenal 5229 omits Chapters CLXXXV–CCXXIV; Rome, Vatican Library MS. 1687 breaks off after Chapter CCXII; Venice, Bibl. Marciana XXIX and Chantilly, Musée Condé 644 (1081) also both lack this part of the narrative.

[8] Summarized by Paton, vol. I, p. 388, epis. 8.

[9] Summarized by Paton, vol. I, p. 374, epis. 3.

[10] This episode has been summarized by Paton, vol. I, pp. 389–90, epis. 6c and 6d. Brit. Mus. Add. 25434 lacks this part of the narrative. The beginning of the episode not preserved in Modena III runs as follows in B.N. fr. 350, f. 415c: Or dit li contez que Sagremor li Desrees qui auquez estoit bon chevalierz fu garis de sa maladie, il prist le roi Artu .i. jor par le main et le trait autre part et li dit: —'Ha, sire, qu'estez vous devenu? Certes, l'en vous deüst honnir du cors. Ou sunt voz barons? Ou sunt li grant tornoiement que vous soliez maintenir parmi le roiaume de Logrez? . . .'

whole of Modena III fragments A and B, it is not possible to arrive at a definitive classification of the manuscripts. Several facts, however, stand out. In the first half of Fragment A, Modena II (N) alone appears in one sentence to have preserved the correct reading. When the lord of the Tower vanquished by Perceval asks for mercy, Perceval agrees to spare him provided that for the rest of his life he will refrain from seizing women by force. The knight laughingly agrees. Modena III (M) has the following reading:

> Et Pricival respont et dist que en lius de prison li comande il que dusque au jors de sa vie se garde de prendre feme a force. Et li chevaliers comence a rire et dist que bien s'en gardera (§ 2.23–25).

The reading of B.N. fr. 350 (f. 413d–414a) is badly truncated and does not contain anything not in M:

> Et Perceval li respont [f. 414a] que en leu de prison se gart tous les jours de sa vie. Et li chevalier conmenche a rire et dit que bien s'en gardera.

It is rather surprising that the knight should laugh on hearing Perceval's request. The reading of Modena II (N) would appear to explain the knight's mirth. Here Perceval adds that 'even if the lady is in agreement when you take her she will cause enough trouble':

> Et Perchevax li respont que en liu de prison li commande il que tous les jours de sa vie se garde de femme prendre a force, 'car quant vous la prenderés au miex que vous porés tout par sa volenté, si vous fera ele assés de wisques'.[11] Et li chevaliers commence a rire et dist ke bien s'en gardera d'ore en avant se Diu plaist.

It is very probable that the common source of Modena III and B.N. fr. 350 omitted this additional sentence, and that the scribe of 350 subsequently further truncated the passage.

There is another example of a common error in Modena III and 350. On hearing Meleagant's suggestion that they should fight a single combat in order to decide the wardenship of the castle at Dover, Gauvain agrees, but on the condition that if they are both unhorsed he should have the right to give away the castle:

> Mes tant voil ge que vos li dites de par moi que se nos cheons andox, ge donerai le garde dou chastel (M, §. 19.134–5).

---

[11] Wisques is the Northern form of guisques.

The reading of 350 is the same as that of *M*, and there can be no doubt that both have omitted after *chastel* a few words stating to whom the castle is to be given.[12]

But *M* and 350 are by no means identical. Neither can in fact be based on the other, as each has individual readings and accidental omissions not in the other. Often when other manuscripts are available for comparison, *M* agrees with these against 350, or vice versa.[13] They must, therefore, be collateral copies of a common source.

The language of the fragments published here is on the whole the 'normal Francien' of the later O.F. period, but it includes a number of features characteristic of texts copied in Italy. Some of these features are found also in Northern, North-Eastern and Eastern documents, as well as being frequent in Franco-Italian texts, and quite possibly figured already in the French manuscript copied by our Italian scribe. Other features, however, seem almost certainly to have been imported into the text by an Italian.[14] Most of these are isolated, occurring only

[12] The only other MS. which contains this part of the narrative is the Bodmer MS., and this is not available at present.

[13] For erroneous omissions and other errors in Modena III (*M*) see variants to §§ 15.61–2; 17.91–2; 6.76; 7.81–2; 7.92; 12.18; 12.23. For erroneous omissions and other errors in 350 (*E*), see variants to §§ 1.6–7; 18.109–10; 3.29–30; 12.10 (first variant).

[14] In attempting to determine which linguistic peculiarities are characteristic of Franco-Italian, one comes up against the same difficulty encountered by any dialect student endeavouring to isolate the distinguishing features of a particular dialect, namely the fact that many features are common to more than one region (cf. L. Remacle, *Le problème de l'ancien wallon* [Bibl. de la Faculté de Philosophie et Lettres de l'Univ. de Liège, fasc. CIX], 1948; C. T. Gossen, *Französische Skriptastudien* [Österreichische Akademie der Wissenschaften Philosophisch-Historische Klasse, Sitzungsberichte, 253. Band], Wien, 1967). In the case of a prose text copied many times over and each manuscript having behind it a long scribal tradition, there is the added difficulty that we do not know which of these 'common' linguistic peculiarities featured already in the French manuscripts copied by the Italian scribes. That many of the Northern, North-Eastern and Eastern features found in so many French texts copied by Italians were not necessarily introduced by the Italian scribes, but were already in the manuscripts they transcribed, is all the more likely as a number of these so-called dialectal features had become by the thirteenth and fourteenth centuries part of the normal literary language of Central France (cf. G. Wacker, *Über das Verhältnis von Dialekt und Schriftsprache im Altfranzösischen*, Halle, 1916). Other Northern or Eastern features not usual in 'normal' O.F. are probably due to the fact that the French manuscripts copied by the Italian scribes had passed through the hands of regional scribes.

in one or two words, and can be found side by side with the 'normal Francien' forms.[15]

For a full bibliography on F -I , see:

J. Monfrin, 'Fragments de la *Chanson d'Aspremont conservés en Italie*', *Romania*, LXXIX (1958), pp. 237–52, 376–88 [*Monfrin*].

H. Tjerneld, *Moamin et Ghatrif; traités de fauconnerie et des chiens de chasse, édition princeps de la version franco-italienne*, Stockholm, 1945 [*Traités*].

F. Bogdanow: *La Folie Lancelot*, ZRPh, Beih. 109, Max Niemeyer Verlag, Tübingen, 1965 [*Folie*].

Id., 'A new fragment of the Tournament of Sorelois', *Romance Philology*, XVI (1963), pp. 268–81 [*Sorelois*].

Other works to which I shall refer include:

H. Breuer, *Eine gereimte altfranzösische-veronische Fassung der Legende der Heiligen Katharina von Alexandrien*, ZRPh., Beih. LIII, 1919 [*Kath.-Leg*].

E. Mainone, *Laut- und Formenlehre in der Berliner frankovenezianischen Chanson de geste von Huon d'Auvergne*, Berlin, 1911 [*Mainone*, I].

Id. *Formenlehre und Syntax in der Berliner frankovenezianischen Chanson de geste von Huon d'Auvergne*, Leipzig, 1936 [*Mainone*, II].

M. K. Pope, *From Latin to Modern French*, Manchester, 1934 [*Pope*].

B. Wiese, *Altitalienisches Elementarbuch*, Heidelberg, 1904 [*Wiese*].

I. ORTHOGRAPHY[16]

1. *oi* for *ei* before palatal *l* and *n* in: *mervoille* (§§ 12.15, 12.16, 17.82; cf. 1.8), *voillier* (§ 7.96; cf. 8.100); *poine* (§ 6.71), *ploine* (§ 20.145). This is clearly an Eastern feature (*Pope*, § 1322 xxii) even though similar examples are not unknown in F.-I. (*Traités*, p. 35).

---

[15] The examples listed of each feature are exhaustive unless the last one is followed by 'etc.'.

[16] Graphies in our text which although not 'normal' (in the sense of representing the supposed Francien phonetic norm) are nevertheless common in MSS. of all provenances in this period include: (i) *voil* §§ 15.57, 19.122, 19.134 for *vueil*. It may be analogical on *voillons* or it may be a case of the absence of diphthongization of tonic open *o* before a palatal, a feature common in N.-E. (*Pope*, § 1321 i). Similarly *orgoil* § 19.120 may be an analogical form (on *orgoillos*). Both *voil* and *orgoil* are found also in other F.-I. texts (*Folie*, p. XL § 8; *Sorelois*, p. 271 § 1); (ii) the graphy *o* instead of *eu* (from closed *o* tonic free) in the ending -*or*, e.g. *lor* § 12.17, etc., *monseignor* § 15.53, etc. Absence of diphthongization in -*or* is generally widespread in literary O.F.; it is common also in F.-I. (*Pope*, §§ 1322 xviii, 230 ii; *Traités*, p. 37; *Sorelois*, p. 271 § 2; *Folie*, p. XL § 10); (iii) *aus* § 15.67 for *eus*. Originally a feature of N., N.-E., E. and S.-C. (*Pope*, §§ 501 ii, 1320 xvii, 1322 ix, 1325 xi); (iv) *lius* § 2.29 (N., N.-E. *Pope*, § 1320 vi).

2. *ie* for *e* (from Latin tonic free *a* not preceded by a palatal) is found once in *eschapier* § 1.11. This development is found both in Eastern texts (*Modus*, p. XV) and in F.-I. (*Traités*, pp. 31–2; *Folie*, p. XXXIX § 1).

3. The graphy *a*, representing the regular *ai* before an oral (*fason* § 19.123) and a nasal consonant (*enfrante* § 3.41, *mantenir* § 11.1) is common in N., N.-E., and E. as well as F.-I. texts (*Pope* § 1320 viii; *Traités* p. 33; *Monfrin* p. 243 § 3).

4. In some words the treatment of initial and intertonic *e* reflects the habits of F.-I. scribes:

(i) replaced four times by *a*: *davant* § 6.69 (cf. Ital. *davanti*), *durament* § 10.131, *comencarai* § 14.44 (cf. Ital. *comenzar*), *da* § 9.110. Very common in F.-I. (*Traités*, p. 39; *Monfrin*, p. 244 § 6; *Sorelois*, p. 271 § 5; *Folie*, p. XLI § 19).

(ii) replaced twice by *o*: *domentiers* § 15.53 (cf. Old Ital. *domentre*: *Wiese*, p. 16 § 19), *domande* § 5.59 beside *demander* § 7.84 (cf. Ital. *domandare*. Common in F.-I. (*Traités*, p. 39; *Sorelois*, p. 271 § 3; *Folie*, p. XLII § 23).

(iii) raised to *i* in *Pricival* §§ 2.20, 2.23 (beside *Perceval* § 3.26, etc.). Common in F.-I. (*Traités*, p. 39; *Monfrin*, p. 244 § 13; *Folie*, p. XLII § 25). Note also the Ital. form *si* § 2.20 (=*se* pronoun).

5. An Italianizing *e* is twice appended to a noun and to an adverb: *mercheante* § 6.78, *amonte* § 1.3 (beside *amont* § 1.5, etc.), a trait very common in F.-I. (*Traités*, pp. 40–1; *Sorelois*, p. 271 § 6). Cf. Old Ital. *avante, vestimente*, etc.: *Wiese*, § 10.

6. *eç* is reduced to *e* in: *duré* § 1.12. This reduction is not unknown in F.-I., but is unusual in standard O.F. (cf. *Kath.-Leg.*, p. 269 § 27).

7. Inorganic *n* is found before *z* once in *prelanz* § 12.24. Although this feature is found fairly frequently in N. and N.-E. texts, it is also a characteristic trait of F.-.I. (*Traités*, pp. 48–9; *Sorelois*, p. 271 § 9; cf. C. Balcke, *Der anorganische Nasallaut im französischen*, ZRPh. Beih. 39, 1912).

8. Velar *k* before Gallo-Roman *a* is found in *castellaus* § 18.112 (beside *chastelaus* § 19.130). Although this feature is very common both in N. (*Pope*, § 1320 i) and F.-I. (*Traités*, pp. 44–5; *Folie*, p. XLII § 31) it occurs only once in our text, perhaps under the influence of Ital. *castello*.

9. *s* impura is found without prosthetic *e* in *spee* (§§ 1.5, 1.7, 1.8, 2.20, 9.120, 10.125, 10.127) beside *espee* (§§ 1.1, 1.4, 20.146). Common

in N.-E. (*Pope*, § 1321 x) and F.-I. (*Traités*, p. 43; *Folie*, p. XLIII § 41) this may well reflect Ital. treatment of *s* impura (cf. Old Ital. *spada*).

Enscrit § 5.62 for *escrit* can be an Italianism or a Latinism (cf. *inscritto, inscriptus*).

10. As so often in F.-I. texts (and fairly frequently also in later 'standard' O.F.) final *s* falls occasionally: cil *le* prist § 6.65, *le* mostiers § 11.4, des veves *dame* § 5.50, une des *bone espee* § 1.8, avoit *escrite* § 4.44, en si *leide* meins § 9.116, des *esperon* § 20.143, encontre les *traitor* § 7.86. Cf. *Traités*, p. 44; *Monfrin*, p. 245 § 25; *Folie*, p. XLIV § 42.

11. The graphy ç for *z* or *s* is found twice: *genç* § 17.82, *penseç* § 18.119. This graphy is very common in F.-I. (*Traités*, pp. 51–2; *Monfrin*, p. 245 § 30) and in Old Ital. MSS. (*Wiese*, § 10).

12. Italianized graphy *che* § 9.118 for *que*.

13. *l* mouillée is once represented by the Ital. graphy *gl*: *enteglees* § 4.55 (cf. Ital. *intagliata*).

14. Graphy *ga* § 15.64 for *ja*.

15. *u* is found after *g* in: *guarder* § 3.40 (beside *garder* § 7.91). Cf. Ital. *guardare*. The *gu* spelling is rare in later O.F., but as an Italianized graphy occurs at times in F.-I. (*Lath.-Leg.*, p. 276 § 55).

16. As so often in F.-I., double consonants are often used for single (*Traités*, pp. 44 and 51; *Sorelois*, p. 271 § 11; *Folie*, p. XLIV § 46): *battaille* § 20.146, *obbliez* § 5.56, *esscrire* § 5.62, *esscrie* § 10.132, *esscapez* § 7.83, *copp* § 1.4, de *rechieff* § 10.130, *sspee* § 2.20, *ssont* § 20.150, etc. (There are in Old Ital. MSS. numerous similar cases of doubling of consonants in internal position. Cf. *Wiese*, p. 12 § 11: *parllare, mortto, temppo, blondda, corppo, osste*, etc.).

17. *h*, without phonetic value, is used as an initial in *hoste* § 10.125 (=3rd. pers. sg. of *oster*); to indicate hiatus between two vowels in *mehailles* § 14.43. In contrast to modern Ital. usage, where *h* is practically unused, initial *h* is found both in Old Ital. MSS. (*Wiese*, § 10) and in F.-I. (*Traités*, pp. 46–7; *Folie*, p. XLII § 33).

II. MORPHOLOGY

Features common to our fragments and other F.-I. texts include:

18. (i) *doner-ai* (§§ 7.91, 15.58, 19.135), *-ont* (§§ 5.49, 5.52) as the future of *doner*. The commoner form in O.F. up to the end of the 14th century is *donrai*. Both forms are found in F.-I. (*Folie*, p. XLV § 57).

(ii) The ending *-oe* (beside the normal *-oie*) in the 1st pers. sg. of the cond.: *diroe* §§ 18.99, 18.106, *seroe* § 10. 135, *voudroe* § 12.23. Though -*oe* is the normal ending of the impf. in Western French, in the cond. -*oe* is extremely rare. There are a few examples of it in the South-Western dialects (*Gossen*, p. 73; E. Goerlich, *Die Südwestlichen Dialekte der Langue d'oïl* [Heilbronn, 1882, p. 135) and in F.-I. (*Folie*, p. XLV § 53; *Sorelois*, p. 272 § 17).

19. Frequent non-observance of the declensional system, and especially:

(i) *Articles.* Apart from occasional use of *le* for *li* in the masc. nom. sg. and of *les* for *li* in the masc. nom. pl. as is quite common, both in later 'standard' O.F. and in F.-I., we find: (a) frequent use of *li* for *le* in the masc. obl. sg.: ainz est a monseignor *li* roi § 18.112, pristrent *li* confanon roial § 18.100, avec *li* vaslet § 6.68, desor *li* hiaume § 1.3, dedenz *li* paveillon § 3.27, etc. *Li* for *le* is unusual in 'standard' O.F., but is very common in F.-I. (*Monfrin*, p. 246 § 34; *Folie*, p. XLVI § 60c; *Sorelois*, p. 272 § 20).

(b) Occasional use of *le* and *li* in the masc. obl. pl. beside the normal *les*: *le* m[o]stiers § 11.4; desvalent *li* degrez § 18.101, les homes . . . oblieront . . . *li* orpheni[n]s § 5.48. In some F.-I. texts *li* is quite common in the obl. pl. (*Sorelois*, p. 272 § 21; *Mainone*, II, 3).

(ii) *Masculine nouns.* Here, too, apart from the use of the obl. for the nom. as is very common in later 'standard' O.F. and in F.-I., we find frequently the nom. sg. for the obl. sg.: a *piez* § 18.105, desor son *escuz* § 9.117, done un *cox* a *Golistanz* § 10.128, baoit et *jors* et nuit § 8.98, en *lius* § 2.23, etc. The use of the nom. for the obl. is unusual in 'standard' O.-F., though not unknown—cf. *Twelve Fabliaux*, ed. T. B. W. Reid, Manchester University Press, 1955, p. xix, § 31), but very common in F.-I. (*Monfrin*, p. 246 § 33; *Folie*, p. XLVI § 61, *Sorelois*, p. 272 § 24).

(iii) *Feminine nouns.* The scribe sometimes adds *s* or *z* in the fem. obl. sg.: en sa delivre *poestez* § 3.30, d'une *pars* § 20.151, la nuit orent grant *plantés* § 8.99, etc. This is unusual in standard O.F., but quite common in F.-I. (*Traités*, p. 55; *Sorelois*, p. 273 § 25).

(iv) *Adjectives.* Apart from the use at times of the obl. for the nom.— common both in later 'standard' O.F. and F.-I., the nom. is again found once for the obl. sg.: il l'abati a la terre tot *estenduz* § 1.14. This is unusual in 'standard' O.F., but not uncommon in F.-I. (*Traités*, p. 56; *Sorelois*, p. 273 § 26).

(v) *Tot* and *trestot*. As often in F.-I. the correct forms are not always used. Twice the nom. sg. is again found for the obl. sg.: par *toz* le roiaume § 14.46, *trestoz* vos aage § 13.29. Cf. *Traités*, p. 59; *Sorelois*, p. 273 § 27.

20. *Past participles.* (i) In the case of vbs. conj. with *avoir* having an obj. the scribe frequently ignores normal O.F. usage as regards treatment of the past part.: (a) addition of flectional *z* where in 'standard' O.F. none is required: vos m'avez *delivrez* § 6.71, puis que ge l'ai *quitez* § 7.84, il m'ont si *corrociez* § 12.19. (b) Addition twice of flectional *s* instead of fem. *e*: il ot *donez* la garde du chastel § 20.152, la tor que vos avez *gaaigniez* § 6.73.

(ii) In the case of vbs. conj. with *avoir* having no obj., the scribe contrary to O.F. usage twice adds a flectional *z* or *ç* (=*z*) to the past part. apparently making it agree with the subj.: si ai *mandez* par toz le roiaume de Logres que § 14.46, il a une grant piece *penseç* § 18.119.

There is similar confusion in other F.-I. texts (*Mainone*, I, 41; *Mainone* II, 18).

21. *Possessive adjectives.* Once we find for the 5th pers. sg. *vos* instead of *vostre*: trestoz *vos* aage § 13.29. *Vos* for *vostre* is common in F.-I. (*Mainone*, II, 10).

22. *Possessive pronouns.* Once nom. sg. for obl. sg.: maugrez *miens* § 6.77. Unusual in 'standard' O.F., but in accordance with the practice of some F.-I. scribes to use the nom. for the obl. (cf. *Espagne*, p. CXI).

23. *Personal pronouns.* Once *li* for *le*: Dex *li* face preudome § 8.104. *Li* for *le* is common in F.-I. (*Traités*, p. 58; *Folie*, p. XLVII § 66e).

24. *Relative pronouns.* As so often in F.-I., *que* is frequently used for *qui*: s'adrece vers celui *que* ja le voloit § 1.2, etc. (cf. *Traités*, p. 59 § 4; *Sorelois*, p. 273 § 31).

Once *quoi* is used for *qui*: celui a *quoi* ge bee § 7.89.

SYNTAX

25. *Verb concordance.* The scribe uses occasionally the 3rd sg. for the 3rd pl.: se il *vient* a Vincestre, fait li roi Artu, il se deffandent encontre aus § 13.36, les Sesnes *s'en vient* § 14.41, se andox sentons la terre, andox *s'en aille* § 19.129, se ne fussent lor chevalier que ne lor *soffre*[17] pas § 20.147, etc.

This feature is common in some F.-I. texts (*Traités*, p. 78; *Mainone*

---

[17] As *E* (B.N. fr. 350) has here the same reading as *M*, *soffre* for *soffrent* may already have been in the French MS. copied by our scribe, and so would be another example of a common error in *EM*. Cf. above, pp. 34–35.

II, 41; *Espagne*, pp. CXX–CXXI) and is no doubt due to the influence of the Northern Italian dialects, and especially Old Venetian where the 3rd sg. is frequently used for the 3rd pl. (*Wiese*, § 232, pp. 135–6).

The fragments have been transcribed in accordance with normal practice, all abbreviations except numerals having been expanded and the modern distinction between *i* and *j*, *u* and *v* being observed. Emendations have been indicated by the use of square brackets. All rejected MS. readings are listed with the variants. The critical apparatus includes all variants, apart from purely graphic ones, from all the relevant manuscripts except the one in Dr. Bodmer's Library, which is not available at present. The following sigla have been used: *E*—MS. B.N. fr. 350; *F*—Brit. Mus., Add. MS. 25434; *H*—Brit. Mus. Harley MS. 1629; *M*—Modena fragments published here; *N*—Modena II; *P*—1498 printed edition of the *Prophécies de Merlin*; *R*—Rennes MS. 593.

TEXT

Fragment A

§ 1 . . . devant son vis, puis prant s'espee [. . .] du fuere et s'adrece vers celui que ja le voloit ferir parmi la teste.

Li chevalier giete un copp a Perceval et le feri amonte desor li haume si durement que quant la bone espee em prant,[18] en abat a la terre. Et
5 Perceval que sa spe[e] avoit enpugnee en fiert lui si durement amont desor li hiaume que il [le] fait engenoillier maugrez lui. Et neporquant il fu erraument en estant et en fiert lui amont desor li hiaume. La spee trenchoit auques mervoilleusement, que une des bone spee dou munde estoit, si en trencha a la terre un grant chantiax. Et quant Perceval vit
10 ce, il dist a soi meesme que [se] il ne s'en prent garde il n'en pora eschapier vis. Et neporquant il voit apertement que se il [ne] le prant entre ses braz, il n'avra vers lui duré, an ce que il li fu avis que il estoit chevalier d'aage. Et lors s'adrece vers lui et le fiert de son escuz de tote sa force si durement que il [l'] abati a la terre tot estenduz et puis
15 li saut desor li cors et li arache li hiaume de la teste et le giete en voie.

---

[18] § 1.4 *em prant*, § 10.129 *em prist*. Neither Godefroy nor Tobler-Lommatzsch record any similar uses of 'em prendre'. It perhaps means here 'get engaged with'. Cf. Godefroy, III, 72b *emprenant* (pres. part. and s.m.)—one who attacks.

Puis li abat sa ventaille et li menace la teste coper se il ne quite la damoisele et ne fiance prison.

—Sire, fait li chevalier, la damoisele vos quit ge dou tot et prison vos fianz ge, sauve tant que vos ne me metez en prison a la damoisele.

20 § 2. Et lors prist Pricival la sspee que li chevalier li tendi et puis si lieve desor li cors. Et li chevaliers se fu levez en estant et dist:

—Sire, comandez la prison.

Et Pricival respont et dist que en lius de prison li comande il que dusque au jors de sa vie se garde de prendre feme a force. Et li chevaliers

25 comence a rire et dist que bien s'en gardera.

§ 3. Quant Perceval se fu delivrez dou chevaliers en tel maniere con vos avez oï, si s'entra dedenz li paveillon et comande que la damoisele soit desliee. Et quant cels que en garde l'avoient sorent que li chevaliers estoit outrez, il deslient la damoisele que moult estoit afobloiee. Et

30 lors quant ele fu en sa delivre poestez, ele demande ou est li chevalier que delivree l'a, et l'en li dist:

—Dame, il s'en est montez et mis en un sentiers que conduist en la foreste.

—Ha! lasse, fait elle, adonc m'a lessé il ensint entre les mains de

35 cellui que tant durement me het.

Et lors appelle un sien vaslet, et cil i fu venuz erraument et dist:

—Dame, veés me ci.

—Montez, fait ele, et t'en va a esperon et di au chevalier de par moi que il re[f.1b][tort arrieres et doint ceste tour que il a gaaignie]e a

40 aucun chevaliers que bien la sache guarder. Et se il ne le fait ensint, il a enfrante la costume de Logres.

§ 4. Lors monta li vaslet et s'en vet a esperon et troeve Perceval que desor une piere estoit arestez. Desor cele piere avoit letres escrites que disoient que Merlins li sage avoit[19] escrite de ses propres mains et

45 enteglees les avoit desor cele piere au tens que il estoit en cele foreste avec la Dame dou Lac.

§ 5. Les letres disoient ensint: 'Au tens que les homes et les femes dou siecle oblieront les veves dames et li orpheni[n]s pour cui les aumosnes furent establies a doner et les doneront as novels religieus, Damledex, le

[19] § 4.44. *EN* reads *les avoit*, but *P* agrees with *M*. The order of words in this sentence is peculiar: one would expect to read: 'que Merlins li sage les avoit escrite de ses propres mains et enteglees desor . . .'. It is possible, though not certain, that 'les avoit' which in all the MSS. follows *enteglees* was introduced as a result of contamination with 'les avoit escrite'.

50 gardeor des veves dame et des orphenins, e[n] mostrera signe de corroz.[20]
Les gens embleront les blés et la pluie ensement, por ce que il embleront
les aumosnes as veves dames et as orpheni[n]s et les doneront a cels que
n'en doivent avoir part, ne selonc Deu ne selonc reison, que il seront
assez, preudomes, et poront bien laborer les terres et doner as autres.

55 Et li demanderont ce que il n'en doivent avoir part. Les orphenins
seront obbliez et les veves dames por cels que bien poront gaaigner lor
vitailles'. Et quant li vaslet fu venuz desor lui et voit que il regardoit
les letres si ententivement, il s'areste et fu illec tant que Perceval meïsme
l[i] domanda que il queroit. Et li vaslet dist tot ce que la damoisele li

60 mandoit.

—Amis, fait Perceval, retorne arriere et aporte moi engre et
parchemin, que je voil esscrire ces letres que li sage Merlins enscrit de
ses propres mains.

§ 6. Et lors retorne li vaslet ariere au ferir des esperons et prist engre

65 et parchemin et les aporta a Perceval. Et cil le prist et mist dedenz cele
carte tot ce que il trova desor cele piere, et puis la mist en s'amosniere.

Quant Perceval ot mis en escrit tot ce que ge vos ai dit, il s'en retorna
avec li vaslet. Et lors quant la damoisele le voit venir, ele s'en vet a
l'encontre et puis se mist a genouz davant lui et li dist:

70 —Ha! sire, l'ore que vos fustes nez soit beneoite. Vos m'avez
delivrez de peril de mort. Que Damedex vos delivre des poines d'enfer.
Sire, por Dex, puis que tant de bien m'avez fait, ge vos pri que ceste
tor que vos avez gaaigniez soit donee a un tel chevalier que bien la
sache garantir [f. 1c] encontre les traïtors de celui païs. Et sachiez cer-

75 teinement que ge ne les ai refusé a prendre por mariz fors solement que
je les conois a traïtors et a robeors des chemins. Et se ge en eüs[se] pris
aucun il eüst la tor [aba]tue maugrez miens. Et si vos dirai por quoi.
Sire, il ne vivent d'autre chose fors que il derobent les mercheante, et

---

[20] § 5.50. One would expect after *corroz* some example of God's anger—such
as the remark 'la terre en tranblera' which we find in *ENR*. But the reading of
ENR is not correct either as it stands, for the 'wheat and the rain' cannot also
tremble as they seem to do in *ENR*. Perhaps originally we had a combination of
the reading of *M* and *ENR*: 'Damledex . . . en mostrera signe de corroz: la
terre en tranblera. Les gens embleront les blés et la pluie ensement . . .'. *P*, or
rather the MS. on which it is based, omitted, it seems, as a result of a *saut du
même au même* the words 'en tranblera les gens', and a later scribe changed 'la
terre' into 'les terres' on account of the pl. vb. 'embleront'. The phrase 'les gens
embleront les blés et la pluie ensement' may seem odd at first sight, but I take it
to mean that 'widows and orphans being deprived of the alms which are given
to those who do not need them' is as if 'people remove both the wheat and the
rain'.

por ce que les mercheant se herbegerent ici dedenz, si la he[e]nt il et
80 moi avec.

§ 7. —Damoisele, fait Perceval, se lor[s] quant [je] me combatoie
a celui que vos fist lier si cruelment me fust tesmoignez sa desloiautez
en tel maniere com vos le dites, il ne fust de ligiers esscapez de mes
mains, mes puis que ge l'ai quitez, ge ne li ai plus que demander. De
85 l'autre part que vos me dites que vos done ceste tor a un tel chevalier
que bien la sache garantir encontre les traïtor de cestui païs, je ne
conois les ques sunt traÿtors ne les autres, se vos ne le m'ensegnez.

—Sire, fait la damoisele, il vos estuet ceste nuit herbergier ici
dedenz, et si vos dirai por quoi. Celui a quoi ge bee et qu'est loiaus et
90 deboneire n'est pas chevalier. A l'endemain le faites chevalier, et puis
li donez mon cors a fame et la tor por garder. Et ge li donerai un si
tres grant tresor por endoaire²² que un rois coronez en [s]eroit bien
apaiez.

Lors descent Perceval de son cheval et dist:
95 —Ma damoisele, puis que la costume de Logres en gist, ja ne sera
par moi fausee. Viegne li vaslet avant, que ceste nuit li estuet voillier
en l'eglise, et a l'endemain le ferai ge chevalier.

§ 8. Et lors envoie la damoisele por son vaslet a cui ele baoit et jors
et nuit. Et cil i fu venuz erraument. La nuit orent a soper grant plantés
100 de viandes, et li vaslet voilla en la chapele dusque au lever des estoilles
jornal.²³ Et quant li [jours] fu venuz se leva Perceval et puis s'en ala

---

²¹ § 7.81. The reading of *M* 'lore quant il me combatoient' is clearly an error.

²² § 7.101. *endoaire*. Godefroy (III, 133c) records the vb. *endouairer* (to provide
with a dowry), but the noun *endoaire* is not recorded in either Godefroy or
Tobler-Lommatzsch, the normal word for dowry being *douaire*. The form
endoaire is however attested by another MS. (see *Sorelois*, p. 280, l. 125: *por
endoaire*).

²³ § 8.101. *au lever des estoilles jornal*. The *estoilles jornal* are the morning stars
or planets which precede the dawn. Cf. Philipe de Thaün's *Cumpoz* (ed. E. Mall,
1873) l. 2795-808:

> *De Terra et Planetis*
> *E es altres reiuns*
> *Ai enposez les nuns*
> *Des esteiles reials*
> *Qu'apelum principals,*
> *Que en Latin numum*
> *Planetes par raisun.*
> La terre dedenz pent,
> L'airs tut entur s'estent,
> Si cum truvum lisant

oïr le servise. Et li provoire en[24] beneïst les armes dont li vaslet en[24] fu adobez. Et lors li ceinst Perceval la spee et puis li dona la colee et li dist que Dex li face preudome. Et quant il fu chevalier, il li dona la tor et la damoisele a feme. Que vos diroe je? Tant prierent trestuit Perceval que il remest avec aus. Mes atant lesse li contes a parler de ceste aventure, que bien i savra retorner et parole de Golistanz li Fort, li filz li bon Morholt d'Irlande [f. 1d].

§ 9. Ci endroit dit li contes que tant erra Golistanz li Fort, li filz li bon Morholt d'Irlande, aprés ce que il se parti da la damoisele quant il trencha la teste au jaiant et que il li dist qu'ele fust donee a Lamorat, que la nuit vint. Et lors se herberja desoz un arbre. Il aloit cerchant Seguranz li Brun por ce que de sa main voloit estre chevalier. Endementiers que il s'en voloit endormir avint que il oï une voiz que crioit: 'Aïe, aïe!, Dex aide', disoit la voiz, 'cheï onques mes nulle damoisele en si leide meins com ge sui cheüe?' Et quant Golistanz li Fort que ja estoit couchiez desor son escuz oï ce, il leve la teste et escoute. Et bien li fu avis que c'estoit une damoisele et que celui che la tenoit la conduisoit cele part. Il se lieve erraument en estant et prist sa spee que il avoit reponue en un erbois,[25] et puis prist son escuz par les enarmes et regarde au rais de la lune et voit que il estoit un home que trainoit une damoisele par les treces, et cele damoisele crioit tote voies.

Lors escrie Golistanz a haute voiz et dist:

—Ha! mauvés home, vos estes venuz a vostre mort.

§ 10. Et quant celui oï la voiz, il leisse la damoisele et hoste sa spee del fuere et s'adrece encontre Golistanz li Fort que ja li venoit a l'encontre, sa spee levee encontre mont. Li home que la damoisele avoit trainee done un cox a Golistanz si dur et si aspre que quant la bone espee en prist[18] de li escuz que Golistanz li gita encontre, en trencha tot

> En Ovide le grant
> Enz es devisemenz
> Qu'il fait des elemenz.
> *Les esteiles reials*
> *Que apelum jurnals*

Cf. also Book of Job, XXXVIII, 7: 'When the morning stars sang together, and all the sons of God shouted for joy'.

[24] § 8.102. *EN* have neither the first nor the second *en*. The first *en* may mean 'consequently', 'as a result of this', but the second is pleonastic or due to a scribal error.

[25] § 9.120. *en un erbois*. Either this is another case of wrong flexion (*erbois* for *erboi*), or we have here the noun *erbois* of which only a very few examples are recorded in Godefroy (IV, 458a) and Tobler-Lammatzsch (fasc. 23, p. 752).

130   contreval la terre. Et puis li voloit doner de rechieff, mes Golistanz ne
      li soffre pas, ainz se fiert en lui si durament que il [l']abati a la terre tot
      envers. Et la damoisele li esscrie et dist:
      —Ha! sire, por Dex, trenchiez li la teste.
      —Non ferai, fait Golistanz, que ge ne sui pas chevalier. Et se il fust
135   chevalier, adonc seroe ge honiz.

                              Fragment B

      § 11. [f. 2a] . . . Ou sont les [. . .] [sol]iez mantenir parmi le roiaume
      de Logres? Ou sont les puceles orphenines que vos soliez marier? Ou
      sont les noveaux chevaliers que vos soliez adober? Certes, vos n'estes
      pas celui rois que le m[o]stiers soliez estorer parmi les forestes. Ou sont
   5 li chapelains que estoient acostumez de aler environ vos et les evesques
      et les arcevesque et les abbés et les autres prelaz? Certes, il vos vont
      trestuit fuiant. Quant vos entrez en sainte gleyse trestuit s'en fuient
      hors. Vostre grant cort est remesse a Danguenet. Et neporquant, il est
      si deboneire que l'en i trove a grant plantee les viandes.
  10   § 12. —Sagremors, ce dit li roi Artu, se ma grant cort est empiree,
      ele n'est pas empiree par moi solement. Mes compaignons en ont
      grant corpes, que combien que ge n'eüsse a cestui point volentez de
      joie demener, il ne me deüssent ensint dou tot deguerpir, que l'en solt
      dire em proverbe que au besoing conoist l'en son ami, et dusque la ne
  15 le puet l'en conoistre. Il est voirs que il n'est mervoille de estre corociez,
      mes il seroit mervoilles de estre a toz jors mes en celui corrox. Mes amis
      et mon linage me troverent corociez, dont il lor fu avis que ge i
      deüs[se] estre corociez a toz jors mes, et por ce s'en aloient il en lor
      païs. Dont il m'ont si corociez que ja mes ne serai liez. Se Danguenot
  20 est sire de ma cort, il m'est moult bel puis que il done a mangier a
      trestoz, ensint con la costume de ma cort le requiert. Et autresint
      voudroie ge que il donast mariz as orphenins del tresor de ma chambre.
      Et les vaslet voudroe ge que il adobas[t], et bien le poroit il fere, que il
      est assez gentix home. De l'autre part, se les prelanz me vont fuiant, il
  25 ne sont pas sages, que il en perdent les offrendes de ma chambre; que
      vos savés apertement que il avoient chascun jors une mars d'arjant sanz
      la despense que il avoient de ma cort.
         § 13. —Adont, fait Sagremors, volez vos tex estre con vos estes
      orendroit trestoz vos aage?

30 —Oïl, ce dit li roi Artu, puis que mon linage le veut.

—Dex aide, fait Sagremors li Desreez, ne savez vos li grant destorbiers que nos cort audesus?

—Et quex destorbiers? ce dit li roi Artu.

—Sire, fait Sagremors, les Sesnes s'en vont a Vincestre a si grant
35 plantee des paiens que trestoz li roiaume de Logres en est en aventure.

—Se il vient a Vincestre, fait li roi Artu, il se deffandent encontre aus, que ja ne metrai mon piez cele part.

§ 14. Quant Sagremors oï ce, il commence a plorer trop durement. Et lors s'en entre li roi Artu e[n] sa chambre. [f. 2b] Grant piece plore.
40 Il s'en vient em mi la sale la ou il troeve Danguenet, si li dist:

—Danguenet, les Sesnes s'en vient a Vincestre. Que baez vos a fere?

—Sire, fait il, ge ai mis en les coffres roial les mehailles por doner la soldee, dont ge vos di apertement que a l'endemain en començarai
45 ge a paier les chevaliers que vivent d'armes et les autres homes, et si ai mandez par toz le roiaume de Logres que trestuit soient appareilliez petiz et grant des armes et des chevax.

—Por saint croix, fait Sagremors, vos en avez tant fait que vos en devez estre loez de totes parz et li rois blasmez.

50 —Taisiez, fait Danguenet, ne tenez parlement de lui, que il est a moi. Il m'ot donez le roiaume aprés sa mort. Ge em porterai corone, que il ne vivra longement.

§ 15. Et domentiers que il parloient entr'aus avint que monseignor Gauveins vint a cort entre lui e Mordret son frere, et avoient conduit
55 avec aus une grant chevalerie dou roiaume d'Orchanie. Mult li fist grant joie Danguenet et grant feste et dist:

—Sire, puis que vos estez venuz, ge voil que vos vos en alez a Vincestre en la compaignie de maint preudomes. Et ge en donerai la soldee a voz chevaliers, se il la volent prandre.

60 Et lors commence monseignor Gaveins a rire et dist:

—[Daguenet, estes vous connestables?]

—[Oïl, ce dit] Daguenet.

—Puis que vos l'estes, ce dit monseignor Gauveins, dahait ai ge se ga pour moi en serez ostez. Et a l'endemain en soit donez la soldee,
65 que l'en me vet contant que li Sesnes vient a Vincestre.

§ 16. A l'endemain fist crier Danguenet le comandement dou roi Artu que trestoz les chevaliers et les homes a piez que vivent d'arm[es] [v]iegnent prandre la soldee et s'en aillent a Vincestre avec monseignor Gauveins. Et lors s'en vient trestuit prandre la soldee et s'en vont a

70 Vincestre. Et monseignor Gaveins parla au roi Artu son oncle anceis
que il s'en alast et dist:

—Sire, que baez vos a fere? Les Sesnes nos vient veoir.

—Se il vient ceste part, fait li roi Artu, ge deffendrai moult bien
ceste ville entre moi et mes amis.

75 —Avez vos point d'amis? ço dit monseignor Gauveins.

—Oïl, assez, fait li roi Artu.

§ 17. Et lors crolla monseignor Gauveins la teste et s'en ala devant
lui moult corociez. Les chevaliers estoient appareilliez pour monter et
les autres genz que a lor despense devoient aler selonc lor pooir, que

80 auques par tans li avoit fait Danguenet li commandement que il fussent
appareilliez et des armes et de viandes. Et quant monseignor Gauveins
fu aval descenduz, il troeve mervoilles [f. 2c] de genç que l'atendoit.
Et quant il le virent venir, il s'escrient et dient:

—Sire, ou est li confanon roial? Certes, ja de ci ne departirons se

85 vos ne le faites aporter devant vos.

Et il respont et dist:

—Seignors, li roi Artus n'est pas en bone memoire. La cort est a
Danguenet.

—Et puis que ele est a Danguenet, font il, et Danguenet viegne et

90 vos done li confanon roial.

Et lors commencent trestuit a rire et ap[elerent] Danguenet que la
soldee fesoit doner:

—Ven[e]z, venez Danguenet et aportez li confanon roial por
doner a monseignor Gauveins.

95 Lors se lieve Danguenet delez Sagremors lez cui il seoit et dist:

—Sagremors, ne vos poise dusque ge reviegne.

Et il respont:

—Alez. A Dex vos commant!

§ 18. Que vos diroe ge? Danguenet entra en la chambre et avec lui

100 grant compaignie des genz et pristrent li confanon roial et puis desvalent li degrez et s'en entrent en la maistre eglyse. Et illec s'en vient
monseignor Gauveins et prist li confanon roial que Danguenet fist
metre desor l'autel ensint com monseignor Gauvein le requist. Quant
li roial confanon dou roiaume de Logres fu aportez devant, lors

105 montent les chevaliers et s'en vo[nt] aprés les homes a piez que ja
estoient mis el chemin que conduisoit a Vincestre. Que vos diroe ge?
Tant errent par lor jornees que il furent venuz au chastel de Doivre ou
Meleaganz estoit. Et lors quant monseignor Gauveins se voloit herbergier dedenz, Meleaganz li mande et dist [au] message que il n'en

110 puet herbergier [et que] il s'en aille en autre part.

—En [n]on Deu, fait monseignor Gauvein, c'est outrage. Li
castellaus[26] n'est pas a lui, ainz est a monseignor li roi Artu.

Et lors se mist environ le chastel que grant peor avoit que Meleaganz
n'en face aucune traïson ou par mauvestié ou par aucun grant tresor
115 que li Sesnes li donassent. Il le conoist a traïtres et a felon et a home de
mauvese foiz. Quant Meleaganz voit celui forfait et que monseignor
Gauvein se herberjoit environ le chastel, il s'apuie desor un dois et
commence a penser moult durement. Et quant il a une grant piece
penseç, il parole et dist a ses homes:

120 § 19. —Seignors chevaliers, que vos semble de l'orgoil de Gavein,
[f. 2d] li neveu dou roi Artu? Certes, il nos tient a traïtres et a desleals.
Fason le bien. Ge voil que entre moi et lui soit une joste tres devant
cestui chastel. Se il me pora abatre de mon cheval, il se herbergera ici
dedenz, et se ge abat lui, il s'en aille a Vincestre et vos leisse ici dedenz.
125 Et la joste soit ma[in]tenue d'une liace de gleive por chascun.

Et lors respont un chevalier de Goret et dist:

—Sire, se vos chaez andox?

Et Meleaganz respont et dist:

—Se andox sentons la terre, andox s'en aille a Vincestre et li
130 chastelaus soit donez en autre garde.

Ensint com il le dist ensint le manda Meleaganz a monseignor
Gauvein. Et quant il oï ce, il commence a rire et dist au message:

—Beaus amis, puis que Meleaganz veut la joste, ja de par moi ne
sera refusee. Mes tant voil ge que vos li dites de par moi que se nos
135 cheons andox, ge donerai la garde dou chastel [. . .].

§ 20. Et lors s'en retorne li message ariere et conte les convenances a
Meleaganz. Et quant il oï ce, sachiez certeinement que il demande ses
armes. Et celui les li aportent que les avoient en garde. Quant Meleaganz
fu armez, il monte en son cheval tres devant le chastel de Doivre et
140 fist aporter .ii. liaces de gleive et envoie l'une a monseignor Gauvein
que ja estei[t] armez et montez desor un cheval que auques estoit fort
et ysnel. Lors prist chascun un gleive et l[ei]ssent core li un encontre
l'autre au ferir des esperon; si durement s'entrefier[en]t desor lor escus
que andox s'entrebatent a la terre par desor les cropes de lor chevax.
145 Et lors se lievent andox corociez et ploins de mautalanz et eüssent
encomenciee illec la battaille as espeez trenchanz se ne fussent lor

---

[26] § 18.112 and § 19.130. *castellaus, chastelaus*. Neither Godefroy (IX, 58) nor
Tobler-Lommatzsch (fasc. 10, p. 306) record *chastelaus* as a variant form of
chastelet. *E* has *chastiaus*.

chevalier que ne lor soffre pas.

—Meleaganz, Meleagans, fait monseignor Gauvein, trop estes orguilleus.

150 Et lors fait Meleaga[n]z crier son banz que trestoz cels que a lui ssont s'en viegnent aprés lui. Meleaganz s'en vet d'une pars a tote sa gent et monseignor Gauvein de l'autre aprés ce que il ot donez la garde dou chastel a un chevalier de la citez de Londres. Et lors se herberge monseignor Gauveins en Vincestre auques pres de Meleaganz. Mes atant
155 lesse li contes a parler de ceste aventure et parole de Perceval li Galois.

VARIANTS

§ 1.1. Lors prent Percheval son escu par lez enarmes et le gete devant son vis, et puis oste s'espee du fuerre *E*; s'espee—*the top of the line has been cut away in M, but from what remains it is clear that there are in M two words after* espee

2. teste a plain cop *E*

4. en prent et abat *E*

5. Perceval qui *E*

5. en *om. E*

6. [le] *om. M*

6–7. que il [le] fait engenoillier . . . desor li hiaume *om. E* (*saut du même au même*)

10. [se] *om. M* que se li ne prent garde de soi que il *E*, que se il ne se prent garde de ses cols il n'en *N*

11. vis et avoec çou il voit *N*

11. [ne] *om. M* se il ne le prent *E*

12. duree a ce que *EN*

13. de grant aage *E*

13. *after* lui *M has deleted* et dist

13. et lors s'adrece vers lui *om. E*

14. a toute *E*

14. [l'] *om. M*

14. de tote sa force *om. N*

14. l'abat *N*, l'abati *E*

16. la ventaille *EN*

16. a cauper *EN*

16. ne li quite *E*

17. et ne fiance prison *om. N*

18–19. et vous fianche (*N* fiancerai) prison sauve *EN*

19. me *om. E*

19. prison de *E*, en la prison a *N*

§ 2.20. prist maintenant Perceval *N*

20. li rendi *N*

21. desour lui et li chevaliers *N*

21. *after* dist *M has deleted* que en lius de prison li comande

20–21. et puis se lieve en estant. Et li chevalierz fu levez de desous lui et dit a Perceval *E*

23. Perceval li respont *EN*

23. et dist *om. EN*

23–24. en leu de prison se gart tous les jours de sa vie et li chevaliers *E*, commande il que tous les jours de sa vie se garde de femme prendre a forche, car quant vous la prenderés au miex que vos porés tout par sa volenté, si vous fera ele assés de wisques (=guisches) *N*

25. dit *E*

25. gardera d'ore en avant se Diu plaist *N*

§ 3.28. fust desliee *N*

28. ceus qui *E*, cil ki *N*

28. orent *N*

29. deslient atant *N*

29–30. qui moult estoit fort liee. Et quant la damoisele fu *E*, ki mout durement estoit afebloiee. Et quant la damoisiele fu *N*

31. ki *N*, ou est celui qui *E*

32. damoiselle il est montés *E*, il s'en est tournés et s'est mis *N*

32. qui conduist a la *E*, qui conduist a aler a la forest *N*

34. fet elle, me laisse il dont entre *E*, fait ele, me laissera il dont ensi entre *N*

35. a celui qui tant me het durement *EN*

36. apele errammant *N*

36. cil fu *N*

36. dit *E*

37. veest *M*

38. monte *EN*

38. ele or t'en va *E*, ele erraument et t'en va *N*

39. si doinst *N*

39. re[tort . . . gaaignie]e. *The top of M has been cut away. The words in brackets have been supplied from EN*

40. que que bien *M*

40. qui bien le sache *EN*

40. il en a enfrainte *E*

41. coustume du païs et du roiaume de Logres *E*

§ 4.42. monte *E*, monta erranment li v. *N*

42. trouva *N*

42. qui *EN*

43–§ 6.66. *The substance of this section has been preserved in Rennes MS. 593 [R] (ed. L. A. Paton, pp. 260–1) and in the 1498 printed edition of the*

Prophécies de Merlin [P]. *The latter begins this portion with the following*
rubric: 'Des hommes et des femmes qui oublieront les veufves dames
et les orphelins'

43. Ci dit li contes que Percheval s'estoit arestés sus une pierre, ou il
avoit letres escriptes *R*, Or dit le compte et la vraye histoire le
tesmongne que dessus celle pierre avoit lettres escriptes *P*

43–46. que disoient . . . Dame dou Lac *not in R* (*P agrees with M*)

43. qui disoient *ENP*

44. les avoit *EN* (*P agrees with M*)

44–5. sez mains propres et entabletees *E*, se propre main et entabletees *N*

45. avoient *M*, avoit il seur (*N desor*) *EN*, avoit dessus *P*

45. au tans que il vivoit et que il estoit *EN*, au temps qu'il estoit en la
forest *P*

§ 5.47. ces letres *N*

47. au tens *om. P*

48. dou siecle *om. ENRP*

48. veves famez *E*

48. orphenins et les povres pour *N*

49. furent establies a donner quant la chose qui jadis nasquit es parties de
Jerusalem avra mil deux centz dix huit ans et les donneront *P*

49. donront as religious et aus noviax religieus *E*, donront as nouvieles
relegions *N*, donront as nouveles religious et as noviaus religeus *R*
(*P agrees with M*)

49. relegions Damedius lor guerdounera li gardeors *N*, religieux Nostre
Seigneur gardeur *P*

50. veves fames *E*

50. e mostrera *M en ENRP*

50. signes de courous. La terre en tranblera lez blés *ENR*, signe de cour-
roux. Les terres embleront les blez et la pluye semblablement pour
ce qu'ilz *P*

51. ensement puis que il *E*

52. veves fames *E*

52–3. donront qui ne les doivent pas avoir ne contre Dieu ne contre
raison *E*, donront a chiaus ki nes doivent pas (*R mie*) avoir ne selonc
NR, donneront a ceulx qui n'y doivent avoir part selon *P*

54. et doner as autres *om. E*

55. demanderont ce ou il ne doivent *ENR*, demanderont ce qu'ilz ne
doyvent pas avoir part *P*

55. part orphelins *P*, nule partie et les orfelins *R*

56. orfelins et les veves fames seront oubliees pour ceus qui *ER*, veufves
dames par ceulx qui *P*

56–7. gaaignier leur terres *E*

57–66. vitailles. Lors quant Percheval ot leues ces letres que Merlin avoit
escriptes de sa main, si les mist en escrit Percheval en une chartre, que

il mist en s'aumosniere. Mes atant se test li contes de ceste aventure et retourne as profecies de Merlin le sage R, vitailles. Mais tant vueil je que les nouveaulx religieux saichent de par moy que si celle envie ne fust entr'eulx que moult fust a louer sa bonne vie et sa bonne penitence et son conseil. Mais celle le trestournera et fera les gens du siecle parler de soy et d'eulx. Mais atant laisse le compte a parler de ceste prophecie et retourne a parler d'une aultre prophecie de Merlin P

57. fu desor lui venus N
57. et il vit EN
59. la M, li EN
59. demanda ki il estoit et que il queroit N
59. li dist EN
61. dist Perceval N
61. et m'aporte anque EN
62. escrit EN
§ 6.64. li vallés retorne arrieres EN
65. l'aporta E, le porta N
65. i mist M, et il la prist et mist EN
66. tot cele que—the scribe of M has expunged the last two letters of cele
66. trouva escrit seur E
67. mis om. E
67. vous ai conté il s'en N
69. se met EN
69. dit E
70. ha! sire, beneoite soit l'eure que vous fustes nés, car vous m'avés E
71. vous voille delivrer E
72. proi que vous ceste tour que vous N
73. a tel N
73. qui bien EN
74. cestui EN
75-6. jou ne sui refussee a marier fors seulement pour çou que N, refusés a maris fors seulement pour ce que je les sent traitors et robeors E
76. eust M, eusse EN
77. tor tue M, abatue EN
78. sire saciés vraiement que il ne N
78. fors que de desrober N
79. et om. E
80. moi autresi N
§ 7.81-2. lore quant il me combatoient M, lors quant je me combatoie a celui qui EN
82. fist aler lier E
82-3. sa desleauté si cruelement conme vous me dites, il ne me E
83. ainsint de legier EN

83. des mes *M*, de *EN*
84. ge les ai quitez *M*, l'ai quité *EN*
85. part de çou que *N*
86. qui bien *EN*
86. sace garder encontre *N*
87. les ques sont boins ne lez ques sont malvais se vous *E*
88. nuit a h. *N*
88. il convient que vous herbergiés annuit mais ci dedens *E*
89. qui ge bee et (*N om.* et) qui *EN*
91-2. donrai si tres *N*, donrai si tres grant douaire de tresor que .i. grant rois *E*
92. en feroit *M*, en seroit *N*, s'en tendroit a bien *E*
95. coustume est tele ja ne sera *E*
95. i gist *N*
96. avant de par Diu car puis que ensi est iceste nuit *N*
97. l'eglyse et le matin le ferai chevalier *N*, nuit li converra veillier en l'eglize et demain le ferai *E*
§ 8.98.–9 et jour et nuit et jour *E*
99. cil i vint *N*
99. a grant *E*; orent a grant plenté a souper, mout de boines viandes *N*
100. veilla la nuit en la capele *N*
101. des estoiles jornax *EN*
101. quant li rois fu *M*, quant il fu jour se leva *EN*
102. en *om. EN*
102. en *om. EN*
103. adoubés. Et Percheval li chaint l'espee *EN*
104. preudoume, et puis li douna la tour *N*
105. Perceval *om. E*, proierent Percheval trestout que *N*
106. avoec iaus la nuit *N*
107-8. et parole de Morgain la fee et de Sebile l'enchanteresse et de Breus Sans Pitié *EN*
§ 9.109. filz au bon *FHE*
110. departi *FHE*
111. quant il ot caupé la teste *E*
111. Lamorat de Galez *E*
112. qui la nuit *FHE*
114. se vouloit *FHE*
114. qui crioit *FHE*
115. aide aide Sainte Marie Dieus aide *FHE*
115. faisoit la vois car onques *H*
116. mauvaises mains *H*
117. qui ja *FE*, ki la *H*
118. bien *om. H*
118. qui la tenoit *FHE*

119. en estant *om. FHE*
119. prent *E*
120. reposte *FE,* reprise *H*
121. que c'estoit *FHE*
121. qui trainoit *FHE*
123. a haute voiz *om. E*
123. dit *E*
124. home a haute voiz vous estez *E*
124. a la mort *H*
§ 10.126. qui ja *FHE*
127. l'espee *FHE*
127. l'oume qui *FHE*
128. Golistans si grant et si aspre que quanquez *E*
129. em prent de l'escu Golistanz que il geta *FHE*
130. a la terre *FHE*
130. redonner *E*
131. pas *om. F;* mie *H*
131. [l'] *om. M* l'abati *EF,* l'abat *H*
131-2. tout estendu *H,* du tot enverz *E*
132. esscrie et *om. E;* et dist *om. H*
133. por Dex *om. FH;* copez li la teste *E*
134. dist *H,* ce dit *FE;* mie *E*
135. se il est *H,* se il estoit *E*
§ 11.1. [. . .] *the top of M has been cut away;* ou sunt li grant tornoiement que vous soliez *EH*
4. rois Artus *E*
4. mestiers *M,* qui les moustiers *EH*
5. chapelain qui soloient aler et venir (*H om.* et venir) environ vous et les evesquez *EH*
6. et li autre prouvoire et li prelat *H*
7-8. eglise il (*H* tout *for* il) fuient hors. Certes (*H om.* certes) vostre cort qui moult estoit grant est remese *EH*
8. Daguenet *EH* (*this is the form found throughout EH*)
9. des viandes *E*
§ 12.10. segnor, ce dit *E* (*H has the correct reading* Saigremor)
10. Artu *om. EH*
11. mais mi compaignon *H*
11. i ont *E*
12-13. point point de joie ne volenté de leesce demourer *H*
13. deussent mie du tout guerpir *E,* deusse mie avoir pour ce dou tout deguerpit *H*
13-14. set (*H* seut) dire en reprovier *EH*
14. au besoi[n]g voit l'en son ami *EH*
15. connoistre son ami *E*

5

15–16. que ce n'est mie mervelle . . . mes il est nerveille d'estre tous
   jors en courouz *E*, que çou n'en est pas merveille se jou estoie cou-
   rouciés et çou n'est pas bon d'estre tous jours courouchiet *H*

17. courouchiés par coi il lor *E*

18. deust *M*, je deusse *EH*

18. s'en vont *E*, s'en sunt il alét *H*

19. dont *om. H*

19. sera il liez *M*, serai liés *EH*

20. il n'en est *E*

20. mangiers *M*

21. coustume de cort *H*, coustume est et que ma cort le requiert *E*

21. et tout autresi *H*

22. voudrai que il mariast les orfelins (*H* les autres orfenes) *EH*

22. orfenes et pucelles a qui il est besoins dou tresor *H*

23. lez chevaliers voudroie *EH*

23. adobassent *M*, adoubast *EH*

24. d'autre *E*

25. *after* perdent les *of H breaks off on f.* 69a *H continues with the adventures
   of Palamedes and Saphar.*

27. de cort *E*

§ 13.29–30. comme vous avés esté tous les jors de vo vie. Oïl, fet li rois *E*

32. qui vous cort sus *E*

33. fet li rois *E*

34. s'en vienent *E*

35. plenté de *E*

35. tous *E*

36. vienent *E*

36. Artus si se *E*

37. n'i metrai *E*

39. e sa

§ 14.39–40. e sa lors s'en va li rois en sa chambre et le lesse illuec. Et quant
   Sagremor vit ce il s'en vient en mi la sale et la *E*

39. ploreç *M*

41. vienent ceste part a Vincestre. Que en *E*

43. en mez coffres reaus mes maailles *E*

45. qui vivent *E*

46. tuit soient aparlié *E*

47. d'armes et de *E*

50. a lui *E*

51. m'a *E*

§ 15.53. endementiers que il parloient ensanle vint monsigneur Gauvain a cort
   entre et lui et *E*

54–5. aconduit une grant compaignie de chevalerie *E*

55. lor fist *E*

59. les soudees a vos chevalierz *E*

60. dit *E*

61-2. Daguenet, estez vous connestablez?—Oïl, ce dit Daguenet. Puis que vous l'estes *E* (*saut du même au même in M*)

64. par moi en estez *E*

65. s'en vienent *E*

§ 16.67. Artu *om. E*

67-8. arm[es] [v]iegnent—*there is a hole in M*

69. lorz vienent tuit *E*

70. Artu *om. E*

70. oncle a l'endemain avant qu'il *E*

71. dit *E*

72 *and* 73. vienent *E*

73. moult *om. E*

75. vous nus amis fet mesire *E*

§ 17.77. en crolla *E*; la teste *om. E*

77. s'en parti de devant *E*

79. qui *E*

81. apareilliez d'armes *E*

82. gens qui l'atendent *E*

85. porter *E*

86. dit *E*

87. mie *E*

90. nous donne *E*

91. riere *M*

91-92. rire et a parler *M*, rire et apelerent Daguenet qui lez soudeez fesoient donner venés *E* (a parler *is undoubtedly a scribal error for* apelerent)

93. venz *M*

95. et lors *E*; Daguenet qui delez Sagremor seoit *E*

96. seigneur ne *E*; jusques atant que je *E*

97-98. respont et dit, alés de ci *E*

§ 18.101. degrés et se metent en la *E*

102. roial *om. E*

105. vos *M*, vont *E*

103-6. requist. Quant li roiaumez ot baillié le gonfanon a monseigneur Gauvain il se mist au chemin entre lui et li chevalier et home a pié s'en vont aprés et s'en vont le droit chemin qui conduisoit a Vincestre *E*

107. que il vindrent a Douvre *E*

109-110. herbergier dedens, et lorz si voit autre part *E* (*saut du même au même in E*)

109. Mealeaganz *M*—*the scribe has expunged the first* a

109. [au] *and* 110. [et que]—*there is a hole in M*

112. li chastiaus *E*
113. ot *E*
114. par ve *M—the scribe has expunged* ve
115-16. il le sentent a si desloial et a si felon et a homme de mauvaise foi *E*
116. vit *E*
118. penser trop d. *E*
119. dit *E*
§ 19.121. neveu au *E*
123. ce *E*
123. puet abatre *E*
124. l'abat il *E*
124. dedenz *om. E*
125. des gleive *M*
125. maintenue d'une lanche, voire d'une liache toute entiere por cascun *E*
126. Gorre *E*; dit *E*
128. *first* et *om. E*; dit *E*
129. aillons *E*
130. chastiaus *E*
130. a autre *E*
131. dit le manda *E*
132. dit *E*
133. ja par *E*
134. diez *E*
135. *both M and E appear to have omitted some words after* chastel
§ 20.136. lors en retorne arrierez li mesage *E*
137. couvenenches, celes que mesire Gauvain avoit dit. Et quant il oï ce, sachiez *E*
137. que *om. E*
138. gardent *M—the scribe has expunged the last two letters;* les i aporte qui en garde lez avoit *E*
139. monta *E*
139. Douvre *E*
140. des gleive *M*, de glaves et en voie *E*
141. qui *E*
141. estoie *M*, esteit *E*
141. montez en *E*
141. qui *E*
142. pristent *E*
142. liessent *M*
143. s'entrefiert *M*, esperons et lors s'entrefierent si durement deseur les escus *E*
144. des chevals *E*
146. eussent iluec commenchié la meslee as espees *E*

146–47. li autre chevalier qui *E*

147. *E has the same reading as M:* suefre

148. ce dist *E*

150. fait crier Meleagant que tuit li chevalier qui a lui sont *E*

151. aprés lui. Et lorz s'en va Meleagant a toute sa gent d'une part et mesire *E*

Some Observations on the Style of the Grail Castle Episode in Chrétien's *Perceval*

A. D. CROW

Fellow and Tutor of Oriel College, Oxford

The Grail Castle episode, if we regard it as beginning at the moment when Perceval takes his leave of the procession of monks and nuns he had encountered on the outskirts of Belrepeire, covers a timespan of exactly twenty-four hours, from early morning on one day until dawn on the next. In this respect it might be said to resemble a much later masterpiece of French fiction, Flaubert's *Hérodias*, likewise a story of a man who, in the course of a night, and of a banquet, is faced with a dilemma, and makes the wrong decision. The times, incidentally, are as precisely noted by Chrétien as they are by Flaubert. The Fisher King opines that Perceval must have set out before dawn, (ll. 3126–7)[1] but Perceval assures him that it was after 'prime' (ll. 3128–9). When he woke up on the following morning in the Grail Castle 'l'aube del jor fu crevee' (l. 3357). *Hérodias* opens 'un matin, avant le jour . . .' and ends 'A l'instant où se levait le soleil'.[2] Flaubert, of course, was writing an independent *conte*; Chrétien simply one episode, if a major one, in a long *roman*. Even so he is obviously just as concerned as Flaubert to pinpoint for the reader the limits of the story. Flaubert would be aware of the concentration to be achieved by imposing on himself the unity of time which he had eschewed in the other two *contes*. Chrétien, who had never heard of the unity of time, nevertheless observes it too and achieves similar concentration. But then he too was not unfamiliar with the techniques of the short story— a form which was developing alongside of the *roman* in his own time (witness the *Lais* of his contemporary Marie de France and his own *juvenilia*). The apprenticeship which Chrétien had served in the

[1] References are to the edition of Alfons Hilka (*Der Percevalroman von Christian von Troyes*, Halle, 1932).

[2] *Hérodias*, in *Oeuvres complètes*, vol. 6 (Conard), pp. 138 and 190.

Ovidiana probably stood him in good stead when it came to composing a strictly limited *nouvelle*-like episode such as that of the Grail Castle, itself the culmination, aesthetically as well as thematically, of a process which began with the poet's first use of the 'invitation au château' motif in *Erec et Enide*. This is evident in the skilful engineering of this episode.

Within the twenty-four hours time span there is a quite clearly marked division into three contrasting stages or acts corresponding to the normal divisions of this span, viz. (a) day: the account of Perceval's journey to the river, his conversation with the Fisher King and his first sight, in the evening, of the Grail Castle; (b) night: the account of his night in the castle, the meal and the procession; (c) morning: the account of his awakening after dawn on the following morning, his fruitless search of the now apparently deserted building, and his undignified departure. In short it is an action which is complete in itself, which has a beginning, a middle and an end. This triptych arrangement is characteristic of Chrétien, and is found on a bigger scale in *Erec* and *Yvain*.[3] Here it is much more concentrated and much more dramatic. It is important to stress this, because it is from this rigour and spareness of the form that certain qualities of the style derive.

The first section is dominated by three motifs, which have their reflection in the style. The first of these is the increasing anxiety felt by Perceval about his mother, his prayers for her safety, his desire to find her. Chrétien had already been at pains to stress Perceval's preoccupation with his mother in the three successive speeches (the second in reported speech) in which the hero turns down the appeals of Gornemant, of Blancheflor and her household, and of the monks and nuns of Belrepeire, to remain with them (ll. 1580–92, 2917–32, 2952–71). This repetitive technique, with its recurrence of refrain-like phrases (Que pasmee la vi cheoir (l. 1584) Que il vit pasmee cheoir (l. 2919)) is almost certainly an adaptation to the purposes of the romance of the well-known epic device, plus variation and accretion of detail rendered, however, less mechanical by alternation of direct and indirect speech. In the account of Perceval's journey to the river, Chrétien continues to employ this technique, as he twice, again alternating indirect and direct

---

[3] For a dissenting view see however J. P. Collas, 'The Romantic Hero of the Twelfth Century' in *Medieval Miscellany presented to Eugène Vinaver*, Manchester University Press, 1965, pp. 84 and 94.

presentation,[4] shows Perceval praying to God that he may find his mother safe and well, and that he may be able to cross the river, on the other side of which he is convinced he will find her. Prayers, as Hilka points out,[5] are a common feature of epic style, but are very infrequent in the romances of Chrétien. His insertion of brief prayers (ll. 2980–4, 2970–93) at this point may perhaps be a pointer to his intentions, following as they do on the scene with the religious community of Belrepeire. In that scene Chrétien, using a parallel quite remarkable in its associations:

> Quand il fors de la vile issi,
> I ot autel procession
> Con s'il fust jorz d'ascension
> Ou autel come au diemoinne;   (ll. 2938–41)

had given Perceval the grave stature of a Christian knight and liberator.[6] His prayers, as he anxiously presses on through the utterly silent landscape, show his mind still turning towards Divine aid.

Effectively contrasted, however, with this forward-thrusting anxiety of the hero is the second motif, one of almost nightmarish frustration. Stylistically this is conveyed by repeated use of negation or of negative constructions. Perceval travels all day without meeting a soul:

> Qu'il n'ancontra rien terriiene
> Ne crestiien ne crestiiene
> Qui li seüst voie anseignier.   (ll. 2978–80)

The terms employed are interesting, and show the poet endeavouring to create an impression of a lonely pilgrimage through a landscape bereft of man and bereft of God. The style thus adumbrates the two themes of the hero's guilt towards his mother and of the stricken land which will be explicitly linked in the explanation given later by his cousin (ll. 3582–95). The river Perceval eventually reaches is so 'roide et parfonde' (l. 2988) that he dare not attempt the crossing:

> Si ne s'ose metre dedanz.   (l. 2989)

---

[4] On this alternation see A. Hilka, *Die direkte Rede als stilistisches Kunstmittel in den Romanen des Kristian von Troyes*, Halle, 1903, pp. 154–7.

[5] Ibid., pp. 98–9.

[6] Leo Pollmann has drawn attention to the importance of this passage in his *Chrétien de Troyes und der Conte del Graal*, Tübingen, 1965, pp. 112–14.

The Fisher King's boat, which he now sees coming downstream towards him, also frustrates him by halting out of his reach in midstream (ll. 3002–05). Quite at a loss, Perceval, described now by Chrétien as

> Cil qui ne set que feire puisse
> Ne an quel leu passage truisse   (ll. 3011–12)

rides along the bank, but even here his path is blocked:

> Et l'eve a cele roche atoche
> Si qu'il ne pot aler avant.   (ll. 2996–7)

He receives from the Fisher King a completely negative reply to his request for information about a crossing. The river, he is told, is impassable; there is no bridge, no ferry, no ford; it is impossible to get a horse across; there is no boat bigger than the one he sees for twenty leagues either way.

However, the Fisher King offers him a lodging for the night. Yet again there is frustration for Perceval. When, following his host's directions, he reaches the summit of the rock, instead of the house he had been told he would see, he finds, stretching 'mout loing devant lui' (l. 3038) the same desolate landscape as before:

> Et ne vit rien fors ciel et terre.   (l. 3039)

Thus, by this constant use of negation an atmosphere is created of solitude, frustration and anxiety. This impression is further heightened by the sinister appearance of the river, and by the suggestion that there is here a kind of barrier between the living and the dead,[7] cf. Perceval's

> 'Ha! sire Deus puissanz,
> Se ceste eve passer pooie,
> De la ma mere troveroie
> Mien esciant, se ele est vive.'   (ll. 2990–93)

At the same time, and this is the third stylistic, as well as thematic, feature to which we would draw attention in this first section of the episode, Chrétien is clearly concerned, here as in the *Charrette*, to suggest that some supernatural power is at work in this desolation edging the hero away from his immediate goal (unknown to him, his mother is already dead) towards a more numinous, if not unrelated, destiny. How does he achieve this effect, stylistically? Not by recourse

---

[7] Pollmann, op. cit., p. 115, suggests a classical parallel ('Das Bild des Acheron').

to rhetoric, as in the foreboding chorus device in the *Joie de la Cort* and the *Pesme Aventure* episodes,[8] but by more negative yet, in their quiet way, equally effective procedures. The first is one to which he is particularly addicted and which he had used in the *Chevalier de la Charrette*, namely the withholding of the names of the protagonists,[9] and the deliberate veiling of their identities, at this stage, in imprecise terms of reference. For, although for the sake of clarity we have been referring to them as Perceval and the Fisher King, it is important to remember that these names are not revealed to the reader, or to Perceval himself, until the subsequent episode. In the passage we are concerned with Chrétien refers to these characters either by a simple demonstrative cum relative pronoun construction or by an appropriate substantive. Thus the Fisher King is 'cil qui pesche' (l. 3016) or 'un bel prodome' (l. 3086); in Perceval's apostrophe he is 'Peschiere' (l. 3047). Perceval himself is 'Cil qui ne set que feire puisse' (l. 3011) or 'li vaslez' (l. 3058). It is an elementary device of mystification, but viewed historically it is a remarkable anticipation of *roman policier* technique in a period in which writers had little grasp of the notion of suspense. The second device is the creation of surprise by apparently artless juxta-position of events. There is the sudden appearance of the Fisher King's boat at the moment when Perceval's way is blocked by the rock, as it some mysterious agency had answered his prayer; the Fisher King's reference to a cleft, a 'freite' (l. 3029) not previously mentioned by Chrétien, by which Perceval may climb up the hitherto impassable rock; above all an effective, even amusing, double anti-climax— Perceval's disappointment on seeing no sign of the promised lodging, his angry apostrophe of the Fisher:

> Peschiere, qui ce me deïs,
> Trop grant desleauté feïs
> Se tu le me deïs por mal!   (ll. 3047–9)

the sudden appearance, as if in answer to his complaint, but without comment by Chrétien, of the Grail Castle, and finally the equally

---

[8] *Erec et Enide*, ed. Mario Roques, Cfmâ., Paris, Champion, 1952, ll. 5461–77, 5655–63. *Yvain*, ed. T. B. W. Reid, Manchester University Press, 1942, ll. 5115–35.

[9] For a discussion of the device of the 'verspätete Namensnennung' see Wilhelm Kellermann, *Aufbaustil und Weltbild Chrestiens von Troyes im Perceval-roman*, Beihefte zur Zeitschrift für romanische Philologie, LXXXVIII Heft, Halle, 1936, pp. 60 ff.

sudden transformation of Perceval's anger, now that he is sure of a lodging for the night, into its opposite:

> Le vaslez cele part avale
> Et dit que bien avoiié l'a
> Cil qui l'avoit anvoiié la
> Si se loe del pescheor,
> Ne l'apele mes tricheor
> Ne desleal ne mançongier
> Des que il trueve ou herbergier. (ll. 3058–64)

Two further stylistic points call for comment in the above passage. First the indirect reporting of the hero's thoughts, as distinct from the direct speech method of his apostrophe of the Fisher. We have already noted how Chrétien rings the changes on these two methods, and we shall have occasion to comment further on his practice in this respect when we deal with the Grail Castle procession section. Secondly, as Peter Haidu points out in his study of 'Aesthetic distance in Chrétien de Troyes',[10] we have here a psychological 'turnabout' of an amusing kind, and Chrétien underlines this, as we have seen, with a comment of his own. That this is deliberate is shown by the repetition, with variation, in lines 3059–60, of the rich rhymes (anvoiié-avoiié) used shortly before in Perceval's outburst, and also by the recapitulation of the notion of 'desleauté'. This technique, frequent in Chrétien, and no doubt a consequence of the fact of oral delivery, is, however, not just one of unaesthetic, if helpful, emphasis; it is accompanied by stylistic variation and linguistic enrichment. Thus in this case, as Peter Haidu notes, the rhymes, at their second occurrence, are inverted and enriched.[11] We may add that the notion of deception, earlier expressed by a trio of substantives (musardie, bricoingne, (l. 3041) desleauté (l. 3048)) is now echoed by a trio of adjectives (tricheor, desleal, mançongier (ll. 3062–3)) of which one (desleal) provides the link with the original speech. A similar technique may be observed in the first conversation between Perceval and the Fisher King, in which there is not only repetition with inversion:

> 'Anseignez moi, "fet il", seignor
> S'an ceste eve a ne gué ne pont?' (ll. 3014–15)

. . . . . .

[10] Peter Haidu, 'Aesthetic Distance in Chrétien de Troyes. Irony and Comedy in *Cligès* and *Perceval*', Droz, Geneva, 1968.
[11] Ibid., p. 169, note 137.

> 'Nenil, frere, an la moie foi,
> N'il n'i a nef . . .   (ll. 3017–18)
> Si n'i puet an passer cheval;
> Qu'il n'i a bac ne pont ne gué':   (ll. 3022–3)

but also, once again, progressive enrichment of vocabulary, two other forms of river crossing (nef, bac) being added in the Fisher King's reply to the two enquired about by Perceval.

To conclude our analysis of the third stylistico-thematic feature which we distinguished in the first section, it must be admitted that the external description of the Grail Castle, itself the goal towards which the hero's steps have been mysteriously drawn, is, stylistically, disappointing. A few lines suffice:

> Lors vit devant lui an un val
> Le chief d'une tor qui parut;
> L'an ne trovast jusq'a Barut
> Si bele ne si bien assise:
> Quarree fu de pierre bise,
> S'avoit deus torneles antor.
> La sale fu devant la tor,
> Et les loges devant la sale.   (ll. 3050–7)

Modest introduction indeed to one of the great themes of imaginative literature! As Peter Haidu notes,[12] this description recalls that of Gornemant's castle (ll. 1322–5). In particular the sudden appearance of the tower echoes a detail, both realistic and poetic, in the earlier passage, viz:

> Si con l'eve aloit au regort,
> Torna li vaslez a senestre
> Et vit les torz del chastel nestre;
> Qu'avis li fu qu'eles neissoient
> Et que fors del chastel issoient.   (ll. 1324–8)

Gornemant's castle, as we know, had so impressed Perceval that he had at first proposed, to their dismay, to send his defeated opponents Anguingeron and Clamadeu there. It may be, then, that in the description of the Grail Castle we have an intention, on the part of Chrétien, to 'signal' (as Peter Haidu suggests)[13] a repetition of the

---

[12] Ibid., p. 169.
[13] Ibid., p. 169.

Gornemant theme. Certainly Gornemant's advice will be only too much in Perceval's mind as he watches the procession in the Grail Castle. It must be said, however, that if the description is a signal it is stylistically a very weak one. What was the reason for Chrétien's at first sight surprising failure to exploit a stylistic opportunity? Partly, no doubt, a desire not to bore his audience. Chrétien, as some of his utterances show,[14] was as conscious of the stylistic virtue of *abbreviatio* in the *narratio* as he was of the attractions of *amplificatio*.[15] To use the latter approach here, i.e. another lengthy display of descriptive technique, might have preempted something of the literary effect he proposed to draw from the strange scenes his hero would witness within the Grail Castle. Our minds are perhaps being carried forward to an inner splendour which will contrast significantly with the outward grandeur of Gornemant, the representative of the 'siècle'.

If we turn now to the middle section of the episode, the strangest and most compelling passage in the whole of Chrétien's work, what stylistic features strike us?

First, the basically straightforward, realistic narrative style, flowing on, without evidence of constraint, through its unobtrusive octo-syllables, presenting a sequence of events and objects which, however, mysterious, have yet a solid background of medieval reality.[16] The granting of hospitality to a benighted traveller, clearly a man of rank, servants dressing and disrobing him, the host receiving him, chatting politely with him about his journey, entertaining him to a meal, excusing himself for having to retire early, giving the visitor directions about his sleeping quarters—these would be familiar enough phenomena in a medieval castle, and they are familiar enough, with variations, in the romances of Chrétien. To convey them the writer employs a vocabulary which is, as we shall see, preeminently concrete.

Secondly, the very limited use of direct speech. This is, however, characteristic of the entire Grail Castle episode, in which direct speech amounts to little more than one seventh of the whole, and it may be appropriate at this point to consider this feature in respect of all three sections and not merely of the second. The forms which direct speech

---

[14] For example in *Erec et Enide*, ll. 5523–31.

[15] On these concepts see E. Faral, *Les Arts poétiques du XIIᵉ et du XIIIᵉ siècle*, Paris, Champion, 1924, pp. 61–85, and E. R. Curtius, *European Literature and the Latin Middle Ages*, 1953, Excursus XIII.

[16] Cf. A. Fourrier, *Le Courant réaliste dans le roman courtois en France au moyen âge*, Paris, Nizet, 1960, vol. I, pp. 111 ff.

takes in the episode are of three kinds, viz. (a) dialogue; the two conversations between Perceval and the Fisher King, the first at the river, the second in the hall of the castle, whither the Fisher King, despite his lameness, has been transported, unobserved by Perceval, with uncanny speed—perhaps another suggestion of the *merveilleux* at work: to this may be added Perceval's parting and unanswered question to the invisible drawbridge raiser (b) the more formal speeches by the 'vaslet' and the Fisher King about the sword which the former bears into the hall and which the latter presents to Perceval (c) monologue; this occurs only in the first section, in the shape of one of the brief prayers of Perceval to which we have already referred (ll. 2990–3) and in his apostrophe of the Fisher King.

The passages of dialogue, though short, well illustrate the poet's skill at rendering the tone of natural, even colloquial conversation, as well as at unobtrusive conveyance of details significant for both narrative and characterization. Thus, while the Fisher King is addressed by Perceval and his own retainer as 'seignor' or 'sire' (ll. 3013, 3110, 3122, 3145) not only when he is seated in state on his bed, but also—a significant pointer to the respect he inspires—when he is engaged in the more homely activity of fishing from his boat, the terms in which he addresses Perceval on the other hand show interesting and, we suggest, intentional variations. First, the familiar, slightly contemptuous 'frere' indicates that Chrétien wishes us to see Perceval once again as his brash, youthful self rather than as the victor of Anguingueron and Clamadeu, the liberator of Belrepeire who had, that very morning, been given such a solemn send-off by the religious of the town. Later, in the Grail Castle, the terms of address show an interesting up-grading from this familiar 'frere' to 'amis' (used on three occasions, ll. 3107, 3115, 3120, in the opening polite exchanges) rising to a respectful 'biaus sire' (l. 3167) when the Fisher King invests Perceval with the sword, and declining again to 'amis' (l. 3336) at the end of the meal. Through such small but significant details of style, more significant of course to his own class-conscious contemporaries than to us, does the poet plot the rise in estimation and expectation of the hero as he approaches his supreme test, and the disillusionment when he has failed. This disillusionment will be underlined, symbolically, by the drawbridge incident in the last section of the episode, which in its mockery seems to represent a return to the original, quizzical attitude of the Fisher King.

Noteworthy, too, in the first conversation between the protagonists, is the ingenious use of time signals which, as we saw, serve the purpose

of anchoring the narrative. But these—the references to the watch-
man's dawn call and to the bell—also insinuate poetic as well as realistic
associations:

> Trop grant jornee avez hui feite;
> Vos meüstes, enz que la gueite
> Eüst hui main l'aube cornee.
> Einz estoit ja prime sonee,
> Fet li vaslez, jel vos afi. (ll. 3125-9)

One might see here an echo, on the part of a writer who was a lyric
poet as well as a romancer, of the *genre* of the *aube*. Perceval had, after
all, left Blancheflor, 's'amie, la jante Mout correciee et mout dolante'
(ll. 2935-6), as well as Belrepeire. No doubt the Fisher King, who later
shows himself so well-informed about Perceval (in respect of the
sword) knew this, and he may be teasing the young man: we have
noted already a hint of irony in his attitude to Perceval, whose naiveté
tends to elicit this reaction in his interlocutors. A more serious under-
tone is perhaps the adumbration, in the choice of the time references,
of the alternatives which will dog this particular hero, the world of
secular chivalry, symbolized by the *gueite*, and the world of the spirit,
symbolized by the bell. It is striking that Chrétien has Perceval prefer
to speak in terms of the latter. . . . He had, as we have noted, been
addressed with quite unusual respect by the religious of Belrepeire, and
had spoken to them with a solemnity we do not associate with the
brash youth who later tucks in at the Fisher King's table and is nearly—
literally—laid by the heels as he leaves the Grail Castle. Was the Fisher
King's question a kind of test, part of some ritual? It is possible. At
least we may note, and this is our particular concern here, the ability
of Chrétien de Troyes to suggest through his style, and through a quite
realistic vocabulary, the bigger issues of his romance.

The speeches about the sword (ll. 3145-57, 3167-70) are more formal.
The sword scene, indeed, constitutes a kind of second investiture,
reminiscent of and parallel to the earlier ceremony performed by
Gornemant before Perceval's departure from his castle. It is noteworthy
that, alone of the mysterious objects which appear to Perceval in this
episode, the sword is the only one with which he comes into actual
physical contact, the only one specifically addressed to him, and,
stylistically speaking, the only one for which Chrétien provides,
through the mouths of the denizens of the castle, an explanation and a

background. When he passes on to the Lance and the Grail, as we shall see, he employs a different technique.

Chrétien makes little use of monologue in this episode. A brief prayer of Perceval when he contemplates with apprehension the apparently insuperable obstacle of the river (ll. 2990–3); an angry outburst against the Fisher King when he thinks the latter has tricked him (ll. 3040–9); fourteen lines in all. The ten line outburst shows a certain artistry of construction in its sequence of rhetorical question and answer, curse and apostrophe. This composition is, however, very elementary in comparison with the elaborate artifice of the monologues used by Chrétien in, for example, *Cligès* and the *Charrette*.[17] Perceval, it is true, is not in the *courtois* situation which is the *raison d'être* of those earlier soliloquies, but nevertheless he has something—his mother's fate—on his mind already in the first section, and he has a further problem to exercise him when confronted with the procession. What is interesting, stylistically, about Chrétien's handling of the hero's reaction to the Grail procession is that he has preferred not to have recourse here to the time-honoured device of the psychological monologue, but rather to use the technique of indirect analysis. Under the superficialities of polite conversation:

> Que qu'il parloient d'un et el   (l. 3190)

Perceval is shown, on three successive occasions, ruminating on what he sees and deciding, in view of Gornemant's earlier instruction:

> Et gardez que vos ne sooiez
> Trop parlanz ne trop noveliers: (ll. 1648–9)

to keep his mouth shut at this stage. There is a certain implausibility about this decision, for after his friendly reception and the gift of the sword one might have expected Perceval not to be inhibited from putting a polite enquiry about all three objects. If we overlook that, however, then we cannot but admire this procedure of burrowing into the mind of one of two non-communicating partners confronted by a common experience. It is a device worthy of Flaubert. Yet alongside this modernity are features which mark the man of the Middle Ages.

---

[17] *Cligès*, ed. A. Micha, *Cfmâ*, Paris, 1957; see especially ll. 618–864 (Alexandre), 889–1038 (Soredamors), 4366–526 (Fenice).

Le Chevalier de la Charrette, ed. Mario Roques, *Cfmâ.*, Paris, 1958, especially ll. 4318–96. Chrétien's use of the monologue is fully discussed by A. Hilka, op. cit., pp. 64–108.

The triple use of the indirect analysis (ll. 3202–12, 3243–53, 3290–3311), the obviously planned balance and gradation of these three passages, so strongly reminiscent of *laisses similaires*, the repetition of the motif, remind us once again how much the writer of romance, even when seemingly in full flight towards the modern novel, remains still very much a poet, and a poet in the medieval sense, a purveyor of verse for aural rather than visual consumption, a contemporary of the *chanson de geste* and of the early lyric, and one reared on their tradition. The respect of the period for authority, its attachment to the 'idée reçue', is also illustrated by Chrétien's own sententious intervention in the second repeat of the motif:

> Si criem que il n'i et domage
> Por ce que j'ai oï retreire
> Qu'ausi bien se puet an trop teire
> Con trop parler a la foiiee.   (ll. 3248–51)

This is to be compared with his tendency elsewhere in his romances to cogitate in terms of such moral saws and proverbs, including, incidentally, one conveying the opposite view to that expressed in *Perceval*, viz.:

> Ainz boens teisirs home ne nut,
> Mes parlers nuist mainte foiee.

This, however, is not an intervention by the author, but is placed by him in the mouth of a character (Enide), who had experienced the unpleasant consequences of 'la parole'.[18] The question was obviously one of great interest in courtly circles, and differing views might be held. Chrétien conceals his own, characteristically, if disconcertingly, behind the shifting facade of popular pragmatism.

Little use, then, of direct speech, but, despite certain traditional medieval characteristics, a remarkably advanced application of indirect notation to psychological analysis, and a building up of the principal character from the inside.

The third notable feature of the style of this, the climactic, section of

---

[18] *Erec et Enide*, op. cit., ll. 4592–3. Cf. J. Morawski, *Proverbes français antérieurs au XVe siècle*, Cfmâ., Paris, 1925, nos. 1254 and 2428. For convenient lists of proverbs, etc., used by Chrétien in *Erec et Enide*, *Cligès* and *Yvain* see the 'Index des mots relatifs à la civilisation et aux moeurs' in the Cfmâ. editions (Roques, Micha) of these romances.

the Grail Castle episode is, not surprisingly, the application by Chrétien of descriptive techniques on a much greater scale than in the first.

It is, however, almost entirely a question of description of objects. Description of persons, a favourite field of the twelfth century theorists and stylists,[19] and not least of Chrétien himself, witness the descriptions of Blancheflor (ll. 1795–1829) and the Loathly Damsel (ll. 4611–37) in this very romance, is conspicuous by its absence. This is hardly surprising in the case of Perceval, who has been with us since the start of the romance, although even he, unlike his predecessors Erec and Cligès, is nowhere clearly depicted, *au physique* that is to say, for his moral portrait is abundantly filled in. One might however have expected a detailed physical picture of the Fisher King, who appears only in this episode, and is such a key figure in Perceval's destiny. But all we learn of his appearance is that he was a 'bel prodome' (l. 3086), that his hair was greying ('de chienes meslez' (l. 3087)) and that, like his counterparts, perhaps his prototypes, Bademagu in the *Charrette* and the lord of the *Château de Pesme Aventure* in *Yvain*, he was leaning on his elbow (l. 3092).[20] The injury which has incapacitated him, the nature of which will be elucidated in the next episode, is here only discreetly indicated (l. 3107–9). Again Chrétien, often so willing to display his literary and linguistic virtuosity, has rejected an opportunity to show his paces. The reason? Partly, no doubt, the fact that a 'noble vieillard' appeared a less interesting subject to the courtly portraitist than the types of extreme beauty or extreme ugliness; partly because of the need for economy in this episode; above all, one suspects, a sense, and a very proper one, of the advantages, for the creation of an atmosphere of mystery, of saying too little rather than too much.

Broadly speaking, this last consideration would appear to have weighed with him in the description of objects too. As we saw, the external description of the Grail Castle suggested a comparatively modest kind of building, certainly not one comparable in dimensions and site with the castle of Gornemant de Goort, of which Chrétien had drawn an impressive picture. Similarly, the description of the interior is short on architectural features. We are told that the 'salle' was

---

[19] Cf. Alice M. Colby, *The Portrait in Twelfth-Century French Literature*, Droz, Geneva, 1965.

[20] *Charrette*, ed. Roques, ll. 3143–4, *Yvain*, ed. Reid, ll. 5362–3. The significance of this position, which has parallels in medieval iconography, might be worth investigation. Was Chrétien influenced by the art of his time? Cf. Roques, *Le Graal de Chrétien et la Demoiselle au Graal*, Romania, LXXVI, 1955.

square, that there was a great fire burning between four massive bronze columns supporting a chimney-piece (*cheminal* (l. 3100)), that in the centre of the room stood the bed of the Fisher King, and later the table from which he and Perceval dine. Opening out of the hall are the doors leading to the mysterious 'chambres' from which emerge and into which disappear the persons and objects of the procession and, later, the Fisher King himself, doors which, on the following morning, Perceval finds locked and silent. A good deal is, then, left to the imagination. Two features, however, which Chrétien stresses, are, first, the fire—and we shall note further insistence on this idea of illumination— and second, the huge dimensions of the fireplace and the surrounding area. The vocabulary, admittedly very spare and basic, underlines this. The fire is 'mout grant' and 'bien ardant' (ll. 3093–4), the columns are 'mout forz' (l. 3099),

> D'arain espés et haut et lé.   (l. 3101)

The fireplace is so vast that four hundred men could have sat round it (ll. 3096–7). As far as the internal architectural features are concerned, then, the style creates an impression of regularity, massiveness, spaciousness and height somewhat unexpected after the modest appearance of the exterior. Perhaps the poet's intention was to emphasize further, by this surprising juxtaposition, that aura of illusion which the first non-view of the castle had already suggested, and which the final disappearing trick of its inmates was later to reinforce.

With reference to Chrétien's use of colour it must be said that his palette is, by the standards of more modern masters of descriptive French, very limited. He uses here the simplest colours—black, red, white, the first two sparingly, if strikingly: thus, the sable headdress of the *prodome*, 'noir come more' (not, admittedly, an original image—he had already used it in *Erec et Enide* and *Cligès*[21]) with its overlaid 'porpre', and the similar colours of his robe (ll. 3088–91); the scarlet drops of blood from the lance (l. 3201); the ebony trestles of the ivory table; and later in the poem there is a further striking instance of his ability to evoke a memorable scene through just such a simple opposition of colours (Perceval contemplating the three drops of blood on the snow (ll. 4186 ff.). On the other hand, many references emphasize the

[21] *Erec et Enide*, op. cit., l. 6735. *Cligès*, op. cit., l. 4616.

quality of whiteness or luminosity; the light from the huge fire 'qui cler ardoit' (l. 3181); the brilliant lighting of the hall;

> Et leanz avoit lumineire
> Si grant con l'an puet greignor feire
> De chandoiles an un ostel;   (ll. 3187–9)

and the light from the many candles (ten at least to each chandelier) borne by the *vaslet* who precedes the Grail procession; the whiteness of the lance, stressed by the triple use of the adjective, with however stylistic variety from inversion and noun gender change (une blanche lance (l. 3192, la lance blanche et le fer blanc l. 3197)) within the space of six lines; the whiteness of the sheets on Perceval's bed (l. 3355), the incomparable whiteness of the napery, with the suggestion, in the comparison which Chrétien employs to emphasize this, of ecclesiastical associations:

> Legaz ne chardonaus ne pape
> Ne manja onques sor si blanche;   (ll. 3278–9)

above all the supreme light of the Grail itself, given particular force by the use of the one major image in the entire episode, and that a beautiful and memorable one derived, like so many images of Chrétien, from a simple phenomenon of nature:

> Une si granz clartez i vint
> Qu'ausi perdirent les chandoiles
> Lor clarte come les estoiles
> Quanz li solauz lieve ou la lune.   (ll. 3226–9)[22]

Lumineire, clartez, solauz, lune, estoiles, chandoiles, ardoit, cler, blanc, blanche —through such substantives, verbs and adjectives and their associations does Chrétien hammer home an impression of overwhelming light, relieved only by the scarlet of the blood, or the black of the fur and the ebony. It is not our business here to speculate on the symbolism of this coloration,[23] but we can at least say, I think, that the stylistic evidence points to a strong desire on the part of the poet to suggest that the mysterious castle and its objects are associated with qualities of purity

---

[22] Chrétien had, however, already used a similar image in the coronation scene in *Erec et Enide*, ll. 6774–91, in speaking of the blinding light from the carbuncles adorning the two crowns.

[23] See D. D. R. Owen, 'The Radiance in the Grail Castle', *Romania* LXXXIII (1962) and Leo Pollmann, op. cit., pp. 118 and 123.

and sacrifice, contrasting perhaps, though this is only touched on in one line, or by implication:

> Li vaslez vit cele mervoille
> Qui leanz ert la nuit venuz;   (ll. 3202–3)

with the darkness of the silent and sinister landscape through which Perceval had just passed. It is, stylistically speaking, difficult to believe that Chrétien did not have in mind here a Christian presentation of his theme. Yet, if this is so, it is worth noting that his symbols are drawn from the hard realities of medieval experience, and that the brilliant lighting of the Grail Castle is the realization, in the world of the imagination, of what must have seemed an unattainable dream in the ill-lit, smoky castles of the twelfth century. Warmth, good lighting, good clothes, good food—the Fisher King is a great personage and a 'riche home' because he enjoys, to a superlative degree, these simple priorities of the medieval economy. These are, in this era, attributes of wealth and power, and Chrétien, realist that he is, uses them as his aesthetic media.

The impression of wealth and luxury is further conveyed by a stylistic technique familiar enough in the metrical romances of the twelfth century, namely by references to precious metals, precious stones, particularly in the shape of, or worked into, tableware and weapons; rich fabrics, fine furniture, rare food and drink and, of course, smooth service. All of these, would in the lifetime of Chrétien have been most uncommon outside of great churches or monasteries or the dwellings of the greatest princes. The first category would indeed have represented a major form of capital. The Fisher King is thus further established, in terms of the medieval economy, as a lord, whether spiritual or temporal, of the highest standing. The Grail itself is of pure gold (l. 3233) and is decorated with precious stones (ll. 3234–9); so too are the pommel of the sword (ll. 3162–3) and the chandeliers, the latter inlaid with niello (l. 3215); the scabbard of the sword is of gold brocade (l. 3164); the wines are served in golden goblets (l. 3283); the *tailleor* is of silver (ll. 3231, 3283); the columns supporting the *cheminal* are of bronze (l. 3101); the table on which the meal is served is of ivory (l. 3261); the trestles are of ebony. The Fisher King wears, as we saw, sable and purple; Perceval is arrayed in a 'un mantel d'escarlate, fres et novel' (ll. 3073–4); the 'ranges' of the sword 'valoient un grant tresor' (l. 3161). Staffing and service are lavish. Four 'vaslet' meet

Perceval on his arrival. Four 'serjant' carry the Fisher King to his bedchamber. Others remain to wait on Perceval and put him to bed. Others wait at table, carry the various objects (except the Grail, of course) in the procession. The recurrence of the figure 'four' is curious (cf. in addition to the examples just given, ll. 3095—quatre colomes— and 3096—quatre canz homes), and suggests that Chrétien wishes to stress some significance of this numeral. Perhaps it is the quality which he ascribes to the four-square hall of the castle:

> qui fu quarree
> Et autant longue come lee,   (ll. 3083-4)

and in which Leo Pollmann sees eschatological significance.[24]

To reinforce the effect of splendour which all this evokes, Chrétien uses a device frequently found in his and other romances, namely the technique of what Professor Colby has called 'hyperbolic comparison',[25] i.e. of asserting, by comparison, the superior quality, quantity, size, richness or variety of the object or phenomenon he is describing, as in the statement that the precious stones adorning the Grail were the finest ever seen on land or sea:

> Totes autres pierres passoient
> Celes del graal sans dotance;   (ll. 3238-9)

or, of the table cloth, the assertion already cited that no ecclesiastical dignitary ever ate on one so white (ll. 3278-9): or, of the ebony trestles, the assurance that this wood has not the defects which no doubt he and his audience normally associated with their own furniture (inflammability, liability to rot (ll. 3268-74)). These two latter comparisons take the form of a simple rhetorical question and answer device, thus:

> Mes que diroie de la nape?
> Legaz ne chardonaus ne pape
> Ne manja onques sor si blanche;   (ll. 3277-9)

---

[24] Pollmann, op. cit., p. 118. 'Chretien legt Werf darauf, festzuhalten, dass dieser Saal eschatologischen Ansprüchen genügt, er ist quadratisch wie bei Prudentius der Tempel der Sapientia, wie im Bereich keltischer Literatur der Fest- und Turniersaal'.

[25] Colby, op. cit., p. 179.

or, of the trestles, more elaborately:

> Don furent eles?—D'ebenus.—
> D'un fust a quoi?—Ja n'i bet nus
> Que il porrisse ne qu'il arde;
> De ces deus choses n'a il garde.   (ll. 3271-4)

Such an intrusion of rhetoric, which is of course at the same time an intrusion of the author, is common enough elsewhere in Chrétien, but it is unusual in this particular episode, where the poet seems to be applying a more detached, a more impersonal technique. The momentary breaking of this impersonality in favour of rhetorical artifice, however modest, indicates both the naïve scale of material values of the twelfth-century poet and at the same time the importance he attaches to creating a particular impression through his stylistic emphasis of these values, and their associations. Similar hyperbole is seen later when Chrétien, speaking of the meal, tells us that it included 'toz les mes que rois ne cuens Ne anperere doie avoir' (ll. 3316-17). Again we note that *procédé* of linguistic enrichment we spoke of earlier. It is however not otiose but meaningful and balanced enrichment, in that the grandeur of the Fisher King, which in the napery comparison was linked with that of the Church, is also equated with that of the secular medieval hierarchy.

Another familiar technique, often found associated with the former, is the dropping of names of exotic countries and places to evoke an aura of mystery and romance, such as the references to Beirut in connection with the tower of the Grail Castle:

> L'an ne trovast jusqu'a Barut
> Si bele ne si bien assise;   (ll. 3052-3)

to Arabia and Greece (l. 3163) in connection with the gold of the sword hilt, to Venice (l. 3164) in connection with the scabbard, to Alexandria (l. 3328) in connection with the 'gingenbrat' served at the meal. The similar reference to Limoges

> Puis l'an menerent jusqu'as loges,
> Et bien sachiez jusqu'a Limoges
> Ne trovast an ne ne veist
> Si beles, qui les i queist;   (ll. 3075-8)

is less atmospheric (though to a twelfth century Champenois, in an age of rudimentary communications, and of the Angevin Empire, within whose bounds Limoges then was, it may not have seemed so) and may owe its insertion to the need to find a convenient rhyme. In fact Chrétien had already used this rhyme in *Erec et Enide* (ll. 2623–4). Metrical considerations probably were a factor in Chrétien's choice of *Barut* (rhyming with *parut*) and the rhyme *Grece-Venece* also. These names, however, with their Mediterranean or near-Eastern flavour, would have, it should not be forgotten, particular associations, not only military but also commercial, in the age of the Crusades, especially for Chrétien's patron Philippe D'Alsace. The walls and towers of Beirut, for example, had in 1182, i.e. in the very decade of the composition of the *Perceval*[26] successfully sustained a siege by Saladin himself.[27] Could Chrétien, who speaks of Beirut in relation to a feature of military architecture, have heard from Philippe about the fortresses of *Outremer*?[28] It is perhaps significant that, with the exception of one reference to India (l. 1604) these are the only references to the Orient in the whole of the *Perceval*. They may then be seen (like the references to Mediterranean fruits and spices in the account of the meal (ll. 3325–6) as stylistic ornamentation designed to give a specifically Oriental air to the Grail Castle and its inmates. But it is an ornamentation based on realism.

Noteworthy, stylistically, is the obvious predilection with which Chrétien dwells on the description of the meal of which Perceval and the Fisher King partake with such gusto, a description notable for the richness, even quaintness, of its vocabulary, e.g.

> Dates, figues et noiz muscates
> Et girofle et pomes grenates
> Et leituaires an la fin
> Et gingenbrat alixandrin
> Et pliris aromaticon,
> Resontif et stomaticon.
> Aprés si burent de maint boivre:
> Pimant, ou n'ot ne miel ne poivre,
> Et bon more et cler sirop.   (ll. 3325–33)

---

[26] See A. Fourrier, *Encore la chronologie der oeuvres de Chrétien de Troyes*, BBSIA, No. 2, 1950, pp. 87–9.

[27] This siege is vividly described in the *Livre d'Eracles*, ed. P. Paris, vol. 2, Paris, 1880, Book 22, chaps. XVI and XVII. Saladin lacked siege engines 'par que il poïst les murs ne les torneles deshorder' (p. 441).

[28] Philippe was in *Outremer* from August 1177 until Easter 1178. For a (highly critical) account of his activities see *Eracles*, op. cit., pp. 381–99, and R. Grousset, *Histoire des Croisades*, vol. 2, pp. 633 ff. He was to return to *Outremer* and die there, during the Third Crusade, in 1191.

Mr. Haidu[29] sees here a comic intention, and he compares a passage from *Cligès*, viz. that in which Thessala boasts of her medical skills:

> Je sai bien garir d'itropique
> Si sai garir de l'arcetique
> De quinancie et de cuerpous;
> Tant sai d'orines et de pous
> Que ja mar avroiz autre mire[30].

A further example might be adduced from the *Chevalier de la Charrette* where Lancelot places more faith in the powers of Guinevere's hair than in the medieval pharmacopœia:

> Dïamargareton desdaigne
> Et pleüriche et tirïasque[31].

That there is an element of irony here seems likely. Linguistically and stylistically there is a hint of the kind of comic effect which five centuries later Molière was to extract from the rebarbative medical terminology of his time.[32] In the case of Perceval, Chrétien has been at pains throughout the romance to stress his naiveté. It may well be that he intended to raise a smile at the picture of the young man post-poning the clearing-up of the mysteries of the Castle and concentrating on the food and lodging about which he had been so anxious and which now is so lavishly provided for him. As Chrétien puts it;

> Einsi la chose a respitiee,
> S'antant a boivre et a mangier. (ll. 3310–11)

The scene would appeal to a medieval audience. At the same time one should not, I think, over-emphasize the element of comedy, which is by no means explicit. But had Chrétien a deeper purpose? Did he, as has been suggested, intend us to see the hero placed between two alternatives, the worldly values represented by the physical food, the spiritual values represented by the Grail, which passes before him like a silent reminder as each course is served (ll. 3229–3301)? And does his decision, as Leo Pollmann suggests, represent the beginning of a 'dinglichere Perspektive'[33] in the work, one which increasingly affects

---

[29] Haidu, op. cit., pp. 174–5.
[30] *Cligès*, ed. A. Micha, Cfmâ., Paris, 1957, ll. 2983–7.
[31] *Le Chevalier de la Charrete*, ed. Mario Roques, Cfmâ., Paris, 1958.
[32] Cf., for example, *Le Malade Imaginaire*, Act II, Sc. 6.
[33] Pollmann, op. cit., p. 32.

the vocabulary, and is already apparent in the passage, with its 'Fülle kulinarischer Dinglichkeit'[34] which we have cited above? The juxta-position of Grail and meal certainly suggests an antithesis, and would be in line with the technique of implication rather than plain statement, insinuation rather than straight comment, to which we have already drawn attention. Nor can we shut out from our minds the later triple criticism of Perceval by his female cousin (ll. 3580 ff.) by the Loathly Damsel (ll. 4646 ff.) and by his Hermit Uncle, especially the last (ll. 6392 ff.). It is obvious from the tenor of their pronouncements that Chrétien intended us to see Perceval as having sinned in some way; it is also clear from the remarks of the Hermit that the content of the Grail is something of a higher order than secular food:

> Mes ne cuidiez pas que il et
> Luz ne lamproies ne saumon:
> D'une sole oiste li sainz hon,
> Que l'an an cest graal li porte,
> Sa vie sostient et conforte.   (ll. 6420–24)

On the other hand, if we confine our attention to the Grail Castle passage account, 'we do not', as Peter Haidu points out, 'see two kinds of food, nor is there any way during this scene that we can guess that two kinds of food are available'.[35] Nor is there any suggestion in the description of the meal that to partake of it is at all reprehensible. On the contrary, Chrétien has nothing but praise for it:

> Li mangiers fu et biaus et buens.   (l. 3315)

Apart from the fact that he speaks of this food, as distinct from the napery, in secular terms, it would appear that Chrétien has no objection to Perceval nor, it should be remembered, to the Fisher King, enjoying terrestrial food in the presence of the Grail. All he criticizes, explicitly, is Perceval's failure to ask about the recipient of the other kind of food. As for the vocabulary, it is certainly unusually rich and detailed by the standards of this episode, but is it in principle more 'dinglich' than what has preceeded it? It is difficult to be clear about the poet's inten-tion at this point and discussion of this is beyond the scope of this essay. Suffice it to say that in the light of the style of this passage as it stands there would seem to be a case for regarding the description of the meal as in the first instance a further embellishment of the picture

---

34 Ibid., op. cit., p. 32.
35 Op. cit., p. 172, note 145.

of the Fisher King's grandeur. It gave the poet an opportunity for a set piece of description, even for a display of culinary erudition, and the realist, the pedant, and, perhaps, the snob in him enjoyed this.

The third section of the episode provides a sharp contrast to the second. It takes us back, stylistically, to the manner of the first, since its most striking feature is the use of the device of negation which we noted there. When Perceval wakes up at dawn on the following day he finds himself, after the company, the rich food and wine, the strange yet lavish entertainment of the previous night, thrust back into the same state of utter loneliness as that in which we had seen him during his journey to the river:

$$\text{Mes il ne vit leanz nelui.} \qquad \text{(l. 3359)}$$

The servants who, the night before, had waited on him and seen him to bed, have vanished. He has to look after himself:

$$\text{Si l'estut par lui seul lever;} \qquad \text{(l. 3361)}$$

and dress and arm himself 'sans aïe atendre' (l. 3365). A youth brought up in the 'gaste forest' (l. 75) might have been expected to be accustomed to this, and Chrétien's observation may therefore seem surprising. However, he clearly intends us to note this as an unusual departure from custom, and certainly a guest of knightly rank entertained in a château by a personage as important as the Fisher King would in the twelfth century have expected at least to be assisted into his armour. And so through this and other details the poet recreates around his hero the same atmosphere of frustration and obstruction which had hampered him earlier. The doors of the mysterious rooms leading off the hall of the castle, which he had seen open the night before, are now closed (l. 3372-3). He batters on the doors and calls out, but all remains silent and closed against him—a scene effectively conveyed by two lines in which the verbs portraying violent sound and action are contrasted with the negative formula which follows:

$$\text{S'apele et bote et hurte assez:}$$
$$\text{Nus ne li oevre ne dit mot.} \qquad \text{(ll. 3374-5)}$$

He then goes out into the courtyard, finds his arms and his horse, rides 'par tot leanz' (l. 3383) but sees no member of the lord's retinue:

$$\text{Mes n'i trueve nul des serjeanz}$$
$$\text{N'escuiier ne vaslet n'i voit.} \qquad \text{(ll. 3384-5)}$$

One door, however, remains open, the door of the castle itself. Beyond it the drawbridge stands lowered, as it had been when he arrived, so that, observes Chrétien, he might be free to leave at any time (ll. 3386–91). To leave, but not, apparently, to return, for as he rides out of the castle over the drawbridge he feels the bridge being lifted beneath him and only escapes serious injury by a great leap of his horse (ll. 3406–8). Perceval calls out, but

> nus ne li respont.   (l. 3413)

A further appeal to the mysterious and invisible porter to show himself—this the only passage of direct speech in this otherwise completely narrative section, and in form an apostrophe reminiscent of, and no doubt intended to be parallel to, Perceval's address to the Fisher King at the end of the first section—remains unanswered. Chrétien's comment indicates his view of the hero's behaviour at this point:

> Einsi de parler se *foloie*;
> Que nus respondre ne li viaut.   (ll. 3420–21)

The effect of these negative formulae, with their variations (e.g. nus . . . ne dit mot (l. 3375) nus ne li respont (l. 3413), nus respondre ne li viaut (l. 3421) and enrichment through synonym (bote et hurte l. 3374 nul des serjanz N'escuier ne vaslet ll. 3384–5) is enhanced by their application to a realistically observed background, by the wiping out, as it were, not only of all the bustle of the night before, but by the stressing of the complete absence, in the morning light, of all those everyday activities and sounds which would have been normal at that moment in any castle of the twelfth century. Exploiting this incongruity, Chrétien creates an atmosphere of suspense all the more remarkable as he keeps the setting quite realistic and familiar; propounds, through his hero, a perfectly plausible explanation which might well be in keeping with the daily routine of a castle:

> Et panse que an la forest
> S'an soient li vaslet alé
> Por le pont qu'il voit avalé
> Cordes et pieges regarder;   (ll. 3392–5)

an activity on which of course a garrison would depend for its daily supply of game and venison; then shatters this illusion of normality by one final and surprising negative effect—the premature raising of the drawbridge which concludes the episode and leaves the hero out in the cold. The effect is all the more telling, stylistically, as Chrétien had not,

until this moment, shown us the drawbridge as other than lowered.
The terms he applies to it at the departure of Perceval, viz. 'le pont
abeissié' (l. 3387) and 'le pont qu'il voit avalé' (l. 3394) echo, in the
manner, unobtrusive yet suggestive, already noted, those he had used
of it on his arrival, viz. 'un pont . . . torneïz, qui fu avalez' (ll. 3066–7).
These terms, especially when we bear in mind the normal purpose of
a drawbridge in a medieval castle, would appear to indicate the
friendliness of the Grail Castle, a friendliness which is now, however,
turned into a mocking rebuke. The lowered drawbridge had been a
symbol of accessibility; now it has become something hostile, something more like the portcullis which so nearly finished off the hero in
Yvain.[36] Of course there is an element of farce in this final scene (cf.
Perceval's naïve appeal to the porter) just as there was an element of
the grotesque (the bisected horse) in the corresponding episode in
Yvain. Chrétien, a great *remanieur* of his own themes, may well have
been mindful here of the earlier one. But there is also something
sinister about an action deliberately intended to put the hero at risk, in
sharp contrast to the kindly reception of the previous evening. Even
allowing that Perceval had been guilty of a grave sin of omission, was
this send-off the behaviour one would have expected from the guardian
of the Grail? The style has indicated a malicious streak in the Fisher
King. His final gesture suggests that Chrétien does not want us to take
him too seriously. Whatever the interpretation to be put on this
passage, however, one characteristic feature of style is again visible
here, namely the underlining of a motif through the exploitation of
realistic contemporary detail.

The atmosphere of enigma in which the Grail Castle episode ends is
further enhanced by Chrétien's persistence with the technique of
presenting the castle and its denizens only through the puzzled eyes
and mind of the hero. There is only one exception to this, namely, his
assertion that the drawbridge had been left lowered for Perceval 'Por
ce que riens nel retenist' (ll. 3388–9). Otherwise he continues to use the
more sophisticated technique of indirect reporting which he had used
in conveying Perceval's train of thought in the procession scene, thus:

> Et panse que an la forest etc.   (ll. 3392 ff.)
>
>   . . . . . .
>
> Na cure de plus arester,
> Einz dist qu'aprés aus s'an iroit
> Savoir se. . . .   (ll. 3396–9)

[36] *Yvain*, ll. 907–55.

These formulae establish a stylistic link with the second section, and at the same time recapitulate and reiterate those themes and questions which the author wishes his audience—as well as his hero—to keep in mind, namely the problems of the Lance and the Grail:

> Einz dist qu'apres aus s'an iroit
> Savoir se nus d'aus li diroit
> De la lance por qu'ele sainne,
> S'il puet estre por nule painne,
> E del graal ou l'an le porte.   (ll. 3997-3401)

There is no reference here—nor had there been in the second section—to the other question which had been so very much in Perceval's mind, as we saw, at the start of his quest, namely the fate of his mother. This is a surprising omission, with which, I think, we must fault Chrétien. Granted the absorbing nature of the objects in the Grail procession, it seems implausible that the earlier preoccupation, which Chrétien himself had so heavily underlined, should have gone so completely out of Perceval's mind. It is true that the author has not forgotten it, as will be made clear in the next episode, but the sudden dropping of it after the first section is a narrative weakness.

To recapitulate the results of our observations, I think the first thing that stands out in the style of this episode is a meaningful, even artful, simplicity, exemplified by the severe limitation of description, of the use of direct speech or soliloquy, of authorial interventions, so often vehicles for medieval prolixity. The reduction to a minimum of authorial comment, the reliance on implication rather than explanation, contributes greatly to the atmosphere of tension and, as we have seen, on occasion, of irony, even comedy, which pervades the whole.

Yet, if Chrétien has resisted, to a large extent, the blandishments of amplification in favour of brevity, he has nevertheless made effective use, within his chosen limits, of the linguistic and stylistic resources available to the twelfth century French poet. Very characteristic of the *roman* in this period, is the fusion of realism and romanticism in the style; on the one hand exotic vocabulary, imagery, colour and allusions, creating an atmosphere of wealth, luxury, mystery, even spirituality, appropriate to the mysteries of the Grail Castle; on the other a factual, even technical terminology describing many familiar objects and phenomena of twelfth century life—buildings, furniture, weapons, clothing, transport, food and drink—the backcloth against which the mystery is played out. The one spurs and teases our imagination; the other, as in the remarkably unrhetorical, even colloquial passages of direct speech, and the suggestions of grotesque humour, keeps our feet as firmly planted on the ground as those of the young Perceval. And it is precisely the mixture of a *stylus gravis* and a *stylus humilis*,[37] together with the limitation or suppression of comment, which gives the narrative so much of its force.

The Grail Castle episode is, however, not simply concerned with the unfolding of an enigmatic adventure. The author of the *Charrette* is as mindful here as he was in his earlier romance of the importance of giving his 'matière' a 'sen', i.e. of propounding or at least implying some underlying moral or psychological significance. In the case of the Grail romance, even more than in the earlier romances of Chrétien, one major theme is obviously the educational one,[38] in this case the development of the hero's personality from his naïve beginnings to his Good Friday experience. In this development the visit to the Grail Castle is clearly a major *étape*, one in which we see the hero, when thinking of his mother's fate, assailed with anxiety, perhaps already remorse, and when confronted with the Grail procession, with puzzlement and uncertainty. Chrétien seems to have wished to remind his readers that there was a deeper significance to the adventure without—lover of mystification that he was—at this stage revealing his hand. Stylistically, he has chosen to do this, as we saw, by presenting the adventure almost entirely through the eyes of his hero, and by using the sophisticated technique of indirect reporting rather than the device of the psychological monologue more commonly found in his time, not least in his own romances. This may have been imposed on him by those considerations of brevity and concentration to which we alluded earlier. Lengthy monologues would hardly have been in place in an episode which relies so much on narrative and visual effects. Whatever the reason for his choice of means it is evident that the near-Flaubertian technique employed represents a remarkable anticipation of more modern stylistic developments in the French novel, as well as, of course, contributing to the aura of mystery surrounding the Grail Castle.

Finally, if Chrétien's method of psychological exploration is in advance of his time, we have been reminded that we are also dealing with a peculiarly medieval form, and one still strongly linked to

---

[37] On these terms see Faral, op. cit., pp. 86–9.

[38] See A. Micha, 'Le Perceval de Chrétien de Troyes (roman éducatif)', in *Lumière du Graal*, les Cahiers du Sud, Paris, 1951, pp. 122–31.

conditions of oral delivery, by the extensive use, in this episode, of the epic technique of repetition. The purpose of this is still, as in the older form, to recapitulate and emphasize important motifs for the audience, and yet, at the same time, to make an aesthetic virtue out of a necessity by the addition of stylistic gradation and variation. An effective example of this is, as we noted, the repeated and cumulative use of negative formulae in the first and final sections. Perhaps, however, the most striking instance occurs—and the combination is piquant—in the otherwise highly modern account of Perceval's mental deliberations at the sight of the procession to which we referred above. The deliberate exploitation of repetition as a narrative device in this way, comes over more naturally in verse than in prose, is indeed inherent in the rhetoric of verse. The octosyllabic couplet as used by Chrétien and his contemporaries is by its very nature so unobtrusive a medium that one tends to overlook its poetic, as distinct from its prosaic potentialities. Our final stylistic point might then be a reminder that the passage we have been examining is the creation not of a modern novelist but of a medieval poet writing to be read aloud, no longer of course with quite the *panache* of the *chanteur de geste*, but nevertheless with a still keen sense of the effects to be derived from a poet's rhetoric.

Laurent Joubert's System of Orthography between 1578 and 1580

A. H. DIVERRES

Carnegie Professor of French at the University of Aberdeen

The importance of Laurent Joubert's works to our knowledge of the French language in the second half of the sixteenth century has long been recognized.[1] One of the leading medical doctors of the century and the author of Latin treatises on medicine, he also wrote works in French which brought a knowledge of hygiene and medical matters to a far wider public than previously and in which one finds a number of medical terms attested for the first time.[2]

Joubert was also one of those who attempted to reform French orthography during the sixteenth century. In her recent *L'Orthographe française à l'époque de la Renaissance* (Geneva, 1968), Nina Catach has tried to show that his contribution in this field is not original. Since her account of it is incomplete and in one or two respects misleading, however, it seems worthwhile taking a further look at his reforms. He introduced modifications in his own system of spelling at various times, and so I shall concentrate on the end of Joubert's career and limit my study to the 1578 edition of his *Erreurs populaires et propos vulgaires touchant la medecine et le regime de santé* (printed by Millanges of Bordeaux), the 1579 edition of his *Traité du Ris . . .* (printed by N. Chesneau of Paris), and the 1580 edition of the *Erreurs populaires . . .*, *Segonde partie* (printer unknown, but published by both L. Brayer and A. L'Angelier of Paris).[3] These three editions used Joubert's own system of spelling, and the author is stated on the title page of *Erreurs*

---

[1] See F. Brunot, *Histoire de la langue française des origines à 1900*, II, pp. 52–5, 119.

[2] The most recent account of Joubert's career is to be found in 'L. J. chancelier de Montpellier' by L. Dulien in *Bib. d'Hum. et Ren.*, XXXI (1969), pp. 139–60.

[3] The copy of this last work used in preparing this article was published by L'Angelier.

populaires . . ., *Segonde partie* to have personally revised the text. Since the three editions, produced by different printers as far as is known, offer the same characteristics, Joubert may well have revised the other two as well, and so we should find in all three Joubert's system in its final form.

One of the main criticisms levelled at Joubert's reforms has been their inconsistency. There is substance in this criticism, for he used more than one transcription for certain sounds, while conventional spellings mingle in nearly every line with the reformed orthography. As Mme. Catach's book clearly shows, the works of most of the sixteenth-century reformers reveal conventional and reformed spellings side by side, and she rightly puts it down to the printers' hostility to reform. One of Joubert's printers readily admits this, stating that his compositors had experienced considerable difficulty with the system and had often infringed it by reverting to conventional spellings.[4] What I shall try to do in this article, therefore, is to describe Joubert's reforms as he would have wished them to be applied, not as they were applied in practice. The 1579 edition of the *Traité du Ris* and the 1580 edition of the second part of the *Erreurs populaires* offer valuable evidence for this purpose in the form of articles explaining features of Joubert's system, the one by his nephew C. de Beauchatel, which follows the *Traité du Ris*, being particularly significant, since it gives by far the more detailed account.[5]

Although Beauchatel states in his 'Annotacions sur l'orthographie de M. Ioubert' that his uncle's maxim was 'il faut ecrire, tout ainsi que l'on parle & prononce',[6] Joubert did not attempt to revolutionize

---

[4] 'Amy Lecteur, ie dois bien estre excusé enuers toy, attendu ma bonne volonté, si i'ay en plusieurs endroits fally contre l'orthographie de M. Ioubert, d'autant qu'elle m'ha esté fort nouuelle à ceste foys, et difficile à imiter. Dequoy ie t'ay bien voulu advertir, affin que tu n'imputes à l'auteur, quelque deffaut en l'observacion de ses reigles, ou de n'estre par tout semblable à soy. I'espere de faire mieux vne autre fois. . . .' (*Erreurs populaires . . . Segonde partie*, 'L'Imprimeur au lecteur de bonn'ame', opposite p. 1 of the 'Advertisement sur l'orthographie de M. Ioubert'. A statement to the same effect by C. de Beauchatel is to be found on p. 407 of his 'Annotacions'; see note 5.

[5] 'Annotacions sur l'orthographie de M. Ioubert, par Christophle de Beauchatel', *Ris*, pp. 390–407; 'Advertisement sur l'orthographie de M. Ioubert', *Erreurs populaires . . Segonde partie*, a three-page account placed just before the text and not included in the main pagination. Beauchatel states: 'dez long tams j'ecris sous luy, & ay transcrit beaucoup de ses evures (*sic*) Fransaises' ('Annotacions', p. 390).

[6] 'Annotacions', p. 390.

orthography by inventing a phonetic alphabet and using it for all his transcriptions. He was no more than a fairly conservative reformer whose aim, essentially reader directed, was to rationalize French orthography by the consistent use of available letters and the retention of the traditionally accepted values of the great majority of them. He sought to reduce the number of alternative transcriptions of sounds, but his reforms revealed his awareness that a revolutionary change of system would only bewilder his reader. Wherever he felt that a modification could lead to confusion, he did not hesitate to retain the conventional orthography of a word. That is why the possessive adjectives were transcribed as *noz*, *voz* in the plural, though they were pronounced in the same way as the personal pronouns *nous*, *vous*,[7] and possibly why he spelt the third person singular present indicative of *avoir* as *ha*, while the other persons were transcribed without *h* (e.g. *ay*, *avons*, *ont*). He made no attempt to reproduce varying pronunciations of the same word according to its position in the sentence, except occasionally to indicate elision of the final [ə] by replacing the *e* by an apostrophe.[8] The presence or absence of liaison is never shown by the deliberate inclusion or omission of a final consonant as the case warrants, each word having a fixed spelling.[9]

Among the most striking of Joubert's innovations is the elimination of a superfluous *e* (e.g. *assuré*, *emu*, *sur* (adj.), *eau*, *lieu* (=*league*)), and of certain unsounded consonants (e.g. *astinance*, *sutils*, *instint*, *infet*, *respet*, *suspet*, *aministrer*, *pois* (*poids*), *ners* (*nerfs*), *vint*, *doit* (*doigt*), *cayers*, *melancolique*, *mante* (*menthe*), *sou* (*soûl*), *pous* (*pouls*), *cu*, *set*, *cors*, *tams*,[10] *exangues*, *et* (*est*), *taite* (*tête*), *plu-tost*, *gate*, *ote*, *puis* (*puits*)). This does not mean, of course, that the final consonants maintained in these examples

---

[7] 'Annotacions', p. 406.

[8] Spellings such as *un' ame*, *com' est*, *habil' homme* are quite common throughout the works studied and seem to be due to the author, in spite of Beauchatel's statement: 'Il ne touche point l'e, nommé feminin, cõme font aucũs: d'autãt qu'il ęt si frequant que rien plus' (Annotacions', p. 391).

[9] The dedicatory 'Epitre' to the *Traité du Ris* seems to bear this out, since we come across the following forms within the space of the first page: *tres-auguste*, *træ-excellante*, *tres-humble*, *træ-affeccionné*, *tres* being the conventional spelling and *træ* the reformed one. The degree of the printer's responsibility for this inconsistency is difficult to measure, but it is considerable, and almost certainly explains the form *træs-heureus* on p. 16 of the 'Epitre'.

[10] Beauchatel tells us that Joubert favoured changing *m* to *n* when *p* had been omitted, e.g. *tans*, *pront*, *ront*, *donte*, *conte* ('Annotacions', p. 404). In the texts *m* is far commoner than *n* in these cases.

were necessarily sounded.[11] When a noun or adjective is used in the plural, final *t* or *d* is omitted (e.g. *androis, espris, vans, chaus, drois, galhars, piés, lours*). On the other hand, initial *h* is always included (e.g. *heure, heureus, hyver, honneur, huile*).

In view of this search for simplification, it is surprising that, with the exception of *s* and *ss*, Joubert not only had no consistent policy with regard to single and double consonants, but that he should have shown a preference for the latter, for no apparent reason (e.g. *robbe, succer, succre, proffit, affin, aggreable, aualler, facillemant, homme, honnorer, appellee souppe, iarret, garderrobes, dittes, toutte*). Beauchatel states that Joubert favoured the use of *u* for the vowel and *v* for the consonant,[12] but this distinction is rarely observed in the text, where in nine cases out of ten one finds *v* indifferently for the vowel or the consonant in an initial position, and *u* for either medially in the word. The use made of the diæresis to clarify this source of confusion will be discussed later. The situation of *i* and *j* is similar, for *i* is far commoner as a consonant than *j* in all positions. Again we learn from Beauchatel that his uncle recommended the use of *j* for *g* before an *a*,[13] yet *i* is far more frequent and indicates the printers' responsibility for many of these anomalies. *x* is eliminated as the final consonant of a word (e.g. *sis, soupsonneus*), and *s* is generalized to the exclusion of *z* (e.g. *accidans, petis, chaus*), except after *e*, when both are used about equally (e.g. *accés, accez; vantuosités, vantuositez*). In spite of Mme. Catach's statement to the contrary,[14] Joubert continued to make wide use of *y* in three ways, firstly to replace an *i* contiguous with *m, n, u*, apparently to assist the compositors who had to read the manuscript, since it can have been of no help to the readers of the printed page (e.g. *syncerité, amys, dimye, poyure, hyuer*; see 'Annotacions', pp. 397–8), in the initial position to avoid confusion with *i* consonant (e.g. *yeus* for *ieus, yure* for *iure*), or else in final position after *a, o*, whether it is a diphthong or not (e.g. *fay, vray, moy, pourquoy*; see 'Annotacions', p. 399). In this last case, since there was no danger of confusion, his concern would seem to

---

[11] Beauchatel makes the surprising statement, unconfirmed by anybody else, that the final *t* of *est* (vb.) was sounded before a word beginning with a consonant. 'Le T y æt fort necessaire; car il sonne manifestement audit verbe, ancore qu'il soit devant une consonne' (Annotacions', p. 393). If this is not an error on Beauchatel's part, it must have been a provincialism.

[12] 'Annotacions', p. 395.

[13] 'Annotacions', p. 398. This point is dealt with in greater detail below (p. 95), under *Transcription of sounds*.

[14] Op. cit., p. 442.

have been aesthetic, *y* at the end of the word being of more pleasing appearance than *i*.

Joubert's most radical reform was to simplify the terminations of the third person plural *-ent*, by omitting *n* (e.g. *accablet, calomniet, plaignet, ayet, diret, firet, eusset*). This shows that he was not concerned with accurate representation of pronunciation, but that he sought to simplify the orthography, at the same time avoiding confusion with the third person singular. In the imperfect indicative and the conditional it is the *e* that was left out (e.g. *avoint, etoint, seroint, mourroint*), and the third person plural of the present subjunctive of *être* was treated in the same way (*soint*).

Transcription of sounds. Where Joubert was at his most inadequate was in the precise transcription of vowels, for it was only in the case of [e] and [ɛ] that he attempted to indicate quality, length or articulation. No distinction at all was made between [a] and [ɑ], [ɔ] and [o], and between [œ] and [ø], though the digraph *au* always seems to stand for [o].[15] [œ] and [ø] were transcribed as *eu* unless the preceding consonant was *c*[k], when *œu* is used (e.g. *eul (œil), yeus, meurs (mœurs), peut, cœur*). On the other hand, he made a clear distinction between [e] and [ɛ], transcribing the former in the final position in the word as *è* or, more commonly, *é* (e.g. the past participles *etouffè, travalhé*), and in the initial or medial position as *e* without an accent (e.g. *emu, moderemant*). He had three separate symbols for [ɛ], either *ę, ai* or *æ*, which he used indifferently for each other (e.g. *eté* (< *æstatem*), *æté, baite (bête), effait, cræte (crête), sujæt, laivres*, etc.).[16] This choice may mask a genuine difficulty in distinguishing between [ɛ] and [ɛi], for, after describing Joubert's symbol for [e], Beauchatel continues: 'Il y a vn autre e, qui æt diphthongue, sonant *ai*, comme la premiere syllabe de *aime, maitre, faire*: lequel M. Ioubert marque volontiers ainsi *ę*, ou d'un *æ*: comme an Latin ces caracteres sont pour representer le αι des anciens: qui depuis ha eté changé en *æ*'.[17]

Both Fouché and Pope are agreed that in these three examples the vowel in the stressed syllable was [ɛ] long before the sixteenth century. But in describing Joubert's use of *y* in final position after *a* and *o*,

---

[15] I have found a consistent use of *aage, aagé*, and a single example of *baalher*, but it is impossible to decide in these cases whether the *aa* indicates lengthening, the maintenance of the hiatus or merely an inconsistency.

[16] The occasional use of *ei*, attested in *peiches, reigles, seiche, seize, treize* may be due to the printers' ingrained habits, since *seche* and *treze* are also attested.

[17] 'Annotacions', p. 392.

Beauchatel states that he used it whether it formed a diphthong or not
with the preceding vowel and gives as his examples *fay* (presumably
the imperative singular) and *moy*.[18] Thurot cites several examples of
hesitation in the pronunciation of monosyllabic words ending in *ai* in
the second half of the sixteenth century,[19] and, though we cannot be
sure, Joubert may well have been among those who hesitated between
the pure vowel and the diphthong or had difficulty in distinguishing
between them.

Joubert was consistent with the nasalized vowels, [ã], whatever its
origin, being transcribed as *an* or *am* (e.g. *an (en)*, *anfans*, *amploya*,
angeandra, *jans*, *sandres (cendres)*, *sant (cent)*, *tams*, etc.), and [ɛ̃] as *ain* (e.g.
etainte, *paintre*, *dessain (dessin)*). *Fin* and *vin* are always spelt traditionally,
but one cannot tell whether this indicates that [ĩ] had not been lowered
to [ɛ̃], or whether it was merely to avoid confusion with *faim* and *vain*.
[u] was invariably transcribed as *ou*, [ũ] as *on* or occasionally *un*, [y] as *u*,
and the remaining diphthongs as *ieu*, *oi*, *oui* and *ui*. It is impossible to
be sure what sound is represented by *eau*.

Joubert was more successful in solving the easier problem of the
consonants. The majority of graphemes represent the sounds in an
orthodox way (*b, p, f, ph, t, d, s, l, r, g, m, n*), and there is nothing to
say about them. He attempted to rationalize the transcription of the
following sounds, however:

(a) [s]. In an initial position and medially after a sounded consonant
or a nasalized vowel, Joubert followed tradition by using either *c* or *s*
when followed by *e* or *i* (e.g. *se, ceus, citoyen, farseurs, ulceres, abondance*).
Intervocalic *c* (+*e, i*) was also in free variation with *ss* (e.g. *procede,
simplicité, epissés*), though again tradition exercised a strong influence in
the choice. When followed by *a, o* or *u*, *s* was used initially or medially
in the word after a sounded consonant or a nasalized vowel (e.g. *sang,
soupson, suer, acsan, apersut, Fransais*),[20] and *ss* in an intervocalic position
(e.g. *indessance, fasson, ressu*), *ç* being eliminated from the alphabet.[21]

(b) [sj]. Whether it was preceded by a vowel or a consonant, Joubert
showed a marked preference for *-ci-* than for *-ti-* (< Lat. *-ti-*; e.g.

[18] 'Annotacions', p. 399.
[19] See C. Thurot, *De la Prononciation française* . . ., 2 vols. Paris, 1881–3,
vol. I, p. 302 ff.
[20] The nasal consonant may still have been sounded. 'M. Ioubert aime mieus
les ecrire par un simple S, quand C ęt precedé d'une consone comme an *fiansa,
fransais*' ('Annotacions', p. 402).
[21] See 'Annotacions', p. 391.

racionel, recreacion, condicion, impaciance, concepcion, distinccion, friccions).[22]
-*si*- and -*xi*- were maintained when the etymon had *s* or *x* (e.g. *apprehension, complexion*).

(c) [ʒ]. According to Beauchatel, Joubert recommended the use of *j* in preference to *ge* before *a* and *o* (e.g. *jans, jantil, toujours*),[23] though he made an exception in the case of *mangeant, mangeoit*, etc., to avoid confusion with *manier*.

(d) [ʎ]. This sound was transcribed as *lh* (e.g. *alhe, talher, oualhes, vielhe, euelher, familhe, perilheus, chatoulhe*).

(e) [ɲ]. *gn, ign* and *ngn* are in common use (e.g. *compagnon, chatagnes, ensegner, temogne, craignet, peigner, bangner, yurongne*).

(f) [k]. The conventional use of *c* or *qu* according to the following vowel, was continued. Unlike Ronsard, Joubert did not introduce *k*.

Diacritic signs and abbreviations. We find a certain confusion in Joubert's use of diacritic signs, but he avoided the temptation, to which some sixteenth-century reformers of orthography succumbed, of cluttering his text with them. Like Meigret and Sebillet, he hesitated between the acute and grave accents in order to indicate [e] in the final syllable of a word, though the former is the commoner.[24] In the initial and medial positions in the word the accent is sparingly used. On *a* and *u* one finds the grave accent. According to Beauchatel, Joubert was in favour of the replacement of the unsounded *s* of *tost* by a circumflex accent, though *s* was sometimes included in the text,[25] but elsewhere the accent was very rarely used and the *s* was omitted (e.g. *apre, facheus, lache, ætre, diner, ote*). The *tilde* was commonly placed above a vowel to indicate that it was nasalized, while, in addition to marking hiatus (e.g. *obeïssant*), a diæresis placed above a vowel showed that the preceding *u* was a vowel (e.g. *preuuë (prévue), preuue (preuve), couärd*; see 'Annotacions', pp. 396–7). It was sometimes placed over the *u* (e.g. *joüant, loüé*).

The traditional abbreviations for *qui, que, par, plus, nous, vous* were widely used, while & for the conjunction *et* was general.

Joubert's pronunciation of certain words. In the 'Advertisement sur l'orthographie de M. Ioubert' which precedes the text of *Erreurs*

---

[22] See 'Annotacions', p. 402.
[23] 'Annotacions', p. 398, and 'Advertisement sur l'orthographie de M. Ioubert' in *Erreurs populaires . . ., Segonde partie*. For the confusion between *i, j*, see above, p. 92.
[24] 'Annotacions', p. 392.
[25] 'Annotacions', pp. 404–5.

populaires . . ., Segonde partie, we are told that Joubert had a clear idea of what he considered to be correct French pronunciation, and he defined it as that heard at court or in the 'lieux esquels on parle mieus'. This is what he tried to reproduce, deliberately avoiding provincialisms. Beauchatel is our main source of information about Joubert's pronunciation, and his remarks, taken together with the orthography, allow us to deduce his pronunciation of a certain number of words. A more detailed study of the texts would lengthen the following list considerably.

(a) Final [ə] was no longer sounded in *eau* (*aqua*), while two pronunciations were acceptable for *lieue,* either [ljø] or [lyə].

(b) The vowel in the stressed syllable of *père, mère, frère, mer, amère, clair, claire, effet, respect* was [ɛ]. It was also open in *et* (conj.), *est* (vb.), and in the first syllables of *été* (< *aestatem*), *hémorrhoïdes, équivoque, lézard.*

(c) The vowel in the first syllable of *aime* was open, but that of *aimer* was closed.[26]

(d) Since it is usually transcribed as *ai*, the vowel in the second syllable of *Français* and *pâmoison* was pronounced [ɛ], not [wɛ].

(e) The nasalized diphthongs in *ancien, patient, Italien, chrétienté* were pronounced [jã], since this sound is always represented by *ian.*

(f) The *o* in the first syllable of the following words was pronounced [u]; *bombance, cochon, connaître, corbeau, côté, coteau, coton, formage, montrer, profit* (spelt *boubance, couchon, counoitre, moutrer,* etc.). It was equally closed in the possessive adjectives and pronouns *notre, nos, votre, vos, nôtre, vôtre.*[27] In *témoigner, éloigner, poignée,* the *o* (+ɲ) had not been diphthongized (spelt *temogner,* etc.). Joubert may have pronounced it [ũ], since this is how he sounded it in *rogner* and *soigneux* (spelt *rougner, sougneus*). *o* (+m, n) was pronounced [ũ] in *ombrage, volontiers* (spelt *umbrage, voluntiers*).

(g) [l] was dental or alveolar, not palatal in *bétail, travail, soupirail, oeil, fenouil* (spelt *betal,* etc.). Final *l* was effaced in the plural of *linceul.*

(h) [n] was alveolar in *digne, signe, signification, bénigne, bénignité.*[28]

(i) Except in words of recent origin, præ-consonantal *s* was effaced medially in the word (e.g. *contriccion, plu-tôt, præque, retrainte, rete* (*reste*), *soutraccion*).

---

[26] 'Annotacions', pp. 392–3.
[27] 'Annotacions', pp. 405–6.
[28] 'Annotacions', p. 404.

(j) The orthography *gehener* suggests that the word was still tri-syllabic.

Joubert's system of orthography was therefore a blend of tradition and innovation, in which tradition predominated, and it is clear that he aimed at graphological consistency and economy, not at an accurate phonetic rendering. The list of characteristics of Joubert's orthography drawn up by Mme. Catach on p. 442 of her book gives the impression that they owed much to the work of Ronsard, Meigret, Peletier du Mans, and perhaps of Ramus or De Tournes. In the 'Dialogue sur la Cacographie fransaise' in the *Traité du Ris* (pp. 375–89), Français, who certainly expresses the author's views on his predecessors, states:

'Il æt vray, que Loys Meigret y ha pris peine, & s'æt efforcé de remettre l'ecriture à son devoir. Mais ses reigles plaiset à peu de jans, & on y treuue fort à redire, combien que (à mon avis) il n'ęt pas loin de la verité, qu'il ha diligeãmant recherchee. Puis vous avés M. Iaques Pelletier, & M. Pierre de la Ramee, tous deus grans personnages . . .' (p. 388).

No mention is made of Ronsard, and I can find no positive evidence that Joubert was influenced by his simplified orthography. There is a certain similarity, it is true, between the systems adopted by the two men, but this is because they were both influenced by Meigret and Peletier du Mans, particularly the latter. I feel sure that it is Peletier who exercised the main influence on Joubert, for Meigret's reforms were considered by him to go too far. But Joubert's innovations had no more immediate success than the more radical ones of his pre-decessors, for accepted tradition and printers' habits continued to prove too strong well into the seventeenth century.

The Old Pilgrim's Catch-words: Notes on *Parlant Moralment* and *Quel Merveille* in *Le Songe du Vieil Pelerin*

JANET M. FERRIER

Chaque écrivain a son mot de prédilection, qui revient fréquemment dans le discours et qui trahit par mégarde, chez celui qui l'emploie, un vœu secret ou un faible. (Sainte-Beuve: 'M. de Sénancour' (*Portraits contemporains*, 1832.)

In 1389, in the seclusion of the convent of the Celestines in Paris, Philippe de Mézières completed the writing of his *Songe du Vieil Pelerin*,[1] in a mood of some depression as he contemplated the times he lived in, *lesquelz ne sont pas dorez appellez*. His purpose in writing was to offer to the young Charles VI the fruits of his long and varied experience as statesman, Chancellor of Cyprus, expert on Middle East affairs, friend and adviser of Charles V and founder of the abortive crusading order of the *Chevalerie de la Passion de Jhesu Crist*.[2] In a series of surveys of increasingly narrowed focus, Philippe examines first the moral state of the whole of the known world of his day, then, in great detail, the organization and administration of every aspect of French society, until he comes in the final and longest book to a treatise on kingship, addressed personally to his sovereign. This is an ambitious project even by fourteenth-century standards; it is carried out by means of a series of interlocking allegories and with the aid of a huge cast of personified virtues and vices and of contemporary figures represented in allegorical form. Philippe himself evidently expected his contemporaries to find these difficult to disentangle, and ends his

[1] *Le Songe du Vieil Pelerin of Philippe de Mézières, Chancellor of Cyprus*, ed. G. W. Coopland, 2 vols., 1969. All textual references are to this edition. Professor Coopland's text has no accents, but in quotations in this article I have accented final *é*'s.

[2] See A. H. Hamdy, 'Philippe de Mézières and the New Order of the Passion'. *Bulletin of the Faculty of Arts*, Alexandria University, Egypt, XVIII (1964), pp. 1–105.

Prologue with a *Table figuree* in which the various allegorical figures are interpreted. Charles VI, for example, is from time to time referred to as *le cerf volant couronné, le blanc faucon pelerin au bec et piez dorez, le grant maistre du grant parc, le jardinier du grant jardin des blanches fleurs dorees, le grant maistre des eauues et des forestz de France, le grant marchant du grant change* and *le jeune Moyse couronné*; while Philippe as the narrator presents himself as the Old Pilgrim and is later given the name of Ardant Desir, but frequently steps out of these guises to reinforce his argument with a personal reminiscence.

Yet despite the daunting length and complexity of this work, it shows a surprising degree of coherence and unity. This is due in part to Philippe's skill in manipulating several allegorical themes simultaneously and particularly in keeping the basic one—that of forging true currency as the foundation of a sound moral economy—constantly before the reader. One is aware throughout of the author's plan, and this is the reflection of his own determination to view human affairs at every level *sub specie aeternitatis* and to insist on the relation of cause and effect: no country and no individual, he declares, can prosper whose conduct is not based on Christian principles. Unity is also given to the work by the consistency of the style and in particular by the use of recurrent images, by the frequent and striking use of homely expressions in an exalted context, and by the persistent use of certain phrases: of these by far the most common are *parlant moralment* and *quel merveille*, which are to be found with great frequency throughout the work, with a considerable variety of meaning and emphasis.

Philippe's intention in the *Songe* is both 'moral' in the modern sense and figurative, in that every instance and event he cites has a spiritual purpose; this works in both directions, so that on the one hand the reader is expected to draw a general moral inference from some particular true incident that is cited, and on the other he must be ready to apply to his own conduct the general principles laid down in allegorical fashion. Philippe's use of *moral* reflects both these preoccupations. It is frequently used, as so often in fourteenth-century writing, in the sense of 'figurative', as when Philippe speaks of *nostre royal eschequier figuré . . . mon ouvrage ou dit eschequier et ma moralle escripture* (II. 429). But there are many instances where *moral* appears to have approximately the modern sense. It is very often linked with *divin*, in such phrases as *les loix divines et morales*, or *l'escripture divine et moralle*, where the meaning seems fairly vague. It can also indicate a distinction between the purely practical and matters that have to do more with the mind and the spirit. Thus where Verité is advising the King on the use of spies, she says:

> En toute guerre et doubtance de guerre la premiere et principale chose morale si est d'estre informé de ses ennemis par les vrayes espies. (II. 404)

This appear to mean that it is essential to be mentally prepared, as well as armed, in order to engage successfully in war. In many cases, however, we find *moral* used to mean 'of high moral principle'. Where Verité is advising the King to have the backgrounds of candidates for office carefully investigated, she adds:

> Et soit faicte ceste enqueste, qui n'est pas de petit poix, par certains preudommes qui ja ont refusé les offices et sont saiges et moraulx et de bonne conscience et contemps de leurs estaz. (II. 328)

In another context again, *moral* appears to have the meaning of 'on an ethical level'. After citing the example of Charlemagne, who by contriving good relations with Saracen leaders succeeded in securing tolerance and good treatment for Christians in Saracen lands, Verité urges Charles VI to send an envoy to the Sultan of Babylon with the object of establishing similar relations:

> Le dit escuier . . . dira que tu as bonne voulenté d'avoir bone amitié moralle avecques le souldan. . . . Et se aucun des con-seilliers du souldan vouldra dire que tu ayes mandé le dit escuier pour espie, il pourra respondre clerement que tu le mandes pour vraye amour et honneur et noblesse, et pour acquerre l'amitié moralle, non tant seulement du souldan, mais du Grant Caan de Tartarie et de tous les seigneurs du monde. (II. 426)

These various shades of meaning of *moral* are naturally reflected in the uses Philippe makes of the phrase *parlant moralment*, though the sense of 'figuratively speaking' accounts for the greater part. However vague and general some of the instances of this usage may appear, it is evident from Philippe's statement in the Prologue of the scope, method and purpose of his book that the ideas and attitudes suggested by the phrase are essential to that purpose. He declares:

> Il est ainsi que l'acteur de cestui Songe, c'est assavoir le Vieil Pelerin, en cestui livre parle communement par figures et par paraboles, par similitudes et par considerations ou ymaginations, aucunesfoiz prinses de la sainte escripture et des livres et des diz moraulz des

philosophes, faignant les noms des roys, des princes et des seigneurs, parlant moralment a son advis selon leurs condicions, pays et regions. . . . Et aussi aux vertuz et aux vices il leur baille propres noms, par adventure autresfoiz non usez, selon leurs condicions. (I. 100)

Philippe's equivocal use of *parlant moralment* is interestingly brought out in this passage, where he is bringing to his readers' attention both the allegorical method he intends to use and the moral issues which will be uppermost in his mind. In this he will be following, as he tells us in the next sentence, the example of the 'moralitez aussi des saints docteurs, et par espicial de monseigneur saint Gregoire ou livre de ses Moralitez'.

Parlant moralment occurs often in the course of Philippe's accounts of the comings and goings of the Queens and their attendants, with no particular purpose except to remind the reader that this is indeed an allegory. In the Prologue, where Philippe is expounding the basic allegory of the assay on which the whole work is constructed, it occurs in almost every sentence, sometimes with a particular application but on other occasions with apparently only the most vague and general meaning:

> Et les vertuz germaines de Charité, c'est assavoir Sapience et Verité . . . s'en sont alées empres comme il fu dit dessus, en laissant leurs lieutenans, parlant moralment, telx quelx. . . . Toute la substance en groz de cestui livre ou songe, parlant moralment, n'est autre chose que la venue en esperit de nouvel en ce monde de la royne Charité, Sapience et Verité. . . . Laquelle venue en esperit des dames, parlant moralment, est moult solennelle. . . . Encores est ainsi que parlant en cestui livre par figure . . . de la sainte et faulce arquemie, . . . n'est autre chose, parlant moralment et en figure, que une nouvelle maniere de parler et tracter des vices et des vertuz. (I. 95–6)

As the work proceeds with ever-increasing complexity, introducing and developing new allegorical themes without losing sight of this basic one of the forge, *parlant moralment* is often used in a more particular way. It may be found introducing a new comparison, as when Droicture presents her comparison of France to the human body—a comparison which will be extremely detailed, likening, for example, the digestive organs to the Treasury officials, and the fingers to the King's body-servants—and begins in a business-like way, 'Supposons, parlant moralment, et prenons l'omme pour le royaume de France' (I. 572). Again, when Philippe gives a detailed description of the appearance of the Queens and their attendants, after pointing out that the light of the sun can both illuminate men and blind them, he goes on:

> La clarté doncques de Verité la royne estoit comparee, parlant moralment, a la clarté du soleil, et la clarté des troys dames, Paix, Misericorde et Justice, pouoit estre comparee a la clarté de la lune, qui du soleil prent sa lumiere. (I. 451)

When the ship of State, *Gracieuse*, is introduced, every item of equipment is given its allegorical equivalent, nearly always with the use of this familiar phrase:

> Par cestui tymon petit barionnoys, parlant moralment, puet estre entendu le doulx et reposé gouvernement du roy et des princes, en temps de paix doulcement maroyant. (I. 557)

—and a similarly frequent use occurs in the exposition of the four-wheeled chariot in the Third Book.

This usage appears to be an alternative for *moralisant. Moralizare* is defined by Du Cange as *dicta ad mores aptare*, and *moraliser* is the verb we find in other fourteenth-century writers such as Christine de Pisan and the unknown author of *Modus et Ratio*. Philippe does sometimes use *moraliser*, as when, mindful no doubt of Jacques de Cessoles, he speaks of the ordinary game of chess 'dont la nature est assez clere pour bien moraliser et forgier bons besans de l'ame' (II. 201), or when at the end of the book, he speaks in his own person and says 'Jusques a ores nous avons parlé et forgié les besans moralisant des vertus en figure' (II. 498). In the extended exposition of the theme of the tombs of the prophets the two terms are evidently synonymous:

> A nostre propoz, parlant moralment, il se puet dire par figure que les dessusdiz seigneurs et officiers de justice . . . sont les prestes de la loy et les Pharisees. . . . Moralisant, les sepulcres peuent estre pris pour une memoyre sollennelle et les prophetes pour les justes et vaillans hommes jadis mors. (I. 505)

Some distinction is, however, implied by Cotgrave, who defines *moraliser* simply as 'to moralize, to expound morally, to give a moral sense unto', but who gives for *moralement* 'morally, in a moral sense or fashion; also, doubly, or with a meaning different from his words'.

An interesting use that may be considered under this general heading of 'figuratively speaking' occurs where Droicture is describing the voyage of the *Gracieuse* towards Jerusalem. She explains that some of the passengers and crew do not complete the journey but leave the ship at various ports of call. The first of these is a volcanic island that Philippe identifies as Stromboli:

> Les autres de la dicte nef . . . estoient arrestez en une ysle qui est nommee Vulcan ou le Trouble. . . . Une partie des marchans, des princes et des patrons, des mariniers et des conseilliers s'i finent leur voyage, et s'ilz ont froit ilz treuvent bien pour eulx eschauffer, ne jamais a la sainte cité ne viendront. (I. 548)

But some stay on board a little longer:

> L'autre condicion des personnes de ladicte nef . . . estoient arrestez en une ysle de mer qui est entre Hierusalem et l'isle de Vulcan, qui est appellee, parlant moralment, l'isle de la Touche. En celle ysle a forges sans nombre, esquelles forges, par le commandement du maistre de la monnoye, tous les besans des marchans qui la sont arrestez, a tous essaiz sont bien examinez. (ibid.)

Those whose *besants* pass the test receive an immediate pass for Jerusalem. *L'Isle de la Touche*, which clearly represents purgatory, is evidently an imaginary spot, in contrast with Stromboli whose natural features provide too telling an image to require comment even from Philippe de Mézières. The reader is warned of this distinction between the two islands by the interpolation of *parlant moralment*.

The alternative meaning of *moral*, in something approaching the modern sense, is reflected in some instances where *moralment* clearly seems to mean, in the words of Cotgrave's first definition, 'in a moral sense or fashion'. When, for example, the Queens in the course of their investigation visit Avignon, Ardant Desir begs them to stay:

> Car j'ay esperance, madame, que se en ladicte cité par vostre sainte arquemie et de mes dames aussi, se forgeront bons besans, que, avant qu'il veignent deux ou troys ans, parlant moralment, des catholiques la descripcion se fera et chacun y accourra. (I. 304)

This sense is made even more clear in the following example, where Magnificence, in the course of her analysis of the ills suffered by the people of France, is condemning pillaging by the soldiery under such notorious leaders as Teste Noyre:

Il se puet dire selon la foy crestienne qu'ilz sont pires devant Dieu que Sarrazins. Et certainement il se puet dire moralment que en la guerre des mescreans encontre les Crestiens, les mescreans ne sont pas si cruelx envers les Crestiens, et de l'eglise, des nobles et du peuple, comme sont les dessusdiz pillars. (I. 531)

This sense of 'from a moral point of view' seems to be intended in some cases where, because the expounding of some allegorical detail is involved, it might superficially appear that *parlant moralment* had the meaning of 'figuratively speaking'. Thus Verité speaks of the night creatures and of those who resemble them, and in particular of the bat, which, as we already know from the *Table figuree*, represents Lucifer:

Quant a la chauve souris . . . il vous doit souvenir, moralment parlant, comment la souriz chauve jadis fu un trop bel oyseau, qui pour sa tresgrande faulte elle fu condempné a perdre son beau plumage et estre laide et noyre. (I. 243)

And in another similar passage, Avarice speaks of her pet mole, which is itself, as the *Table figuree* tells us, the symbol of avarice:

'Quant a la taupe noire et aveuglee que je porte pour mon esbate-ment, aucuns dient que je lui ressemble assez', dist la vieille, 'parlant moralment, selon le dit de la gent, et que je suis ville, noyre et terrestre et me delicte es biens de la terre.' (I. 334)

It seems, indeed, possible that both meanings are simultaneously present in these examples, and there are occasional instances where Philippe appears to use *moral* in a deliberately ambiguous fashion. Thus when Verité is speaking of the King's debts and demolishing the excuse that they are so extensive that it is impossible to start dealing with them, she uses the analogy of a knight wounded in so many places that he does not know which to heal first and dies from lack of care. This comparison is introduced by the words, ' "A laquelle contradiction je respons," dist la royne, "en mectant un exemple assez moral" ' (II. 358). The use of the qualifying *assez* here seems to suggest that *moral* is used not only to introduce the parable, but to indicate that the king's immortal soul is at stake in leaving these debts unpaid, so that the example is a 'moral' one in the modern sense.

Parlant moralment is such a favourite expression with Philippe de Mézières, and so closely mirrors his preoccupations as a writer, that it is not surprising to find that he occasionally tends to use it apparently without any very precise intention, perhaps—as we shall see that he does with his other recurrent expression, *quel merveille*—to give a characteristic rhythm to his sentence. It acts, too, as a warning to the too literally-minded reader that every word is not to be taken at its face value, and in these instances might be rendered, perhaps, as 'so to speak'. Many of the examples of this usage are to be found as a parenthetical addition to the homely metaphors and proverbial expressions to which Philippe is so addicted. Thus during the visit to Avignon, Bonne Aventure says:

> En ceste cité, . . . selon l'effect de la relacion des vieilles, je cognois clerement que les ungs sont gras, les autres maigres, parlant moralment; les ungs sont yvres et les autres meurent de fain. (I. 361)

Shortly afterwards, Philippe himself, in the person of Ardant Desir, is commenting on those rulers who take advantage of the schism to retain revenues due to the Church, alleging that they will eventually pay them to whichever papal candidate is finally chosen. He adds sceptically, 'Lesquelles rentes, parlant moralment, ilz rendront quand je fileray' (I. 368). Yet again, where he is speaking of the corrupt finance officers who grow unaccountably rich in the course of their tax-collecting, he contrasts this affluence with their condition earlier in their career:

> Et quant ilz furent mis en l'office, ilz n'avoient ne cheval ne jument ne sergent ne varlet, parlant moralment. (I. 459)

Very often *parlant moralment* is used where Philippe has mentioned, in the course of an illustration to reinforce his argument, some exact detail. It may be a statistic, as when, after telling the story of the *conseillier* who every year presented his lord with an exact list of the gifts he had been offered, and who refused to take undue advantage of the benefits available to him, Droicture adds:

> Car il estoit contempt pour sa marchandise en la nef de gaigner tant seulement, parlant moralment, x pour cent. (I. 578)

Again, it may be a gesture, as in the passage where Verité is telling the King to remember that at Mass he is no more important than any of his subjects, and speaks with disapproval of some princes who

> A pasques recoivent le saint sacrement secretement en une chappelle et puis viennent a la grant messe, la ou tout le peuple et les bonnes

creatures communient communement, et lors ilz sont presens, les bras croisiez, parlant moralment, donnant matiere de mal penser. (II. 265)

These examples seem to indicate Philippe's extreme anxiety not to be misunderstood. He is clearly concerned that the impact of his message should not be spoiled by some niggling critic who may seize on a minor point of detail and by condemning it as inaccurate attempt to invalidate his whole argument.

There remain a few examples of the use of *parlant moralment* that do not appear to fit into any of these categories and indeed seem at first sight paradoxical if not meaningless.[3] Thus where Verité is advising the king of the benefits both to himself and to his subjects of receiving the sacrament devoutly, she ends with the words

Et lors, Beau Filz, ce faisant tu verras visiblement, parlant moralment, descendre la rousee du ciel et la misericorde de Dieu sus toy et sus ton peuple, par telle maniere que chacun, ou la plusgrant

[3] There are some instances of apparent obscurity which may be due to the editor's punctuation. Thus where Magnificence is introducing the bold allegory in which the three estates are likened to the three persons of the Trinity, she says,

Je reciteray . . . une clere figure pour descendre particulierement es contrayres des nobles du royaume de France et de sa chevalerie. Parlant moralment, chacun scet que en tous royaumes des Crestiens et aussi des payens a troys estaz, c'est assavoir les gens de l'eglise, les nobles et le peuple (I. 526).

Parlant moralment seems meaningless here, since what follows is a statement of fact. But if we put the stop after *parlant moralment*, it complements *une clere figure* at the beginning of the sentence; then *chacun scet* introduces the statement of fact on which the figure is based. Again, where Verité is introducing the allegory of the box of spices to be found inside the chariot, we find:

A nostre propoz, les espices dudit coffre en qualité sont diverses, car les unes sont fortes, et aucunement mordans, sicomme gymgembre, cloux de gyrofle et graine de paradis. Les autres sont doulces et alectives, sicomme sucre, canelle et saffron, et les autres doulces espices, parlant moralment. Beau Filz,' dist la royne Verité, 'quant en ton curre proposé tu aras bien combatu et grandement labouré, pour aucune recreation d'esperit, de par mon Pere les espices fortes et mordans premierement te seront presentees, c'est assavoir que tout ce que tu auras fait en combatant jusques a celle journee sera comme nyant ou regart des batailles bien mordans a venir, qui sont des couars redoubtees. . . .' (II. 170).

Here the stop should surely come after *espices*, since this ends the factual description of the box and its contents. *Parlant moralment* then introduces the figurative explanation.

partie, recoignoistra ses deffaultes et la bonté de Dieu, et amandera
sa vie. (II. 263)

Here at first sight *visiblement* and *moralment* might appear to cancel each
other out, if we take *moralment* to mean 'figuratively'—and it is
unlikely that at the climax of this eloquent passage Philippe would
wish to give the phrase only the meaning of 'so to speak'. The end of
the sentence, however, seems to suggest that what he means is that the
spiritual or moral benefits to the kingdom will become visible in the
improved conduct of his subjects.

Another rather curious example occurs in the story of the obstinate
Chief Justice who refused the sacrament of penance to those he
condemned to death:

> Lequel chief de justice au contrayre de cestui cas se trouva si obstiné
> et de si forte cervelle . . . que, parlant a la lectre et moralment, on
> eust plustost fait retourner la roe d'un moulin au contraire que
> l'endurcy susdit de son oppinion rigoreuse il se volust retraire.
> (II. 283-4)[4]

Here it seems likely that *a la lectre* applies to the mill-wheel and *moralment* to the Chief Justice; in this case *moralment* appears to mean 'from
a moral point of view'. Alternatively, the expression may mean 'to
use a figurative example, it would literally be easier. . . .' A more
elaborate instance of the juxtaposition of *parlant moralment* and *parlant
a la lectre* is to be found in the detailed comparison that Hardiesse makes
in the Second Book (I. 505-7) between the judges of Philippe's day
and the Pharisees of the Gospel. After quoting from Matt. XXIV,
27 ff. Christ's words about the tombs of the prophets, she goes on 'A
nostre propoz, parlant moralment, il se puet dire par figure que les
dessudiz seigneurs et officiers en justice . . . sont les prestes de la loy et
les Pharisees.' This is straightforward enough; and, continuing the
analogy, Hardiesse adds that *moralisant* the tombs are memorials, the
prophets the virtuous departed and the paintings the virtues of the dead.
She then says, 'Or venons a la concordance' and pursues the analogy
to point out detailed parallels between the scriptural example and its
modern application. Now comes the climax of the passage:

> Or est a veoir qui sont les peres des dessusdiz glorieux incorrigibles
> et obstinez, parlant a la lectre et sans glose. Ce sont orgueil, pere et

---

[4] Philippe is much given to analogies and proverbial sayings taken from the
working of mills: see I. 231, 381, 508; II. 229, 239.

commaincement de mort, acompaigné a sa dextre et a sa senestre
d'envie et de ire. . . .

Despite the introductory *parlant a la lectre*, Philippe in the person of
Hardiesse thus in fact moves away from the concrete and particular to
the true motivation of the judges, and we are back with the deadly
sins: these are the literal reality, and Philippe makes his final point
clearly and unambiguously without having recourse to any allegorical
figures.

Of Philippe's other favourite expression, Professor Dora M. Bell has
remarked that 'Cette petite phrase, qui se répète avec des nuances
infinies, pourrait servir de signature à Mézières.'[5] There are over two
hundred instances in the *Songe* of the use of *quel merveille*; most
chapters contain at least one example and some have several. This is not
to imply, however, that Philippe uses the expression indiscriminately:
in Book III, for example, *quel merveille* does not occur in the first
seventeen chapters. Here the scene is set for the allegories of the chariot
and the chess-board, which are to be the framework for Philippe's
treatise on kingship, and much space is devoted to the dialogue between
Verité and Charles VI, here identified as the Young Moses. The first
instance of *quel merveille* in this third book occurs significantly where
Philippe, in the person of Verité, is dealing with blasphemy and false
swearing, a subject on which he feels strongly and which, he says,
persists in France because belief in the popular saying *qui bien le jure,
bien le croyt*, is handed on from father to son (II. 144). The phrase does
not appear again during the rest of the exposition of the ten command-
ments: the next instance is not until ten chapters further on, where
Verité is applying the parable of the talents to the King's situation, and
is once more concerned with the question of cause and effect. Similarly,
in Philippe's work setting out the aims and organization of his pro-
jected crusading order[6] *quel merveille* occurs several times in the
preamble, in which he enumerates the philosophical and historical
justification for his enterprise, but not at all in the part dealing with
practical details and with an historical account of earlier crusades. It is

---

[5] Dora M. Bell, *Le Songe du Vieil Pèlerin de Philippe de Mézières*, 1955, p. 43,
n. 13.
[6] See Hamdy, op. cit., pp. 51–104.

not until the end, when Philippe is about to give the text of the prayer for the use of members of the order, that we find the final example:

> Et se puet dire doulcement que apres la Patrenostre ladite oroison est de tresgrant vertu et bien esprovee par le tesmoing de ceulx, qui l'ont acoustumé de dire. Quel merveille, car elle comprent en substance iii choses necessaires à l'omme. . . .

In the majority of instances, the meaning of *quel merveille* appears to be 'and no wonder'. It is most commonly followed by *car*, and sometimes introduces a simple explanation, such as that for the names of the ship of State:

> Ceste nef en beauté singuliere avoit deux noms, c'est assavoir La Gracieuse, et, Souveraine. Quelle merveille, car de tous biens elle estoit plaine. (I. 537)[7]

More often, however, the use of this expression shows Philippe's overriding preoccupation throughout the work: to demonstrate the ineluctable sequence of cause and effect. *Quel merveille* is used to introduce an explanation for what has gone before, either by reference to some universal law of nature or of human conduct, or, more practically, by providing details of historical background or of geographical or biographical interest. Thus as the allegory of the ship progresses, an old sailor is made to remark that in former times it was well commanded, and so gives the author an opportunity to remind the young king once again that good government does not go with dissipation and late nights:

> . . . lors la marchandise multiplioit, et le bon besant lors avoit son cours, . . . lors les vens fortunaux ne tempeste communement en la nef n'avoyent nulle puissance. Quel merveille, car lors les seigneurs ne mangeoyent pas a mynuit, ilz ne faisoient pas du jour la nuyt, comme on fait a present. (I. 582)

Or again, in the Third Book, Verité, with a homely analogy characteristic of Philippe, condemns the marriages of little children for reasons of political or diplomatic expediency:

> . . . desquelz mariages et aliances communement le fruit est nul, petit ou moult amer. Quel merveille! car la loy de nature est pervertie. On cueilt la poyre avant qu'elle soit flourie. (II. 347)

---

[7] I believe that the rhyme here is not fortuitous. Many other examples of vestigial rhyme occur, especially in the First Book; I hope to deal with these in a later article.

This meaning of 'and no wonder' is present even in a few examples where *quel merveille* is not followed by *car*, as in the passage where Droicture condemns the religious orders for love of riches and indifference towards the poor:

> Or venons et brefment aux moisnes et aux religieux de la nef francoise. Ilz ont grans rentes et par leurs pechiez mal revenans, et si meurent les aucuns de fain. Quel merveille, entr'eulx l'arquemie de ma dame l'Amoreuse grant temps a est faillie, celle qui soustenoit et le corps et la vie. (I. 623)

L'Amoreuse, as we learn from the *Table figuree*, is 'la vertu de doulce misericorde': where her currency is not in use, it is no wonder that the riches of the religious orders are misapplied and false values are accepted. Droicture goes on in the next sentence to speak of an abbey she knows of which has involved itself in fifty lawsuits at once, and for this too she has an explanation based on the same principles:

> Quel merveille, des moisnes et religieux de l'ordre de saint Benoist, de saint Augustin, de saint Bernart, et de plusieurs autres, ilz ont lachié le frain a leur benoist reigle, et la guerre et dehors et dedans, l'espee au poing, est seurvenue, et devocion s'en est yssue. (I. 624)

It is characteristic of Philippe's method of composition that he frequently makes use of this expression when he is reinforcing his argument by the use of Scriptural quotations. These are often difficult to disentangle from the rest of his text, since he translates freely, alters the order of the excerpts he includes, and interpolates remarks of his own. These glosses, however, are often given his characteristic signature by being introduced by *quel merveille*, as when Verité refers to Psalm CXI, 10:

> La premiere chose que tu doys avoir si est vraye crainte de Dieu. Car la doubtance de Dieu est le commaincement de sapience. Quel merveille! Qui doubte Dieu, il fera toujours bien. (II. 159)

And a little later, in a passage largely composed of excerpts from the book of Proverbs, he follows a quotation from Prov. III, 24 with his own brief comment:

> Se tu dormiras, tu ne doubteras riens, et repouseras doulcement. Quel merveille! car Dieu sera a ton cousté et te garderas de tous maulx. (II. 160)

We see the same technique at work during the section dealing with astrology, in which Philippe has drawn heavily on Oresme's *Livre de Divinacions* (I. 590–619).[8] This borrowing from his revered contemporary is done with great skill, the argument being interpolated into the dramatic dialogue between Bonne Foy and La Vieille Superstition, embroidered with references to the allegories of the *Songe* and enlivened by reminiscences of places and people Philippe has seen; and the occurrence of *quel merveille* from time to time in this passage gives it the characteristic flavour of Philippe de Mézières's writing.

As we read this long book, it is difficult to avoid the impression that the force of *quel merveille* used with the meaning of 'and no wonder' diminishes as the narrative and the arguments proceed: the sentence as a whole would often lose nothing of its cogency if the phrase were omitted. Some examples from Book III, taken at random, will illustrate this. When St. Cyril's dead nephew appears to the saint at prayer,

> lors il leva les yeulx et veit son nepveu si treshorrible qu'il ne l'osoit regarder. Quel merveille! car il estoit tout noir comme un charbon, lié par tout son corps de chaennes de feue ardant qui rendoyent flambes si trespuans que on ne les pourroit descripre. (II. 215–16)

Verité puts the case against having the scriptures translated into French:

> Car la saincte escripture, escripte et dictee par les sains en latin et depuis translatee en francois, ne rent pas telle substance aux lisans es ruisseaux comme elle fait en sa propre fontayne. Quel merveille! car il y a en la sainte escripture certains et plusieurs motz en latin qui du lisant percent le cuer en grant devocion, lesquel translatez en francois se treuvent en vulgal sans saveur et sans delectacion. (II. 223–4)

—or excuses herself from providing a longer excursus into the question of war and peace:

> Se de la forme et proces de guerre . . . je voulusse entrer en la matiere, cestui point seroit trop long. Quel merveille! car d'une si grant matiere on en feroit un livre plusgrant assez que cestui present eschequier. (II. 380)

---

[8] See G. W. Coopland, *Nicole Oresme and the Astrologers: a study of his Livre de Divinacions*, 1952.

In these examples *quel merveille* does not so much add to the meaning of the sentence as provide a pivotal point on which it turns. The reader, confronted with this characteristic and by now familiar phrase, is able to pause momentarily, knowing that he is about to have Philippe's comment on what has gone before.

A more emphatic meaning seems to be attached to the few examples where *quel merveille* is followed by *se* and where the sense is more interrogatory: 'Is it to be wondered at if . . .?' There are some half-dozen instances of this usage, and all occur in Books I and II—significantly, perhaps, in view of the progressive weakness in meaning that the phrase seems to show during the latter part of the work. The examples with *se*, on the contrary, have considerable force. When the Queens visit Genoa, they set up their consistory with great splendour and summon before them Pope Urban VI and his cardinals. Philippe goes on to explain that the effect they produced on the beholder depended upon whether or not Urban's claim to the papacy was accepted. To some their vestments appeared splendid, shining with jewels and rich colours,

> . . . et aux autres sembloient lesdiz abiz obscurs, derompuz, sales et jaunes, tissuz de la toison d'une vieille brebiz. Et les chapeaux leur sembloient composez de vieil papier, qui longuement avoit trempé ou fumier. Quel merveille! disoient les assistens dessusdiz, se ces cardinaulx estoient vestuz de jaune comme les Juifz, car de grant chaleur d'avarice et d'ambicion leur foye estoit tout entierement pourry. (I. 284)

Again, Hardiesse, in Book II, condemns the excessive number of officials in the Parlement; scarcely a quarter or a fifth of them, she says, have any legal knowledge and qualifications, and she adds

> Quel merveille s'ilz sont nouveaux en l'office et mains cognoissans, car aujourdui ilz sont intrus es offices . . . par faveur de seigneurs et par diverses autres voyes. (I. 503-4)

—or Droicture remarks that corruption among the clergy filters through from the top:

> Quel merveille, se l'arcedyacre, le doyen et le curé en gouvernant leurs brebiz se conforment a leurs prelatz et abbé. (I. 623)

All the instances with *se* are to be found in passages where Philippe's feelings appear to be strongly engaged by some scandal of legal or ecclesiastical mismanagement or corruption, and where his style becomes correspondingly highly charged.⁹ By attaching *quel merveille* not to the explanation which in some cases follows, but to the state of affairs he is attacking, he appears to invite his readers to share his indignation.

It is somewhat disconcerting to find that there remain some examples of the use of *quel merveille* where the meaning appears to be the direct opposite of those we have considered so far. Here, instead of following *quel merveille* by an explanation or a comment intended to justify what has gone before by showing a close relationship of cause and effect, the meaning of the phrase seems to be 'How extraordinary!' What follows is still, in a sense, a gloss on the passage immediately preceding; but here it is not so much an explanation as an expansion, in which the author introduces some new element of wonder, usually at the extravagance or folly of human conduct which can lead to the state of affairs he is describing. Thus Luxure, glorying in her pernicious influence and that of Venus, attributes to it the fourteenth-century epidemic of chorea in Germany:¹⁰

> 'Je puis bien dire,' dist la vieille, que es Crestiens d'occident aujourduy, Venus et moy avons trop plus grant seigneurie, que nous n'avons entre les Tartres, Juifz et Sarrazins. . . . Quel merveille!' dist la vieille. 'Nagayres en Brebant et en Alemaigne, je les feiz tant dancer que, sans dormir et mangier, jour et nuyt ilz dancoient, en dancant ilz mouroient et de la mort ilz ne pouoient eschapper.'
> (I. 343)

Here *quel merveille* seems clearly intended to introduce the reader not to a mere explanation or comment on what has gone before but to a new and surprising statement, providing a particular instance of the general truth already enunciated. The same force is given to the phrase in a passage where Droicture is condemning the way that favourite servants of kings and great nobles are able to line their own pockets:

> Mais aujourduy les serviteurs des grans seigneurs . . . ne sont pas bien contens de leur marchandise . . . de gaigner chacun an x pour

⁹ The other examples occur where Ardant Desir excuses those who elected Urban VI through fear of the Romans, and now regret their decision (I. 371); where Hardiesse is recommending a simplification of the legal process on the lines of the Milanese system (I. 498); and in the description of the *Gracieuse*, where the Captain's imperfect authority is excused by the lack of co-operation from the lower decks (I. 552).

¹⁰ See Douglas Guthrie, *A History of Medicine*, 1945, p. 100.

cent, mais fault qu'ilz en ayent par phas ou par nephas et V^c et
mille. Quel merveille! le filz d'un pauvre homme ou d'un laboureur,
d'un grant patron serviteur, en mains d'un an, ou de deux, ou de
troys, acquestera V^c ou mille livres de terre, et les autres deux mille
ou troys mille. (I. 571)

A very similar instance is to be found where Verité speaks, in Book III,
of corruption among the officials who are concerned with collecting
the *aides*:

Le second inconvenient et dommage publique du royaume si est
l'oppression du peuple gallican par les sergens et officiers royaulx au
liever des dictes aides. Quel merveille! Il est assez notoire que une
ville qui doivra des aides c livres en un an, il se trouvera que tant
montera que au chief de l'an la dicte ville sera dommagee de autres
II^c livres. (II. 393)

In almost every instance where *quel merveille* is used in this sense, the
author's purpose is to emphasise the wickedness or folly of his generation, whether it is manifested in the excesses of private conduct or in
corruption in public life. The last example in the book is in the climactic
passage where Philippe describes how, after their prolonged sojourn on
earth and their exhaustive examination of the state of men's morals,
Charity, Wisdom, Truth and their retinue of attendant virtues depart
in a chariot of fire:

Lors toutes les personnes du consistoire des quatre gerarchies non
pas petitement se trouverent esbahies et a certain temps privez des
divines vertuz, en figure filles de Dieu appellees. Quel merveille!
car le peuple gallican, qui par la divine bonté avoit esté visité . . .
refusans bone monnoye, se trouva en tenebres, les uns regardans a
la terre come devant aux honneurs et couvoitises, et les autres a
luxurier non regardans le ciel, mectans leur joye et leur felicité avec
les Egypturiens es viandes et buvrages delicieux. (II. 494)

The use of *quel merveille* in this sense at this moment of apocalyptic
vision is particularly striking, as indicating Philippe's recognition that
the ills of his country are not to be cured by any words of admonition,
or any shining example, from himself or anyone else.

Among the prose works of the later fourteenth century, *Le Songe du
Vieil Pelerin* stands out not only for its extraordinary scope and

complexity, but for the author's mastery of his material and the consistency of his style, which obviously merits close and detailed study. The recurrent phrases *parlant moralment* and *quel merveille* give this work the unmistakable stamp of its author not by their mere reappearance in so many contexts but by the preoccupations they reveal.

Words and Word Criteria in French

ROY HARRIS
Fellow of Keble College, Oxford

Something about the structure of French—although exactly what is perhaps not immediately obvious—can be pointed to (rather than pointed out) by drawing attention to various queries about the concept 'word'[1] which arise in attempting to describe in general terms the patterns of organization of morphs in the French sentence, and the diachronic movements which have created them.

For some languages, like English, it is noticeable that phonological and grammatical criteria for word delimitation on the whole coincide. French is often cited as an example of a language for which this is not true. In French, we are told, 'whatever congruence there is between phonological and grammatical structure seems to hold over units of higher rank than the word'.[2] At the grammatical level, it is said that

[1] We are here concerned with the 'word' in the sense in which 'the word belongs to the aspectual level of the morph, not to the aspectual level of the morpheme' (C. E. Bazell, *Linguistic Form*, Istanbul, 1953, p. 13). We shall not be concerned with words as lexemes (J. Lyons, *Introduction to Theoretical Linguistics*, Cambridge, 1968, p. 197), nor with criteria for mapping sets of phonological or orthographical word tokens into the set of grammatical words of the language.

[2] Lyons, op cit., p. 205. Cf. also L. Bloomfield, *Language*, London, 1935, p. 181; R. H. Robins, *General Linguistics. An Introductory Survey*, London, 1964, p. 197. Some reservations about the extent to which liaison obscures word boundaries in French are voiced by P. Delattre ('Le mot est-il une entité phonétique en français?', *Le français moderne*, VIII (1940), pp. 47–56). According to Bloomfield, some French word boundaries are predictable on the basis of vowel length, since 'the mere presence of a long vowel in French . . . indicates that the next consonant or consonant-group ends a word' (Bloomfield, op. cit., p. 110). This statement is curious in view of Bloomfield's reference for data on French to the publications of Passy, since for a French speaker of Passy's generation it seems doubtful whether the generalization holds. For example, applying Bloomfield's criterion as it stands to the sample transcripts of French given by Passy in *Les Sons du français* (Paris, 8th ed., 1917, pp. 126–39) would result in the recognition of word boundaries in the middle of such forms as *pensait*, *bêtise*, *choisis*, *attention*, *maison*, *enfant*, *épuiser*, *privation*. (Cf. also Passy's explicit assertion that [ɛ] is always long in the ending -*aison* (op. cit., p. 160.)

many French pronominal forms have only a marginal status as words. It is also a fact, although less frequently commented on, that if occurrence in absolute position is to be our test, many French nouns and some verbs are less 'fully' words than their English counterparts. (Q. *Qu'est-ce que tu cherches?* A. *Du pain.*) (Q. *Tu en as pour longtemps?* A. *J'arrive.*) It is not *pain* but *du pain*, and not *arrive* but *j'arrive*, which qualify as free forms.

Various expedients can doubtless be suggested if we want to keep on counting as 'words' the forms orthography and tradition identify as 'words'. For example, it might be more appropriate for French, Bazell suggests,[3] to replace the criterion of occurrence in absolute position by occurrence in both initial and final position. (This would capture even *y* and *en*.) But if we follow Hockett in thinking that calculation of the synthetic index is 'the easiest rough measure of morphological complexity in a language',[4] it will still be true that either there is, curiously, no easy way of measuring the morphological complexity of French, or else we must say that in the case of French the index has to be calculated in a special way (which, presumably, defeats the purpose of typological comparison).

Typological statements about French are often, unfortunately, couched in the confused and confusing terminology, of nineteenth-century origin, which distinguishes between 'analytic' and other varieties of language. 'The history of French consists largely in the abandonment of flexions in favour of particles and word-order, in the passage from a synthetic to an analytic language'.[5] 'Le français moderne est, avec l'anglais, la langue européenne qui a le plus accentué cette évolution, de l'état synthétique vers l'état analytique'.[6] And so on. Such formulations are usually based, either overtly or implicitly, on a particular definition of the 'word'.

It will, of course, be tantamount to tautology to say that 'French is an analytic language' if we mean by 'analytic' what was meant by von Schlegel (apparently the first to apply this term to the Romance languages):

'J'entends par langues analytiques celles qui sont astreintes à l'emploi de l'article devant les substantifs, des pronoms personnels devant les

[3] Bazell, op. cit., p. 68.
[4] C. F. Hockett, *A Course in Modern Linguistics*, New York, 1958, p. 181.
[5] A. Ewert, *The French Language*, London, 1933, p. 123.
[6] A. Dauzat, *Phonétique et grammaire historiques de la langue française*, Paris, 1950, p. 137.

verbes, qui ont recours aux verbes auxiliaires dans la conjugaison, qui suppléent par des prépositions aux désinences qui leur manquent, qui expriment les degrés de comparaison des adjectifs par des adverbes, et ainsi du reste'.[7] It would be naïve to observe that by these criteria French clearly qualifies as an analytic language; for it is a case of the criteria qualifying to fit the language. Schlegel, having selected French as the model of an 'analytic' language, defines 'analytic' accordingly. 'Analytic' thus means, in effect, 'French-like'.

On the other hand, if we redefine 'analytic' in a more up-to-date manner on the basis of typological indices à la Greenberg,[8] the question arises how to choose between competing definitions of 'wordhood', without prejudging the issue whether the definition chosen makes sense for French. (Greenberg's main criterion is a version of 'separability' which makes it a necessary and sufficient condition of a boundary between morphs being also a word boundary that it be 'possible to insert an indefinitely long sequence of nuclei'. Nuclei are defined in terms of morph substitution classes.)

As a framework for discussion, it will be convenient to treat the surface structure of any sentence as a grouping or groupings of morphs, analysable in terms of the usual relations of position, co-occurrence and substitutability. Both within and between groupings, various kinds of arrangement are theoretically conceivable. Thus, to take an example based on one suggested by Lyons,[9] the sentence

(1) *Normale — ment — il — arriv — ait — à — sept — heures*
    1   2   3   4   5   6   7   8

can be treated as an arrangement of three groupings (12; 345; 678) which are found in a different intergrouping arrangement in

(2) *Il — arriv — ait — normale — ment — à — sept — heures*
    3   4   5   1   2   6   7   8

---

[7] A. W. von Schlegel, *Observations sur la langue et la littérature provençales*, Paris, 1818, p. 16.

[8] J. H. Greenberg, 'A quantitative approach to the morphological typology of language', *Method and Perspective in Anthropology*, ed. R. E. Spencer, University of Minnesota Press, 1954, pp. 192–220.

[9] Lyons, op. cit., pp. 202–3.

9

and again in

(3) *Il — arriv — ait — à — sept — heures — normale — ment*
   3   4   5   6   7   8   1   2

But in (1), (2) and (3) the intragrouping positional relations remain the same. It might have been—but in fact is not—possible to have in French the sentence

(4) *Ment — normale — arriv — il — ait — heures — sept — à*
    2   1   4 3   5   8   7   6

in which the intergrouping arrangement is the same as in (1) but each of the three groupings is internally re-arranged.

To some extent the sequence of morphs we take as constituting a grouping may be arbitrary; but for present purposes that does not matter. Intuitive segmentation will always avoid setting up sequences like 56 (*ait-à*) of (1) as groupings. In any case, surface segmentation into intuitive groupings of the kind illustrated is required merely to provide a context within which we can examine the question 'Which of the elements here are words?'

Now the word, as everyone agrees, can be regarded as determined by various criteria, with marginality of status depending on the satisfaction of some but not all of the criteria chosen. It is also common to say that phonological criteria are less important than grammatical criteria. Robins describes phonological correlates of word segmentation as being 'of necessity, logically secondary considerations in the establishment of grammatical word units. They are seldom, if ever, entirely in agreement with the grammatical criteria over the whole of the vocabulary of a language, and where there is conflict between grammatical criteria . . . and phonological features normally coinciding in delimiting the same stretch of speech, the grammatical criteria must be allowed to carry the day'.[10] Two provisos should be added. The first depends on the fact that there is no virtue in having a criterion, even a grammatical criterion, which leaves too much in doubt. Thus it may be appropriate, as Bazell points out, to let some phonological criterion of approximately the same scope but which resolves more borderline queries 'occupy a superior place in the hierarchy of criteria than the definitional criterion itself'.[11] The second proviso depends on what the

[10] Robins, op. cit., p. 198.

ultimate object of the exercise is. It is perhaps too readily assumed that
the purpose we have in mind—or ought to have—is setting up a unit
for grammatical description. If that is so, then by all means let grammatical criteria take precedence. But if our concern (as happens to be
the case here) lies rather in the detection of linguistic patterns of a more
general kind, we should do well not to worry too much about questions
of precedence, but take from any criterion whatever of interest it can
give us.

Having said that, it should immediately be added that perhaps some
criteria have nothing to give us at all. Can such a criterion, then, 'really
be' a word criterion? To this the answer is: 'No. It is a bogus criterion,
but disguised well enough to look like a genuine one'. That there may
be totally bogus word criteria may perhaps seem surprising, at least
until one inspects closely the most celebrated of these impostors,
namely 'potential pause'.

According to the criterion of 'potential pause' words are segments in
sequences 'separable by means of pauses' (Jakobson and Halle[12]), or
'bounded by successive points at which pausing is possible' (Hockett[13]).
Critics of this criterion sometimes point out that 'speakers do not normally pause between words';[14] but this is an idle objection, since the
criterion appeals not to what pauses do in fact occur, but to what
pauses could occur. The trouble is that, for purposes of the criterion,
not any old pause will do, e.g. not what Nida calls 'hesitations', for
these 'may occur within words, as well as between words'.[15] But what
kind of pause, then, is meant? As soon as one asks the question, it
becomes apparent that what is wrong with the 'potential pause'
criterion is its circularity; i.e. it tells us to look for just those pauses
which can separate words. Unless we know which these pauses are, we
cannot apply the criterion: but that is exactly what the criterion was
supposed to tell us. Such a merry-go-round cannot even be, as has been
claimed for it, 'a procedural help to the linguist working with infor-
mants'.[16] For all it is is a misguided attempt to transfer into the analysis

[11] Bazell, op. cit., p. 67.
[12] R. Jakobson & M. Halle, *Fundamentals of Language*, 's-Gravenhage, 1956,
p. 20.
[13] Hockett, op. cit., p. 167.
[14] Lyons, op. cit., p. 199.
[15] E. A. Nida, *Morphology. The Descriptive Analysis of Words*, 2nd ed., Ann
Arbor, 1949, p. 86, note 15. Surprisingly, this appears to be contested by D.
Bolinger (*Aspects of Language*, New York, 1968, pp. 52–3) who takes possibility
of hesitation as an indication of word boundaries.
[16] Lyons, op. cit., p. 199.

of speech the traditional 'word-divider' of writing, namely the space. In the French grammatical tradition, the confusion is given canonical status in the Port Royal grammar: 'On appelle Mot ce qui se prononce à part, et s'écrit à part'.[17]

Turning to 'genuine' word criteria,[18] it may first of all be observed that the widely acknowledged non-correspondence between phonological and grammatical 'word features' in French is, from a historical point of view, the result of an accumulation of apparently independent phonological changes at various times. What is perhaps remarkable about French is the way in which the development of quite minor phonological features of word demarcation is sometimes counteracted, as for example in the operation of the 'loi des trois consonnes'. Pronunciations like [luʀsəblɑ̃] (l'ours blanc) exemplify this: they may, of course, deliberately be avoided, but that, as Ewert observes, is to be expected in speech which is 'conscious of and guided by the written word'.[19] The syllabification across morph boundaries of the kind which sixteenth-century grammarians illustrate with sentences like *Tou tin si ke tu fai zau zautres, vou zeste zun nome de bien*,[20] and which occasioned Palsgrave's comment that the French pronounce 'as though fyve or syx wordes or sometyme mo made but one worde', can be traced back to the thirteenth century. As early as the ninth, there is enough evidence of the prevalence of proclisis and enclisis to cast doubt on the existence of juncture phonemes as word markers. But these features well antedate the abandonment of the so-called 'tonic accent', which may be regarded as providing a phonological demarcation of certain word boundaries in Old French.

What at least is clear is that if we trace the development of a form like *ille*, which starts out as what Robins would call a 'nuclear member' of the class of 'words', by Early Old French we have to abandon word

[17] *Grammaire générale et raisonnée*, 1660, Ch. IV.
[18] There is a whole family of bogus word criteria about which nothing will be said here, namely semantic criteria. These are usually based on the untenable thesis that features of the word as a segmental unit are merely incidental properties of the expression of a semantic unit. (For a sympathetic account of this position, however, see S. Ullmann, 'The word and its autonomy', in *Principles of Semantics*, 2nd revised ed., Glasgow/Oxford, 1959, pp. 43–65, esp. pp. 50–4.) Since no semantic theorist has ever given a reasoned account of 'word-meaning' which would enable e.g. a commutation test on sentences to be used as the basis of a word analysis, the matter does not merit serious discussion.
[19] Ewert, op. cit., p. 104.
[20] M. K. Pope, *From Latin to Modern French*, Manchester, 1934, p. 219.

stress as a necessary condition of 'wordhood' and begin appealing to syntactic criteria if we want to keep as 'words' those descendants of *ille* which have become definite articles or weak oblique pronouns. To accommodate the Old French definite article we could deploy almost exactly the same arguments as Lyons uses for English *the*, conceding that it is not a minimum free form, nor one that passes the test of 'positional mobility'.[21] For in e.g. *Li rois voit sa fille*, however we permute the groupings in accordance with the freedoms allowed by Old French 'word order', *li + rois* must remain as a block, and in that sequence. But, like English *the*, *li* is saved as at least a 'marginal' word by the criterion of 'interruptability', it being grammatically permissible to interrupt the sequence *li + rois* by insertion of an adjective.

'Interruptability' (or 'separability') is perhaps generally regarded as the most important word criterion in French. It is not open to the objections raised above against 'potential pause'. But it does give rise to reservations of a different kind. In a well known passage,[22] Jespersen took Bally and Dauzat to task for suggesting that certain French pronominal forms had become, or were becoming, agglutinated with the verb, and ridiculed Bally's paradigm: *jèm, tu èm, ilèm, nouzémon, vouzémé, ilzèm*. (Bally's hypothetical travelling linguist, said Jespersen, must have collected his data in a very odd way, presumably by listening in on grammar lessons in which the persons of the verb were rattled off one after the other.) Jespersen was right in that we do not see here full pronominal agglutination of the kind to be observed in some Gallo-Romance areas, e.g. in certain Valdôtain dialects, where Bally's traveller would have reached the conclusion (and would have been wrong not to reach it) that the form of the third singular present indicative of *avoir* is not *a* but *la*. Nonetheless, Jespersen's counter-argument for treating the forms of Bally's paradigm as two-word sequences is not altogether convincing. The contrast he draws between *j'aime, il aime, il a aimé* and *amo, amat, amavit* is particularly unfortunate in that while it is true that *je* can be separated from *aime* (as in *je t'aime, je n'aime pas*, etc.) it is not, strictly, true that 'we never find anything placed between *am* and *o* in the first person, *amo*'.[23] (We find, for example, the future infix, as in *amabo*.) It might be said that the possibilities of insertion are fewer in the Latin examples; but they are not

[21] Lyons, op. cit., p. 204.
[22] O. Jespersen, *Language*, London, 1922, pp. 422–5.
[23] Jespersen, op. cit., p. 423.

all that abundant in the French. *Amo* may be more clearly one word
than *j'aime*; but that does not make *j'aime* clearly two words.

Hardly more convincing is Martinet's contention that '*dorm-ons*
reste un mot, bien qu'on trouve également *dorm-i-ons*, car le signe *-i-*
du subjonctif présent et des divers imparfaits (parmi lesquels le con-
ditionnel) n'existe que dans des combinaisons de ce type, et toujours
dans cette même position'; whereas '*je fais* forme deux mots parce
qu'on peut dire *je le fais*'.[24] For it seems arbitrary to pick on the fact of
the limited distribution of *-i-* as discounting *dormions* as a counterexample to the inseparability of *dorm-ons*, when *je le fais* is allowed to
stand as a counterexample to the inseparability of *je fais*; inasmuch as
although the object pronoun is found in other positions than that
exemplified in *je le fais*, its possibilities of occurrence are nonetheless
extremely restricted in French. Furthermore, if it is maintained, as by
Martinet, 'que l'on peut, sans dissocier le mot, intercaler, entre deux
signes qui le composent, un autre signe, à condition que ce dernier
n'existe jamais que dans ce type de combinaison', what is to decide
whether it is legitimate to count e.g. *le* in *je le fais* and in *faites-le* as
occurring in the same 'type de combinaison'? The application of such
a criterion would require a prior definition of the notion 'combination
type'; but separability itself would seem to be one of the obvious
criteria involved in any such definition.

It is relevant to ask at this point for a somewhat fuller account of
'separability'. The criterion is described, somewhat loosely, by Lyons
as depending on 'the possibility of inserting other elements, more or
less freely, between the morphemes or 'blocks' of morphemes'.[25]
('Morphemes' should be read as 'morphs'.) But there is an important
condition left out here. It is: *salva grammaticalitate*, not merely in the
sense that the resultant whole should be a grammatical sequence, but,
more narrowly, in the sense that in the resultant whole grammatical
relations between the separated elements should remain as they were.
For example, it has nothing to do with whether *je connais* is one word
or two that in the sentence *je connais Suzanne* one can insert a sequence
as long as Tottenham Court Road between pronoun and verb, of the
type *je suis un jeune homme qui . . . et qui connais Suzanne*, and end up
eventually with a grammatical sentence. For in that grammatical
sentence the pronoun is no longer the subject of the verb *connais*.

[24] *Actes du sixième Congrès International des Linguistes*, Paris, 1949, p. 293.
[25] Lyons, op. cit., p. 204.

If we are attempting to analyse the adhesion[26] of a grouping of morphs on the basis of interruption *salva grammaticalitate*,[27] various possibilities must be distinguished. First, it is possible that when XY is a given morph grouping in a language, XMY is the only grammatical sequence which exhibits an interruption of X and Y and does not alter the grammatical relation between X and Y. In such a case, only one other morph (M) may be inserted ('paradigmatic restriction') and that only once ('sequential restriction'). If XMMY, XMMMY, XMMM . . . MY were also grammatical under the same conditions, the separability of XY could be said to be paradigmatically restricted (to M), but sequentially unrestricted. In a case where the separability of XY is paradigmatically restricted to one of the members of the original grouping (i.e. where we can have e.g. XXY, or XYY, but not XMY) there is what may be termed 'internal paradigmatic restriction'. Should the interruption be paradigmatically restricted to a certain set of morphs (e.g. M, N, P, Q), but with restrictions governing the permitted number, order, or co-occurrence of morphs in the interruption, we may say the separability of X and Y is subject to 'place restriction', and distinguish one, two, or more 'places' accordingly. For example if X and Y are separable by (i) either M or N but not both, followed by (ii) either P or Q but not both, we could say there was a 'two-place' restriction with one place paradigmatically restricted to the morphs M and N, and the other place paradigmatically restricted to the morphs P and Q. It would also be possible to have cases of place restriction in which different sequential restrictions applied to different places, so that e.g. XMM . . . MPX was grammatical, but XMPP . . . PX not.

There will be cases where separability restrictions can most conveniently be stated not by reference to morphs but by reference either (i) to distributional classes of morphs, or (ii) to types of construction. The

---

[26] Adhesion is not to be confused with cohesion, i.e. 'the possibility of syntactic substitution of a single word for the whole group while preserving the rest of the sentence structure intact' (Robins, op. cit., p. 234). Cf. also Bazell, op. cit., pp. 35–6.

[27] This narrower sense of *salva grammaticalitate* stands, ultimately, in need of much more clarification than it is possible to give it here, and perhaps of more than anyone has so far been able to give it. To mention only one point, the fact that *red* in the *red Danish house* is only 'indirectly subordinate' to *house*, i.e. that *red* and *house* do not here combine to form a constituent (contrast *the red house*), would not be taken as a reason for denying that in *the red house* the form *Danish* can be inserted *salva grammaticalitate*. (The example is used by Bazell in his discussion of the relation of 'attachment'; op. cit., pp. 36–7.)

terminology proposed above easily extends to such cases. If X and Y
are separable only by morphs belonging to the distributional class *k*, we
may say there is paradigmatic restriction to *k*, and this will be a case of
internal paradigmatic restriction if *k* includes X or Y. If X and Y are
separable only by constructions of the type *ø* we may say there is
paradigmatic restriction to *ø*, and this will be a case of internal paradigmatic restriction if XY is itself a construction of the type *ø*. In all
such cases there may or may not be, additionally, sequential restrictions
and place restrictions.

Thus separability can be treated as a gradation or cline, with complete
freedom of interruption at the top end, and paradigmatic-cum-
sequential restriction to a single morph at the bottom. Its utility as a
criterion in the case of any individual language will depend on whether
and where well demarcated 'breaks' occur on the scale of types of
separability found in that language. In the present context, it will be of
particular interest to see whether a clear distinction is apparent between
separability which is paradigmatically restricted to a few individual
morphs, and separability which admits the members of a large distributional class of morphs, or constructions of a common type. Such
a distinction would reflect the existence of what Hockett calls 'two
basic orders of magnitude in grammatical patterning'.

It might perhaps be objected by traditionalists that all this is so much
terminological camouflage for what we all recognize anyway as the
difference between morphology and syntax. Two observations are
pertinent here. The first is that *if* the traditional terminology were
adequate to the linguistic facts, that would be fine. As Hockett says,[28]
whenever we *can* clearly distinguish two 'basic orders of magnitude',
then 'the traditional terms "morphology" and "syntax" do very well'.
However, 'closer scrutiny often reveals a separate order of magnitude
of grammatical patterning sandwiched between'. The example
Hockett cites is not from French, but it is from another Romance
language, and the point carries over. 'The internal organization of
dando, *me* and *lo* is morphology; the participation of *dándomelo* in
larger forms is syntax: the patterns by which *dando*, *me* and *lo* are
conjoined to yield *dándomelo* are not conveniently classed as either'. The
second observation is that, whether adequate to the linguistic facts or
not, the terms 'morphology' and 'syntax' will not help us here if they

---

[28] C. F. Hockett, 'The Problem of Universals in Language', *Universals of
Language*, ed. J. H. Greenberg, 2nd ed., Cambridge, Mass., 1966, p. 22.

are themselves based, directly or indirectly, on the concept 'word', as, for example, explicitly in the subtitle of Nida's book (*Morphology. The descriptive analysis of words*), or in Bloomfield's definition of 'syntactic constructions' as 'constructions in which none of the immediate constituents is a bound form'.[29] The point of elaborating a cline of separability is to ground a non-circular definition of 'word'.

The next move in that direction might be to point out that conceivably it comes close to being a linguistic universal that where separability *salva grammaticalitate* involves paradigmatic restriction to one or a few individual morphs, there is an accompanying sequential restriction. One might take this fact—if it is a fact—as suggesting a conjunction of conditions which would provide a satisfactory language-neutral 'upper terminus' for word units on the separability cline. For varieties of separability falling above this 'upper terminus' we might reserve the term 'intercalation'. Thus e.g. French *très + grand, très + très + grand, très + très + . . . + très + grand* would count as intercalation, whereas *arriv + ons, arriv + er + ons* (but* *arriv + er + er + ons*), and *le + voi + là, le + re + voi + là* (but **le + re + re + voi + là*) would not.

Reconsidered in the light of these proposals, Jespersen's case for treating *j'aime*, etc., as two words seems weak, since the examples he cites to prove his point come in fact very low down on the separability cline. In *il n'a pas aimé* the place filled by *n'* is paradigmatically restricted uniquely to the negative adverb, *pas* belongs to a limited set (cf. *il n'a rien aimé*), and there is a sequential restriction to a single occurrence in both cases. In *il nous a toujours aimés* the place filled by *nous* is paradigmatically restricted to a limited set of morphs, and also subject to a sequential restriction. Only for *toujours* can a case be made out for treating the interruption as an intercalation. Martinet's argument, judged by the same standard, fares no better.

There are, however, other possible arguments for treating *j'aime*, etc., as two words, which do not rely directly on the criterion of separability at all. Bloomfield allowed not only *je, tu, il*, etc., but also *me, te, le*, etc., as words in French on the ground that their substitution for *moi, toi*, etc., could be treated as a feature of grammatical selection, and the *moi, toi*, series qualified in any case as minimum free forms. Now there is an objection to this which may sometimes be overlooked. It can perhaps be stated most forcefully by pointing out that if *me* is a word in *il me voit* because it 'stands for' *moi*, then *me* in *il me le donne*

[29] Bloomfield, op. cit., p. 184.

may count as something more, since it 'stands for' *à moi*. In short, the argument tacitly commits us to a concept of the 'word' as a more abstract unit which may be 'present' or 'represented' sequentially in sentences in various ways, and hence to the possibility that more than one word may be 'present' or 'represented' in a given segmentally indivisible unit. Evidence for this commitment in Bloomfield's treatment of the 'word' comes in the passage where he describes *au* in *au roi* as a case of 'a single phoneme representing two words'.[30] The striking thing about this analysis of *au* is that neither of what Bloomfield calls 'the two words *à* [a] "to" and *le* [lə] "the"' itself qualifies a ; a minimum free form. Nor can either be treated with any plausibility as a grammatically selected substitute for a free form. It should in this connexion be pointed out that the argument which Bloomfield uses for treating the English definite article as a word will not work for the French definite article. It is an argument from analogy based on the similarity between *the*, *this* and *that*. Thus, as Lyons observes, 'instead of making a stand on his primary criterion and saying that, despite their traditional classification, such forms as *the* and *a* are not in fact words, he introduces a supplementary criterion of 'parallelism' with forms which are classified as words by the first criterion of freedom of occurrence'.[31] But in the case of Modern French there is no parallel which will do the trick. There is a parallel between *le* and *ce* (*le roi*, *ce roi*); but *ce* itself is not a free form. The 'nearest' free form is *ceci*, and we cannot have **ceci roi*, but only *ce roi-ci*. Thus the chain of analogy required to include *le* as a word in French is a conspicuously long and tenuous one. But at least a chain can be traced, which is more than can be said in the case of *à*. For neither in Old French nor in Modern French does *à* ever stand in absolute position; nor does it stand in any suitable relation to a form which does.

Thus it is difficult to exculpate Bloomfield from the charge of confusing, in his use of the word 'word', at least two quite different concepts. If French *au* stands for more than one of anything, it is not more than one word (in the sense of 'minimum free form') but more plausibly what Jespersen would have called more than one 'idea', or what some linguists nowadays would call more than one 'category'. This is not to imply that 'idea' and 'category' are simply synonymous labels, although one might perhaps be forgiven for thinking so if one

[30] Bloomfield, op. cit., p. 179.
[31] Lyons, op. cit., p. 201.

compares, e.g. Jespersen's statement that 'such a word as Latin *cantavisset* unites in one inseparable whole the equivalents of six ideas: (1) 'sing' (2) pluperfect (3) that indefinite modification of the verbal idea which we term subjunctive (4) active (5) third person, and (6) singular'[32] with Robins's statement that 'Latin /amo/(I) love, is morphologically divisible into two morphemes, root /am-/ and suffix /-o/; but this suffix, though morphologically not further divisible, marks five separate categories, each syntactically relevant in different ways to other words in sentences in which the form may occur (and in varying ways correlatable with separate semantic functions): singular number, first person, present tense, indicative mood, and active voice'.[33] An alternative description here would be one which, following Bazell and Lyons, reserves the term 'morpheme' for a distributional factor and employs 'morph' as the term for a segmental unit. Adopting this terminology, we may say that French *au* is a single nonsegmentable morph which represents more than one morpheme; and this state of affairs has obtained in French ever since the monophthongization of [au]. In O.F. *al roi*, the segment *al* is still, as Lyons would say, 'determinate with respect to segmentation'[34] and can therefore still be analysed as the combination of a preposition with the enclitic form of *le*. Here Bloomfield's analysis would be correct (if we granted him that the O.F. preposition and definite article are words), for there is an admissible sense in which *le* is 'represented' in *al*. But we cannot—as Bloomfield would apparently have us do—preserve this analysis when the morphic justification for it has long since disappeared. This would be an error just as bad as the most blatant confusion of diachronic with synchronic description. Once the monophthongization has taken place, then '*à* + *le* → *au*' can have only the status of a morphophonemic rule. And the abstractions in terms of which such rules are formulated are not to be equated with the abstractions which can be called 'minimum free forms'. (The other sense in which *au* might be said to represent two units is the sense in which one phonological or orthographical unit may represent more than one grammatical unit. Thus *au* might be described as representing the different but homophonous grammatical units exemplified in (i) *au roi* and (ii) *au printemps*. But this distinction is clearly not what Bloomfield has in mind.)

Bloomfield's definition of the word as a **minimum free form** is in

---

[32] Jespersen, op. cit., p. 421.
[33] Robins, op. cit., pp. 333–4.
[34] Lyons, op. cit., p. 181.

any case itself open to objection. For it is a matter of chance whether or to what extent the units thus delimited in a particular language do in fact play any consistent and characteristic role in the organization of morph groupings. The point may perhaps best be illustrated by a hypothetical example. Suppose L_1 and L_2 are both languages in which the sequence 'subject pronoun + verb' is determinate with respect to segmentation and forms a grouping corresponding in positional mobility within the sentence to some monomorphic elements. Let us further suppose that in both languages the sequence 'subject pronoun + verb' is uninterruptable and internally nonpermutable, and that the imperative is morphologically identical with the present indicative for all verbs. Let it be the case that in L_1 the subject pronoun is obligatorily expressed with all verb structures, whereas in L_2 omission of subject pronouns is optional with the imperative. In L_2 replies to questions can in appropriate cases by given by the subject pronoun in absolute position (i.e. the subject pronoun functions as what is sometimes called a 'response sentence'[35]), whereas in L_1 the addition of an anaphoric verb is required. Now the languages described will receive quite different word analyses if the definition of the word as a minimum free form is adopted, since in L_1 equivalents of *j'aime*, *tu aimes*, etc., count as one word, but as two words in L_2. Yet in fact the role of these combinations in the syntax of morph groupings is, apart from potentiality of occurrence in absolute position, identical in the two languages. In more general terms, the definition of the word as a minimum free form rests on the tacit assumption that occurrence in absolute position correlates with certain important properties of combinability in sentences.[36] But for some languages this may just not be true, and there is no guarantee that for all languages of which it is true the correlations are approximately comparable. (There would be nothing intrinsically absurd about the notion of a language in which all segmentally

---

[35] Robins, op. cit., p. 224.

[36] The assumption generally made is that 'zero-environment depends very closely on the overt relation of juncture. A morph *otherwise* in close juncture with neighbouring morphs is unlikely to occur in zero-environment' (Bazell, op. cit., p. 68). Bazell adds: 'it would usually be more appropriate to regard the close juncture as primary and the absence of independent occurrence as secondary'. This is, in effect, to concede the point made above; but nonetheless to stop short of conceding that the basis of the assumption is the confusion whereby occurrence in absolute position is treated as the extreme degree of 'separability in combination'. (This is just as nonsensical as to treat being a bachelor as the extreme degree of 'living apart from one's wife'.)

indivisible elements occurring in absolute position never occurred elsewhere within sentences at all, except perhaps as mention-forms.)

To argue that the defects of Bloomfield's definition can always be remedied by appeal to analogy is hardly satisfactory. Doubtless everyone would agree that it is arbitrary that in French *vous allez* should count as two words (on the ground that *vous* and *allez* are minimum free forms) when *je vais* counts as only one (because *je* and *vais* are not minimum free forms). But the appeal to analogy will only give the right result for the wrong reason. What is required is a classification which recognizes the parity between *vous allez* and *je vais* as far as morph grouping is concerned.

One advantage of a criterion based on intercalation is that it does justice to this parity between *vous allez* and *je vais*. Another is that it happens to fit the diachronic facts of French syntax, i.e. the various changes in French 'word order' have brought about restrictions which can be seen as a trend towards reducing freedom of intercalation, while maintaining more or less unchanged the possibilities of separation paradigmatically restricted to limited sets of morphs. For example, in the twelfth and thirteenth centuries, it is permissible to separate *je* + *voi* by various elements, including a direct object noun phrase (e.g. *quant je la demoisele voi*). In the sixteenth it is still possible to have a relative clause or appositional phrase separating *je* from its verb (e.g. *je, qui vous fais ces tant veritables contes, m'estois caché . . .*). None of these constructions is any longer grammatical in Modern French. Intercalation with paradigmatic restriction of the type *je* + *descends*: *je* + *m'* + *arrête* + *et* + *descends*, etc., remains grammatical, but is increasingly limited by the prevalent repetition of conjunct subject pronouns with co-ordinated verbs. Since the sixteenth century intercalation of the type *(je)* + *les* + *entends*; *(je)* + *les* + *vois* + *et* + *entends* has also disappeared: > *(je)* + *les* + *vois* + *et* + *les* + *entends*. Likewise in the noun phrase, repetition of articles, possessives, etc., before the individual members of a co-ordinated sequence of nouns has had a similar effect: *les* + *offenses* + *et* + *afflictions* > *les* + *offenses* + *et* + *les* + *afflictions*. What all these developments have in common is the reduction of intercalation. On the other hand, although e.g. the permissible sequences involving pronoun forms have altered during the history of French, it remains true for Modern French as for Old French that the conjunct subject pronoun can be separated from its verb by other pronouns occupying a 'direct object' place and also an 'indirect object' place, and that both places are governed in Old as in Modern French by a sequential restriction to one morph. Although the positional rules governing the relative order of the morphs have changed, the changes cannot be construed as a 'reduction' in the separability of the subject pronoun from its verb. (On the contrary, Modern French may require both places separating subject from verb to be filled, where Old French allows one to be left vacant; O.F. *je li done* vs. Mod.F. *je la lui donne*.)

If we base an analysis on intercalation, together with positional mobility within and between groupings (in both cases *salva grammaticalitate*), we can describe the major changes that have taken place in the history of French in terms of four classes, which may be labelled 'A', 'B', 'C' and 'D'. These are groupings which have positional mobility in relation to other groupings in a sentence, and

(A) allow neither internal permutation nor intercalation, or
(B) allow internal permutation but not intercalation, or
(C) allow intercalation but not internal permutation, or
(D) allow both internal permutation and intercalation.

In the history of French we observe class changes of various types. $C > A$ is exemplified in the case of adverbs; e.g. in Old French we have *humble + ment* (but not **ment + humble*) and also intercalations of the type *humble + et + douce + ment*, whereas in Modern French only *humble + ment + et + douce + ment*. $B > A$ is exemplified in the case of some compound nouns; e.g. in the sixteenth century we find both *grand + mère* and also *mère + grand*, both without possibility of intercalation, but in Modern French only the former survives. In general, $D > C$ is the typical change for groupings of noun and determiner (V.L. *patrem meum, meum patrem*; O.F. *mon père*); freedom of permutation reappears in Renaissance French (*les premiers exemples et comportements nostres*) but is no longer found to-day. In general, $D > B$ is the typical change for groupings of subject pronoun and verb (*il voit, voit-il?*), but in addition a marked tendency may be noted in the direction $B > A$ with the elimination of inversion as an interrogative device. $D > A$ is found in the syntax of comparative constructions (Mod.F *plus grand que*, as compared with earlier *plus est grand que* or *grand est plus que*). To sum up, the history of morph groupings in French may be said to show a general tendency towards changes in the direction $D \rightarrow C \rightarrow B \rightarrow A$. It is doubtful whether there are examples of permanent changes in the reverse direction $A \rightarrow B \rightarrow C \rightarrow D$.

Finally, we could of course use the 'ABCD' classification for defining the 'word' in French (by agreeing, say, to call all class 'A' groupings 'single words'). But it is questionable whether the grammatical organization of French surface structures offers us, in the final analysis, sufficient inducement to do so. For the 'something' about French which the investigation of word criteria shows up is the fact that French has no unit which corresponds exactly to the 'word' of Latin (or of English). That is to say, it does not use features of separability and permutability to mark out *uniformly* within each major distributional class a type of item which could plausibly be described, in respect of its grammatical behaviour, as a 'minimum version' of the sentence. Rather, French tends, by rules of permutability and separability, to differentiate rather than to standardize the internal grammatical organization of the various types of morph complex which play characteristic roles in the syntax of the language.

The Use of *Tu* and *Vous* in the First Part of the Old French Prose *Lancelot*

ELSPETH KENNEDY

Fellow of St. Hilda's College and Lecturer in the
University of Oxford

Lucien Foulet in *Petite Syntaxe de l'ancien français* confesses his bewilderment at the way in which *vous* and *tu* can alternate in Old French, and, after citing examples from *Courtois d'Arras* and *Male Honte*, he concludes: 'Dans les exemples du moyen âge la plupart du temps l'explication ne se présente pas. Avons-nous affaire à une tradition purement littéraire? Il est plus probable que nous réveillons ici l'écho d'un usage populaire, qui reste a déterminer.'[1] However, if he had been examining the situation in the Prose *Lancelot*, he might well have come to rather different conclusions, for as J. Frappier in his *Etude sur la Mort le roi Artu* has shown, the alternation between *tu* and *vous* in at least one branch of the Lancelot cycle is not haphazard but 'un procédé très conscient de style et un moyen d'expression dramatique'.[2] I thought that it might be useful to explore in depth an earlier part of the cycle in order to see not only whether alternation between *vous* and *tu* is also used there as a deliberate stylistic device, but also whether the pattern of alternation continues to be recognized and maintained over three centuries of a manuscript tradition in which scribes alter forms and constructions freely.[3] Using as a basis the Bibliothèque Nationale MS. fr. 768[4] I have compared all the passages in it in which *vous* and *tu* alternate with the readings in the manuscripts which I list below.

[1] L. Foulet, *Petite syntaxe de l'ancien français*, troisième édition revue, Paris, 1965, p. 201.

[2] J. Frappier, *Etude sur la Mort le Roi Artu*, seconde edition, Paris, 1961, p. 397.

[3] Cf. J. Frappier, *La Mort le roi Artu*, Paris, 1936, pp. XXXVII–XXXVIII, and A. Pauphilet, *Etudes sur la Queste del Saint Graal*, Paris, 1921, pp. XXV–XXVI.

[4] B.N., fr. 768 covers the part of the text to be found in H. O. Sommer, *The Vulgate Version of the Arthurian Romances*, Washington, 1910, Volume III and Appendix 1 of Volume IV.

MS.	Symbol	Date and other information
Bibliothèque Nationale, fr. 768	Ao	2nd quarter of 13th century.
British Museum, Royal 19B VII	B	Early 14th century.
B.N., fr. 96	E	15th century.
B.N., fr. 98	F	15th century.
B.N., fr. 111	G	15th century.
B.M., Additional 10292–4	J	1st half of 14th century. Used by Sommer in his edition.
Bodleian, Rawlinson Q.b. 6	K	1st third of 14th century.
B.N., fr. 110	L	End of 13th or beginning of 14th century.
B.N., fr. 112	M	15th century.
B.N., fr. 113–15	N	15th century.
B.N., fr. 339	O	2nd half of 13th century.
B.N., fr. 344	P	2nd half of 13th century.
B.N., fr. 16999	T	End of 14th century.
B.N., fr. 117–20	Aa	End of 14th century.
Arsenal, fr. 3479–80	Ac	End of 14th century.
B.N., fr. 751	Ad	2nd half of 13th century.
B.N., fr. 1430	Ae	Middle of 13th century.
B.N., fr. 121	Af	15th century.
Arsenal, 3481	Ah	Middle of 14th century.
B.N., fr. 341	Ak	14th century.
B.N., fr. 753	Am	15th century.
B.N., fr. 754	An	13th century.
B.N., fr. 773	Ap	13th century Italian.
Rennes 2427	Ar	Late 13th or early 14th century.
Rouen 1055(06)	At	14th century.
B.M., Royal 20 D III	Au	Early 14th century Anglo-Norman.
B.M., Lansdowne 757	Av	13th century.
Pierpont Morgan 803–7	Ax	14th century.
Printed edition	Ez	Rouen 1488.

I will first examine the use of *tu* and *vous* in Ao, giving the variants from it in the footnotes, and will then attempt to analyse the nature and extent of the divergencies from the pattern to be found in Ao.

As in Modern French, the status of the speaker and his relationship with the person addressed normally determine the form used. It is the plural form which predominates; it is even used between those closely related to one another, for example between husband and wife. King Ban uses only *vous* to his wife in private conversation, and indeed there is no example of husband or wife addressing one another with *tu* in the text. Between father and son *vous* seems also to be the recognized form of address. King Claudas grieves for the death of his son, apostrophizing him with *vous* only, although admittedly in a formal lament.[5] More significantly perhaps, when a squire brings Hector to his father's house late at night, his father addresses him thus: 'Biaus filz, est ce vostre sires?'[6] Between brothers too the standard form seems to have been *vous*. When Agravain is upbraiding in no uncertain terms his young brother Mordret, described as a *vallet*, he still uses *vous*: 'Que est ce, . . . fiz a putain, bastarz, de coi faites vos duel?'[7] On the other hand, a *vallet* coming to Arthur's court is greeted in public by his brother as follows: 'Biax frere, bien soies tu venuz. Quex besoignz t'a aporté a cort?'[8] A squire, as we shall see, is usually although not invariably addressed as *tu* by a knight; it is as a squire that the youth is being received at court, and it is perhaps because his brother is greeting him in this context that he uses *tu* rather than the more usual *vous*.

Again, uncles do not normally *tutoie* their nephews. Arthur always addresses Gauvain as *vous*. The good and wise vassal Pharien almost always uses *vous* to his nephew Lambegue, a brave and headstrong young knight, but he does use *tu* on certain occasions. When he wishes to remind him that he is still a youth and should remain silent in the council of his elders, he says:

'Biaus niés, de *toi* ne me mervoil ge pas se *tu* mez po de raison an *tes* affaires, car l'an ne voit gaires avenir en nule terre que granz sens et granz proësce soient ensenble herbergié en cuer d'anfant. . . .'[9]

[5] Sommer III, pp. 58–9.
[6] Ao, f. 134d; Sommer III, p. 328. Variants: In only two MSS., Ae, Av, does the father *tutoie* his son, yet a few hours earlier the son, as a squire, has been addressed as *tu* by the knights of the lord of Falerne (Sommer III, p. 327). Hector, on the other hand, having spent the night at his father's house, uses *vous* to him (Sommer III, p. 329).
[7] Ao, f 129d; Sommer III, p 315.
[8] Ao, f. 65d; Sommer III, p. 154. Variants: K, P here use *vous*.
[9] Ao, f. 28a; Sommer III, p. 70.

On another occasion Lambegue overhears Pharien's lamentations over the fate of his city, Trebe, which will be destroyed if his nephew is not surrendered to Claudas, and the young man offers of his own free will to go. His uncle, deeply moved, protests:

'Ha biax niés! deceü m'*as*, car por ce, se gel disoie, ne voldroie ge pas *ta* mort, ne ja Dex veoir ne la me laist. Ne ja, se Deu plaist, ice ne *te* loerai.'[10]

Pharien continues to address Lambegue as *tu* during the whole of this conversation.

These passages would seem to suggest that the use of *tu* will often depend not so much on permanent social relationships as on the character of the speaker and on his feelings at any given moment. Hence the change to *tu*, sometimes, as we shall see, even in mid-sentence.

Tu can express, as one might expect, anger and defiance, and here the extent of its use will be influenced by the speaker's temperament as well as his status, that is to say the degree to which he is liable to give way to sudden gusts of anger. King Claudas, who in the full length portrait given of him by the author is presented as a mixture of good and bad, both physically and morally, hence subject to sudden impulses towards violence or generosity, will break into *tutoiement* as soon as his anger is aroused, but, when he becomes calmer, he will return to *vous*. This is well illustrated by his use of *tu* to Lambegue. When the latter, in the heat of battle, hurls insults at him, Claudas, perhaps understandably, replies with *tu*.[11] When Lambegue surrenders to the king and stands unarmed before him, Claudas addresses him as *tu*:

[10] Ao, f. 41a; Sommer III, p. 100. Variants: Four MSS. introduce *tu* at a different point in this conversation: Am, Au use *vous* in this speech but change to *tu* in the next one; Aa, Ac give two speeches from Pharien with *vous*, then move to *tu*.

[11] Ao, f. 40a; Sommer III, p. 96. Variants: G and Am use *vous* throughout; J begins with *vous* and transfers to *tu*: 'Lambegue, Lambegue, ore tout belement ne *vous* covient pas si haster, car par tans m'avrois ataint; et quanque je me puisse de traïson esloiauter, *tu* savras orendroit que je ne sui pas granment entechiés de couardise!' Ap begins with *vous* and changes to *tu* at 'par tens m'avras.'

'Lanbegues, comment *fus tu* si hardiz que *tu osas* çaianz venir? Dont ne *sez tu* que ge *te* hé plus que nul home?'[12]

Then when his anger melts Claudas uses *vous*; and when he lapses back to *tu* it is to express tenderness towards his youthful courage, not wrath:

'D'une chose se puet vanter qui *vos* a a compaignon, qu'il a lo plus hardi chevalier qui hui matin se levast del lit, et celui qui a la durece de toz les cuers. Et se *tu vivoies* par aage, *tu seroies* assez preuzdom.'[13]

Equally significant is the change from *vous* to *tu* which occurs in the scene between Claudas and Pharien, when Claudas rejects Pharien's appeal for peace. At first Claudas addresses Pharien as *vous*. Pharien renounces his allegiance and defies the king, always, of course, using the more respectful *vous* which is in keeping with his character. Claudas, having tried to placate him, still with *vous*, makes a final appeal with *tu*:

'Phariens, *tu ies* fox qui ci m'ahatis de bataille veiant ma gent, mais tu ne t'i combatras ja en tel maniere, car se ge t'ocioie, plus me seroit atorné a mal q'a bien. Mais ge te semoin que tu gardes vers moi ta foi si com tu doiz, ne ne doiz mon homage laissier se ge ne l'ai vers toi forfait, ne ge ne te forfis onques nule rien que ge seüsse.'[14]

When he calls Pharien to the walls of Trebe, reproaches him for leaving his allegiance, and offers terms, he still uses *tu*, and it is only after a reconciliation has taken place that Claudas reverts to *vous*.

Lambegue, more hot-headed and impetuous than Pharien, also uses *tu* to express rage or defiance, even to his lord. He gives Claudas due warning with *vous* that he is going to attack:

'Claudas, Claudas, par Sainte Croiz, tant *avez* chacié que a honte an retorneroiz, o vos savroiz se li aciers de mon glaive set fer tranchier.'[15]

Claudas continues to flee, and Lambegue accuses him of cowardice with *tu*:

[12] Ao, f. 42d; Sommer III, p. 102. Variants: Am uses *vous* in this speech, but in the next one transfers to *tu*.

[13] Ao, f. 43a; Sommer III, p. 102.

[14] Ao, f. 39b; Sommer III, p. 94. Variants: Ap begins with *tu*, but lapses into *vous* for the last part of this speech. Claudas also uses *tu* in an urgent appeal to a brave knight, Banin, who is holding a castle against him (Sommer III, p. 10).

[15] Ao, f. 39d; Sommer III, p. 95.

'Qu'est ce mauvais traitres! Car *tornes* a *ton* anemi mortel qui nule rien ne dessirre autretant comme ta mort. Coart sanz foi, qui mon oncle voloies faire ocirre desleialment.'[16]

He is so fearless that even when he stands defenceless before Claudas, he deliberately uses *tu* to express his scorn and defiance: 'Claudas, or *puez* savoir que po *te* dot.'[17]

Knights can hurl insults and challenges at one another, using vous, as for example Yvain lo Avoutre to a vavassor who has offered him and his companions hospitality only to imprison them: 'Hé! filz a putain, traitres, ja nos aviez vos a foi herbergiez!'[18] But a progression in scorn or anger can be shown by a switch from *vous* to *tu*, as for instance in one of Hector's adventures. He asks an unarmed knight to put on his armour before fighting him. The knight replies: 'Fi! Por *vos* m'armeroie gié!'[19] When Hector once again urges him to put on his armour, he replies still more scornfully: 'M'aïst Dex, ge ne me deigneroie mies armer por *toi*!'[20] He is then, while still unarmed, forced to acknowledge himself as *outré*, but does so defiantly continuing with *tu*:

'Ge l'otroi com hom desarmez, si i *aies* tel honor com *tu* i *devras* avoir. Mais se tu voloies otroier que ge m'armasse et que tu m'atendieses et combatiesses contre moi, lors diroie gié que tu seroies chevaliers. Et lors i avroies tu anor de ce que tu m'avroies conquis.'[21]

Hector, who up till this time has used the more formal *vous*, now replies with *tu*: 'Et ge lo ferai, mais *tu* me *diras* avant por qoi celle damoisele plore.'[22] And the conversation continues with *tu* until they start fighting again. When the knight is defeated a second time, now in full armour, he uses *vous* to Hector, and Hector replies in the same way.

[16] Ao, f. 39d; Sommer III, p. 95. Variants: J uses *vous* with one lapse to *tu*: 'ta mort'; G begins with *vous* and transfers to *tu*; Au has one lapse to *vous*: 'qui vouliez'.
[17] Ao, f. 42d; Sommer III, p. 102. Variants: Ap, E, T, Ah, start with *vous* and then transfer to *tu*.
[18] Ao, f. 68a; Sommer III, p. 159.
[19] Ao, f. 133a; Sommer III, p. 324.
[20] Ao, f. 133b; Sommer III, p. 324. Variant : B uses *vous*.
[21] Ao, f. 133c; Sommer III, p. 325. Variants: N, M use *vous* throughout. Ah begins with *vous*, then transfers to *tu*.
[22] Ao, f. 133c; Sommer III, p. 325.

During battle *tu* is used more often for urgent appeals than to express hatred or ferocity. Impressed by his adversary's courage, Gauvain calls upon a seneschal whom he is fighting in a judicial combat:

'Requenuis *ta* desleiauté et ge metrai poine an toi acorder au duc et au vavasor por cui ge me combat. Et ge ferai tant, o par moi, o par autrui, que tu n'i perdras ne vie ne membre ne annor.'[23]

The seneschal refuses with *tu*,[24] accusing the *vavasor* for whom Gauvain is fighting of being the most disloyal creature ever born of woman. Gauvain replies with counter accusations, now using *tu* in anger. Hector, during his fight with a knight called Marganor, addresses his opponent as *vous* when he suggests that he should surrender. He then sees that Marganor is about to step backwards into water and calls out urgently: 'Ha Marganor, *tu charas* ja ou marés'! *Trai toi* ça !'[25] Marganor again refuses to acknowledge defeat and Hector switches back to *vous*: 'En non Deu! donc i *morroiz vos* toz!' Marganor is again about to fall into the water and Hector warns him: 'Marganor, Marganor, *tu seras* ja morz!' The more courteous the knight, the less easily will he be provoked to use *tu* in anger. Lancelot never does so, but when he tells a knight with *vous* that he is lying, he evokes *tu* in return: 'Commant! Si m'*as* desmanti! Or *te* garde, que ge ne *t'*aseur plus.'[26]

Thus, as one might expect, the normal form of address between knights is *vous*, however well they know one another, or even if they are closely related. To use *tu* will be to move away from the accustomed pattern and will therefore achieve a certain emotional or dramatic effect.

There are, however, certain categories of people who will usually be called *tu*: social inferiors such as porters and watchmen,[27] or those of junior status such as squires and *vallets* (the two terms are often used

[23] Ao, f. 151a–b; Sommer III, p. 371. Variants: N, G, M, Ar use *vous* throughout; L begins with *vous* and transfers to *tu* at 'an toi acorder', and continues with *tu*.

[24] Variant: In G the seneschal begins with *vous* and then transfers to *tu*.

[25] Ao, f. 142a; Sommer III, p. 347.

[26] Ao, f. 171c; Sommer III, p. 424. Variants: N, M, B use *vous* throughout; O, Av, Ax begin with *vous* and transfer to *tu*.

[27] There is an example of an apparent plural form being used to a porter in three/MSS. In Ao, Ap, Ac Lancelot tells the man at the gate: 'Or *gardez* que quant il i anvoiera mais que *tu dies*. . . .' (Ao, f. 71d; Sommer III, p. 167). There does seem sometimes to be a certain confusion over imperative forms such as

almost interchangeably). Squires are, however, not invariably addressed as *tu*. Although it seems to have been more usual to *tutoie* a passing squire from whom one asks for information, Hector asks for news of Gauvain from one with *vous*: 'Biax frere, *savriez* me *vos* novelles d'un chevalier errant qui va en Sorelois'?[28] When a fierce squire comes with a threatening message from his lord to the Lady of Roestoc, her seneschal replies with formal courtesy: 'Biau frere, ce *poez* dire a *vostre* seignor. . . .'[29] Gauvain uses *vous* to a *vallet* who presses hospitality upon him and whom he knights; however, this is no ordinary *vallet*, it was only because he was determined to be dubbed only by Gauvain, that he was not already a knight, and as Gauvain says: 'vos iestes riches hom'.[30] There are sometimes rather unexpected mixtures of *tu* and *vos* spoken to squires. A veiled damsel, who usually addressed Lyonel, a youth but of royal blood, as *vous*, appeals to him to reveal the name of the lord he serves. He refuses and she insists: 'Si *feras*, car ge *vos* praign.':: Here, unusually, the *feras* of Ao would appear to be an isolated reading; all other MSS. have *ferez*. She continues twice more with *vous*, then as she moves away, she makes a final appeal with *tu*, this time in all MSS.: 'Vallez, vallez, *tu* ne me *diras* mies ce de quoi ge te conjure et sor la rien o mont que tu deusses plus amer?', and continues with *tu* until the end of the conversation. Here, apart from the one lapse to *tu*, confined to Ao, the change from *vous* to *tu* corresponds with an increasing urgency in her demand and with an appeal to Lyonel's emotions, for she saved his life and won his affection when he was a small boy. But the switch in the following passage is not so easily explained. Lyonel, watching a battle, has almost ridden on a damsel; a knight forces his horse back, Lyonel asks what he wants, the knight replies: 'Ge voil tant que par un po ge ne *vos* doig

---

gardez, gardes and *garde*. (There is confusion in some MSS. between singular and plural forms in the present indicative, as some scribes use -*es* and -*ez* interchangeably.) In J. Lancelot says on another occasion to the man at the gate: ' "Et bien *sachiés*", fait il, "que se *tu* ne *fuses* si viex je *te* coperoie orendroit la teste par *ta* folie" ' (Sommer III, p. 162). For this use of *sachies* and of plural imperative forms cf. footnotes 40 and 45.

28 Ao, f. 161c; Sommer III, p. 397.
29 Ao, f. 120a; Sommer III, p. 289.
30 Ao, f. 123b; Sommer III, p. 298.
31 Ao, f. 151d; Sommer III, p. 373.

de cest baston par mi la teste, car trop *ies* fox garz et mesafaitiez.'[32] He continues the conversation with *tu*. Here we do not have an isolated lapse, for about half the MSS. support the Ao reading, the knight becoming more unceremonious as he speaks.

Dwarves are usually presented in the romance as deformed, male-volent creatures who readily give and receive a discourteous *tu*.[33] Only Gauvain, who is noted for his great politeness and restraint, keeps to *vous* while being insulted with *tu* by a dwarf who has not recognized him and who, in fact, needs his help.[34] Giants, the large monsters of Arthurian romance, also use *tu*, their manners being as unknightly as their methods of fighting.[35]

Perhaps the most interesting use of *tu* and the most unusual one from the modern point of view occurs when someone comes to the royal court to ask for help or to administer a rebuke. The newcomer, often a stranger, usually greets the king with *tu*, then, having gained a hearing, he or she may change to *vous*. In such cases *tu* and *vous* may be used in the same speech, the pattern is well kept in the manuscript tradition, although there may be slight variations over the exact point at which the transfer to *vous* is made. When a *randu* comes to Arthur's court to rebuke him for not having avenged the dispossession and death of his vassal Ban, he enters the hall without ceremony, strides up to the dais and cries in ringing tones:

'Rois Artu, Dex *te* saut comme lou plus preudome et lou meilleur qui onques fust, se ne fust une seule chose.'[36]

The king, in spite of his bewilderment, replies courteously: 'Dex *vos* beneie, biaus sire!', and begs to be told wherein lies his fault. Then the *randu* proceeds to retail his misdeeds, using *tu*.[37] When Beduier, in his

[32] Ao, f. 151c; Sommer III, p. 372. Variants: (Mixture as in Ao: Av, Ax, M, K, Af, B, J, Ar, O, Ad, P, Ah, F). With *vos* throughout: L, N, G, Ae, Ak, Aa, Ac, E, T, Af, Ez, At,; with *tu* throughout: Au.

[33] Sommer III, pp. 352-3.

[34] Ao, f. 116d; Sommer III, p. 281. Variant: In Ak Gauvain uses *tu* to the dwarf.

[35] Sommer III, p. 206.

[36] An, f. 26a (lacuna in Ao); Sommer III, p. 45. Variants: E, Ah use *vous*.

[37] An, f. 26a; Sommer III, p. 45. Variants: N, G, Aa, Ac, F, M begin the speech with *vous* and then transfers to *tu*: 'et je la *vous* diray il est voirs que tu . . .'; Am, J, T use *vous* throughout the speech; Au uses *tu* with one lapse to *vous*: 'mes trop estes perecuse'.

official position as *bouteillier*, protests at the interruption of the banquet, he is rebuked by the stranger in round terms, but with *vous*:

> 'Bien avez fait samblant d'anfant et contenance, qui devant toz les esprovez preudomes de ceianz iestes venuz contredire que ge ne parol.'[38]

The *tu* must be reserved for the king to have its full effect. Then, when the identity of the *randu* has been revealed by Hervi de Rivel and the king has formally expressed his desire to hear what Adragain, the *randu*, has to say, he proceeds with *vous*: 'Sire, et ge *vos* di. . . .'[39] The damsel who comes to the court of Claudas to procure the release of Lyonel and Bohort uses much the same method of approach. She greets the king with *tu*: 'Dex *te* saut!' She then upbraids him, still with *tu*. He replies with *vous* and begs her to explain what she means. Having caught his attention, she switches to *vous*: 'Tant m'an *avez* conjuré. . . .'[40] A wounded knight who comes to seek an avenger, not to make reproaches, greets Arthur with *tu*: 'Dex *te* saut!' The King returns his greeting with *vous*. Then the knight, in Ao and seven other MSS., continues:

> 'Sire, ge vaig a *toi* por secors et por aide et con a celui a cui l'an dit que nus desconseilliez ne faut. Si *vos* pri que *vos* me secorroiz por Deu.'[41]

Other people, knights, or squires, arriving with appeals for help also begin with *tu*.[42] There is one example of a messenger asking for help who does not begin with *tu*; but here the request is first conveyed in indirect speech:

[38] An, f. 26c; Sommer III, p. 46.
[39] An, f. 26d; Sommer III, p. 47.
[40] An, f. 28a; Ao, f. 19a; Sommer III, p. 49. Variants: Aa, Ac, give a rather different version of the damsel's first speech to Claudas, in which, although *tutoiement* predominates, two plural imperatives are used: 'ne cuidiez mie que vous avez . . . mais sachiez. . . .'
[41] Ao, f. 51c; Sommer III, p. 119–20. Variants: Ak, T, Ez, E use *vous* throughout; Ar, K, P, B, J, Au, Ae, Ap, P, Af, Aa, Ac, while using *tu* for the knight's first speech, use *vous* throughout the second.
[42] For example, a knight sent by the lady of Nohaut (Sommer III, p. 128): a *vallet* asking for Arthur's help against a wild boar (Ao, f. 178d; Sommer IV, p. 376. O, At agree with Ao, but Ax, used by Sommer gives *vous*) in the first sentence and then transfers to *tu*.

'Et li manda que Galehoz, li filz a la Jaiande, estoit antrez an sa terre et tote la li avoit tolue fors deus chastiaus que ele a el chief de sa terre de ça. "Rois Artus," fait li messages, "por ce *vos* mande que vos veigniez deffandre vostre terre, car ele ne se puet longuement tenir, se vos n'i venez".'[43]

Here as the opening speech is only reported, the transfer to *vous* has, as it were, already taken place by the time we have direct speech. Nevertheless this distinction is ignored by four MSS. which do use *tu* to a varying degree in the passage quoted above. When the Lady of the Lake first brings Lancelot to Arthur's court, from the beginning she uses *vous* to Arthur, but she comes to him neither to plead nor to reprove but to make a request as from one equal to another, and she has already attracted his attention and admiration by her own appearance and the richness of her train.[44]

Tu is used for an ultimatum. When Galehot sends a knight messenger to Arthur to announce his intention of invading his land if Arthur does not agree to be his vassal, the knight begins: 'Rois, a *toi* m'anvoie li plus preuzdom qui orandroit vive de son aage.'[45] He continues with *tu* while the king replies with *vous*. *Tu* is also used by announcers of strange tidings or marvels. A *vallet* comes to court to tell Arthur that the Dolorous Guard has been conquered by an unknown knight: 'Rois Artus, Dex *te* saut! Ge t'aport novelles les plus estranges qui onques entrassent en ton ostel.'[46] Having brought attention to himself he then continues with *vous*. But the second time he comes to court with more strange news he again begins with *tu*.[47] A damsel creates a sensation by arriving at court with the crowned lion of Libya and by declaring with *tu* that the king can only learn the name of the lady who sent her from the knight who kills the lion.[48]

[43] Ao, f. 87c; Sommer III, p. 210. Variants: Aa, Ac use *tu* throughout the speech; Ad and F begin the speech with *tu* and transfer to *vous*.

[44] Sommer III, pp. 121–2.

[45] Ao, f. 84b; Sommer III, p. 201. Variants: Ae, begins with *vous*, 'a vos m'envoie', and then transfers at once to *tu*; Aa, Ac has a lapse into *vous* in the messenger's second speech; At uses *tu* except for one phrase: 'sachiez dons . . . que messires vos defie'.

[46] Ao, f. 65d; Sommer III, p. 153. Variants: Ap uses *vous* throughout; Au begins 'jeo *te* porte', but ends the sentence '*vostre* court'.

[47] Ao, f. 66d; Sommer III, p. 156. Variants: K, P use *vous* throughout; Ae in one sentence combines '*vostre* neveu' with '*ton* regne'.

[48] Ao, f. 185b; Sommer IV, p. 392. A damsel uses *tu* to Arthur from a tower in which she is imprisoned in order to draw attention to her plight, and to the

It is interesting to observe that the salutation of a royal personage with *tu* at the beginning of an embassy, etc., is also to be found not only in *la Mort le roi Artu*,[49] but also in Villehardouin. Conon de Béthune addresses the Emperor Alexis as follows:

> 'Sire, nos somes a *toi* venu de par les barons de l'ost et de par le duc de Venise. Et saches *tu* que il *te* reprovent le servise que il t'ont fait con la gent sevent et cum il est apparissant. *Vos* lor avez juré, *vos* et *vostre* pere, la convenance a tenir que *vos* lor avez convent, et *vos* chartes en ont; *vos* ne lor avez mie si bien tenue con *vos* deussiez.'[50]

Thus, where the normal form of address is clearly established as *vous*, the deliberate use of *tu* to an august personage can create an important shock effect; once the point has been made, then the usual movement will be towards *vous*, sometimes even in mid-sentence. However, there is one occasion at the arrival of a stranger at the court of Arthur when the movement is the other way. Arthur's kingdom is in peril; so far he has only been saved by the intervention of an unknown knight, he is fearful of losing his land and disturbed by some strange dreams which he has had. At this moment of crisis he hears of the arrival of a *preudom* full of great wisdom and hastens to him for comfort and counsel; but the *preudom* receives his greeting coldly:

> 'Li preudom ne li randié mis son salu ainz dist come correciez: "Ne de *vos*, ne de vostre salu n'ai ge cure, ne pas ne l'ain; car vos iestes li plus vis pechierres de toz les autres pecheors. Et bien vos parra, car tote enor terriene avez ja aprochié de perdre".'[51]

---

mystery of the *covine* of the castle (Sommer III, p. 170). Damsels also may occasionally use *tu* to knights whom they meet on their journeys to startle them or to convey urgency as does a damsel in the service of the Lady of the Lake, who hails Gauvain in the middle of one of his battles (Sommer III, p. 374). Another damsel's response with *tu* to a polite request from Gauvain for information about Lancelot is less usual; it may possibly be designed to emphasise the mystery surrounding Lancelot (Sommer III, p. 175). In any case, the pattern seems to have been less familiar to judge from the variants: *tu* in Ao, Ad, L, P, N, G, T, Am, F, Af, J, K, At—*vous* in Ae, Ap, Ak, Aa, Ac, Ah, E, Ar, Av, Au, Ax.

49 *La Mort le roi Artu*, § 14 and § 67.

50 Geoffroy de Villehardouin, *La Conquête de Constantinople*, ed. E. Faral, Paris, 1938–9, II, p. 12.

51 Ao, f. 89d; Sommer III, p. 215. Variants: J, Ax, P, T, K, B, Ak, Ap, Ah, Af, Av, E, L, N, G have a lapse into *vous* in the middle of the conversation (Sommer III, p. 216): 'encore venront li conseil a tans se croire les voles. Et je t'enseignerai. . . .'

Then the king and the *preudom* draw apart and ride along together. The king asks why he rejects his greeting and calls him a vile sinner. ' "Gel te dirai," fait li prodoms, "car ge sai assez miauz que *tu* ies que tu meismes ne lo sez".' And he then continues with *tu* throughout several pages of exhortation and instruction. It is only when the *preudom* has been persuaded to accept the role of spiritual counsellor that he uses the *tu* which is to characterize this relationship.[52]

The alternations between *tu* and *vous* in this part of the Prose Lancelot do not, therefore, appear to be arbitrary; the departures from the forms to be expected, given the status of the speaker and that of the person addressed, may seem abrupt to modern ears, but in nearly every case achieve certain dramatic or stylistic effects and can be explained in those terms. Indeed, the pattern to be found in Ao is also to be found with remarkable consistency in the other MSS. There are, however, four passages where the manuscript tradition is divided. In the first of these—the arrival of the wounded knight at Arthur's court (see footnote 41)—there is a slight variation in an accepted pattern for *tutoiement* by people seeking help from the king, that is to say a later change to *vous* in eight MSS. In the second we have, perhaps, an example of a less familiar pattern in the episode where a damsel uses *tu* in reply to a question from Gauvain in thirteen MSS., but *vous* in eleven (see footnote 48). Thirdly, an unusual mixture between *tu* and *vous* used by a knight to the squire Lyonel is regularized in thirteen MSS. (see footnote 32). Finally, there is an unusually well supported lapse to *vous* in the *preudom*'s long conversation with Arthur in which he uses *tu* after a cold beginning with *vous* (see footnote 51). The *preudom* says: 'Encore venront li conseil a tans se croire les *volés*,' in fifteen MSS. It is perhaps possible that the use of *vous* here may indicate a certain reservation on the part of the *preudom* as to the willingness of the king to accept him wholeheartedly as spiritual adviser, a role characterized by the use of *tu*. It is also possible that *vous* has crept in here with the set phrase, 'se croire les volés'.

Most deviations, as can be seen from the variants in the footnotes, are, however, to be found only in very small numbers of MSS. Sometimes they only represent small deviations in the usual pattern, with

---

[52] In *La Queste del Saint Graal*, ed. A. Pauphilet, Paris, 1939, *tu* is used by hermits to knights such as Lancelot whom they are exhorting to repentance. In one episode a hermit counselling Lancelot begins with *vous* (pp. 63–8), and then transfers to *tu* (pp. 68–70) and then returns to *vous* (p. 71), when Lancelot has accepted his advice and renounced his sinful love of Guinevere.

the change to *tu* or *vous* being made at a slightly different point; sometimes they are more fundamental in that they involve the removal of an alternation, usually by the generalization of the form *vous*. There are a certain number of lapses to *vous* amid *tu* which do not appear to be deliberate. For example, in a long narrative of past events given by a dwarf to Gauvain, whom he is addressing as *tu*, three MSS. use in differing places the occasional phrase such as '*que vous onques veissiez de vos iex*', or '*si com vos veistes*'.[53] *Veez ci* is used in a similar way. *Sachiez* may also slip in as a kind of set phrase amongst a series of *tu* forms. In fact, plural imperatives do sometimes appear unexpectedly, sometimes as an accepted formula with which to begin a sentence or speech, sometimes, perhaps, because there seems quite often to be some confusion between the written forms in MSS. which use *s* and *z* somewhat indiscriminately (see footnote 27). An Anglo-Norman MS. such as Au, as one might expect, is particularly uncertain of the verb forms and produces some strange mixtures.[54]

No MS. consistently changes the pattern or contains more than a very small number of deviations from it, although there are slightly more examples of the use of *vous* instead of *tu* in the later MSS. J, an early 14th century MS., gives *vous* for *tu* six times, but none of these represent an elimination of a *tu* and *vous* alternation to the same person. Ap, a 13th century Italian MS., removes one *tu vous* alternation and has five other examples of *vous* for *tu*. Ae, another 13th century MS., has five deviations, all except one towards *vous*, but again, none eliminating an alternation. The other 13th and early 14th century MSS. show very few variations. The highest number of deviations, nine in all, are to be found in Aa and Ac, closely related MSS. of the late 14th century which treat the text with particular freedom. They have four lapses to *vous* amid *tu*, three moves from *vous* to *tu* at a slightly later point than usual and one from *tu* to *vous* at an earlier point than usual, one use of *tu* by a messenger instead of the *vous* to be found in the other MSS. The printed edition is more conservative; it apologizes for 'la crudité et indigestion du langage qui est gros et maternel', and only replaces *tu* by *vous* on five occasions, three of these are lapses to *vous* in set phrases amid a series of *tu* forms, and only one represents an elimination of a *tu vous* alternation in the speech of a messenger. The other 15th century MSS show much the same picture of a pattern

[53] Sommer III, pp. 284–5. K: 'que vous onques veissiez de vos iex'; Ez: 'que vous y vistes'; 'si grant comme vous vistes'; Ac: 'si comme vous veistes'.

[54] For example 'tu ne me deistes', 'tu nel me voudries'.

remarkably consistently maintained, with only five or six deviations towards *vous*.

How far does the pattern of *tu* and *vous* which we have found so well preserved in the romance represent purely literary convention, how far does it reflect medieval conversational usage? This is unfortunately, difficult to determine. Some scenes, such as the arrival of messengers at court, are recurring themes in Arthurian romance and in other literary texts; they are usually treated in a highly stylized way, and certain set phrases recur. In other passages, however, the dialogue would seem to be much more naturalistic, within of course a highly restricted social circle. What does, in any case, seem certain is that the alternation between *tu* and *vous* was a remarkably subtle and well recognized instrument for conveying shades of feeling and for increasing the dramatic tension.

Old French *Trifoire*

FAITH LYONS

Reader in Medieval French, Bedford College, University of London

So far as I know, *trifoire* is the only Old French word in Littré to stand there not as part of the historic background to a modern word but in its own right. Perhaps it slipped in by error, or perhaps being little understood it attracted Littré by its mystery. Appearing first in the Supplément of 1877, it has been incorporated since 1958 into the complete Gallimard-Hachette edition of the main dictionary. The related word *triforium*, listed by Ducange, is excluded by Littré but appears in the *Larousse du XIXe siècle* which neglects *trifoire* altogether. *Triforium* occupies several columns of the Oxford English Dictionary with many examples of its use since 1800. On the grounds that the explanation based on three openings in the triforium-arcade fits ill with the facts at Canterbury, the OED declares its etymology unknown. Though first found in Gervase's late twelfth century history of that cathedral, the term is not therein employed strictly but is applied indiscriminately to both clerestory and triforium passages. But in favour of the rejected etymology *tres fores* (Ernout-Meillet's dictionary, s.v. *bifariam*) Edward Bell[1] has argued that on the clerestory level three inner arches are found at Cérissy-la-forêt, a Norman church built by the father of William the Conqueror. He has further argued that these triple clerestory openings are a general type in early Norman churches of England. Logically therefore it is possible to suppose that *triforium* originated as a name for such galleries. Whatever its origins, *triforium* is in Gervase a synonym of *via* or more exactly of Villard de Honne-court's *voie dedens*, inner gallery. As for *trifoire*, Enlart opened his Grande Encyclopédie article on *triforium* (Vol. 31, p. 391, col. B) with a mention of the Old French adjective. Treating philological consider-ations in a somewhat cavalier manner, the French archaeologist is

---

[1] E. Bell, 'The Origin and Use of the Word "Triforium",' *Transactions of the St. Paul's Ecclesiological Society*, III (1895), pp. 114–30.

helpful on the semantics of the terms under review. From his *Manuel d'archéologie française*, 1902, vol. I, p. 280, I quote some relevant remarks: 'Le *triforium* (v.f. alées, aloirs, alours, coursières; lat. M.A. *alloria, couratoria*) consiste en un rang de baies ou de galeries de moindre importance pratiqué dans les murs latéraux au-dessus des bas-côtés. Ce mot vient de l'adjectif français trifore ou trifoire sorti du latin *transforatum* et qui signifie repercé ou ajouré. . . . Le triforium est, en effet, un chemin de ronde dont la paroi est ajourée.' Enlart omits to recall that in the Middle Ages architectural *triforium* is limited to Gervase. As early as 1845, Professor Willis of Cambridge wrote a long note on this late twelfth century use of triforium 'employed solely in the sense of an upper passage or thoroughfare, perhaps confined to a *covered* passage . . . but it was certainly not confined to passages in the thickness of the wall, because the lower triforium of Canterbury passes over the side-aisle vaults; while the upper one, which would now be called the clerestory gallery, is formed in the thickness of the wall'.[2] When annotating Gervase, Victor Mortet accepted the view of Willis that it was English archaeologists in modern times who restricted the triforium to the galleries over the pier arches of a large church while terming the upper gallery the clerestory.[3] Recently architectural terminology in the twelfth century has occupied Paul Frankl in his monumental *The Gothic*, Princeton, N.J., 1960. On p. 170, he quotes line 7571 of the *Eneas*, 'defors estoit tote trifoire' as indicating that there was a triforium or gallery on the fourth floor of the building crowned by Camille's fantastic tomb. It is impossible to determine if the style of architecture is classical or not. Frankl overlooks a second use of *trifoire* in the same romance, a text which may antedate Gervase by some twenty-five years:

> devers la vile erent trifoire
> li mur, a ars et a civoire,
> O granz pilers de marbre toz.
> Li chemins alot par desoz;
> Grant marchié i aveit toz dis.   (ll. 445–9)

I interpret these lines as describing how the inner side of Carthage city walls possessed a triforium, with arches, vaults and marble columns,

---

[2] R. Willis, *The Architectural History of Canterbury Cathedral*, London, 1845, p. 43. Cf. p. 49.

[3] V. Mortet, *Recueil de textes relatifs à l'histoire de l'architecture*, 1911, vol. 1, p. 216, n. 4.

where a market was held daily. It is again impossible to say that the architecture is classical, particularly since at Canterbury some pillars also were of marble. In conclusion, these few twelfth century uses of *triforium* and of *trifoire* support each other, and are part of the established history of architectural terminology.

However as early as 1843 in his *Architectural Nomenclature of the Middle Ages*, p. 34, Professor Willis had already pointed out that *triforium* 'is also a kind of pierced or open work in embroidery or metal'. Medieval Latin *triforium* or rather the derivative adjectioe *triforiatus* or the phrase *opere triforio* and Old French adjective *trifoire* or the phrase *a trifoire* are all used to describe the decoration by craftsmen of gold and gilded objects. As an art term, Old French *trifoire* has recently attracted the attention of students of literature with particular reference to another expression found in the same semantic field, *l'uevre Salemon*. Dr. Abercrombie, Professor West, Professor Lawton and Dr. Bullock Davies have all examined the significance of Solomon-work, discussing Marie de France's *Guigemar* (ll. 170–82) and the *Eneas* (ll. 4075–8). In their articles, both Professor Lawton[4] and Dr. Bullock Davies[5] have suggested that decoration by means of an arcading design is the primary meaning of *trifoire*. Long ago in his glossary to *Thèbes*, Constans defined *trifuere* (*trifoire*) as an architectural design 'qui offre l'ornement composé d'arceaux'. My objection to this hypothesis is that it offers a solution extraneous to and imposed upon the texts. There is no real evidence of any sort that this transfer of design from architectural decoration to the work of goldsmiths and jewellers has anything to do with Old French *trifoire*. Professor Lawton reaches a finally negative view, since he links both *l'uevre Salemon* and *trifoire* together as 'the imaginary products of fabulous craftsmen endowed with a skill to be found only in such wondrous works as Salomon's Temple'. I myself believe it certain from non-literary textual evidence that both these terms were in current use and based on reality.

In the present article, I propose therefore to confront Old French *trifoire* with reality, through the use of inventories and of art history. An attempt will be made to reach a soundly based definition of the word as follows. First actual uses will be examined of *trifoire* in Old French literature, especially where the examples are self-defining. Secondly the actual objects described or similar objects will be considered in the light

---

4 *Modern Language Review*, L (1955), pp. 51–2.
5 'L'Uevre Salemun', *Medium Aevum*, XXIX (1960), p. 178.

of the archaeological evidence of non-literary texts, and of surviving
art treasures. Thirdly account will be taken of what we know about
metalwork techniques and craftsmanship. If, through the agreement
of all these three criteria, I can attempt to define *trifoire*, then that
definition should be satisfactory or at the very least should furnish a
working hypothesis. Nevertheless I have found it very difficult to
match the word, the object and the technique.

One of the earliest Old French uses of *trifoire* is to describe saddle-
bows:[6]

> La sele est buene, et li arçon
> furent de l'uevre Salemon,
> a or taillié de blanc ivoire;
> l'entaille en ert toute trifoire.

Manuscript D of the *Eneas* has a passage describing the gates of Dido's
castle as follows:

> Les portes sont toutes d'ivuire,
> l'entaille y est toute tassire (sic).
> Mis y a or en tel mesure
> qu'il pert parmi l'entailleure.

Meaningless 'tassire' is surely a corruption of 'trifuire', a reading which
is confirmed by the rhyme. From this description of the ivory and gold
gates one may suppose the *Eneas* saddlebows to have been decorated in
pierced ivory with the resulting openwork backed by gold that shows
through it, in the same way that a carved screen may be backed by
silk. The Old French text is specific since *parmi* means 'right through'.
Moreover an identical technique for the carving of ivory is outlined
by the twelfth century craftsman Theophilus in Chapter 93 of his
celebrated third book:[7] '. . . cum subtilibus ferris campos transfora;
deinde sculpe quam gracilius et operosius possis. Quo facto, imple
foramen interius ligno quercino, quod cooperis cupro tenui deaurata,
ita ut per omnes campos aurum videri possit.' These instructions
relate to carved ivory handles, with pierced grounds through which a
gold backing can show. This particular technique is illustrated by Plate
XVI in a recent English version of the Latin treatise.[8] The photograph

[6] *Eneas*, ed. Salverda de Grave, *Bibliotheca Normannica*, IV (1891).

[7] *De Diversis Artibus*, ed. C. R. Dodwell, 1961, p. 167, with English translation.

[8] *On Divers Arts*, transl. J. G. Hawthorne and C. S. Smith, Chicago, 1963,
facing page 59. See p. 187, note 1.

depicts an Italian tenth-century reliquary of pierced ivory carving, flat, not in bas-relief, with a design of a bird together with flowers and foliage, mounted over gilded copper, as in Theophilus. Under the word *alva*, Ducange associates gold decoration with saddle-making. He quotes from the laws of Frederick I of Sicily:

IN ARZONIBUS SAMBUCARUM IPSARUM POSSIT PONI AURUM . . . ET ALVAE IPSARUM POSSINT COOPERIRI AERE, ET FIERI SMALTAE

The saddle is possibly in wood, the *auves* or side-pieces of which are covered with brass and enamelled, while the pommel and cantle apparently have a gilt overlay. Twelfth century *Ipomedon* (ed. Kölbing and Koschwitz) has carved ivory saddlebows with nielloed gold in pierced work (neelez a or trifoire, 7946).[9]

In the thirteenth-century *Li Chevaliers as deus espees*, two passages associate carving on a saddle or on saddle-bows with gold and ivory:

> S'ot sele u ot archons vautis,
> A esmaus d'or fin et d'ivore,
> Trestoute entaillie a trifoire;
> S'ert d'or et de pieres li frains.

> (ed. Foerster, ll. 1124–7)

Of interest is the reference to enamels, the *smaltae* of the Latin text above. Similar decorated saddlework is briefly described in a later passage of the same romance:

> Et erent li archon trifoire
> De lor siele d'or et d'yvoire
> Moult bien ouvre et entaillie. (ll. 11885–7)

'Li arçon trifoire' echoes 'li mur trifoire' of the *Eneas* (ll. 445–6). In *Li Chevaliers as deus espees* the prominent saddle-bows are like high edifices. But, whereas the walls in *Eneas* have a triforium gallery, the pommel and cantel are of pierced work. In the *Chanson d'Antioche* there is a precious object which lends support to the self-defining

---

9 Cf. *Athis et Prophilias*, ed. Hilka, l. 6943–6 and *Protheselaus*, ed. Kluckow, l. 826.

passage from manuscript D of the *Eneas*, and helps to interpret triforium-work. I refer to a hollow statue in gold of a seated idol:

> Tous fu d'or et d'argent, moult luist et reflambie,
> Sor l'oliphant seoit en la forme musie;
> Creus estoit par dedens et fait par triphorie,
> Mainte pierre i flamboie et luist et esclaircie.
> La dedens n'avoit riens faite par establie,
> Que cil defors ne voient tant est l'ovre polie.
>
> (ed. P. Paris, V, ll. 1028–33)

This is clearly a second self-defining example, in which the polished
interior of the hollow statue can be seen through the open metal-work,
'fait par triphorie'.

Like the decorated saddle-bows belonging to secular life, the reliquary in the church appears as a minor work of architecture. It often
had a decorative edge running the length of its summit, known as a
'cresta' or crest, Ducange's 'apex feretri'. In his *Glossaire Archéologique*
Victor Gay describes it as 'une galerie ajourée qui surmonte la toiture
des édifices ou des châsses'. Under *châsse* Gay pictures a thirteenth
century chest-type reliquary with just such an upper edging in open-
work.[10] Dating from 1245 and 1295, two inventories survive of
church plate and vestments at St. Paul's, London. Both mention the
reliquary of St. Ethelbert whose wooden core or 'heart' is covered by
thick silver plates, set with many precious stones. The 1295 inventory
adds that it was portable, with triforium-work on the crest and on the
circles, 'cum cresta et circulis triphoriatis' (the Dugdale-Ellis edition,
p. 314, column one). While decorative, the open work cresting could
also have provided the convenience of a handle. The frequently
mentioned gold or gilded circles were used to decorate prominent
parts of art objects, and the pierced work would permit the viewing of
relics or reading of inscriptions.

Together with the St. Ethelbert one, there is a second important
reliquary which can help this present examination of triforium-work.
In 1887 when Canon Sparrow Simpson was preparing his own edition
of the 1245 inventory,[11] he collated upon an original manuscript the
1295 inventory. This had already appeared in Dugdale's first edition of

[10] There is in the Victoria and Albert Museum, Number 514–1895, a late
fifteenth century French reliquary with pierced gilt copper cresting.
[11] 'Two Inventories of the Cathedral of St. Paul, London,' ed. Sparrow
Simpson, *Archaeologia* 50, ii (1887), pp. 439–524.

the *History of St. Paul's* (1658), and had been reproduced by Sir Henry Ellis in his version of the same work (1818, pp. 310–36). Discovering many errors in the Dugdale-Ellis edition, Sparrow Simpson published a few corrections (*Archeologia* L^{ii}, pp. 460–3). The omission which concerns the present inquiry into art terminology is the correction to the Ellis edition, p. 314, column 2, where after line 8 one should insert:

> Item Brachium Sancti Melliti magnum ornatum platis et sexdecem cristallis et anterius continet circulum triforiatum et deauratum qui continet unum lapidem sculptum et quatuor alios majores et vj minores et deficiunt quinque.

No doubt the arm of St. Mellitus had a wooden core or 'heart'. This possessed a covering of silver plates and sixteen cristals, with in front a gilded circle of pierced work and sixteen gems. Writing about one stone, curiously carved, Sparrow Simpson (p. 445) stated that it was probably an antique gem; I will return to this point later. As for the gilded and triforiated circle it originally held sixteen gems which correspond in number to the sixteen cristals. The fact that the circle was pierced would allow the faithful to read an inscription or *titulus* about the relic, and perhaps the cristals also permitted viewing.

The above reliquary may be compared with the first of four mitres in the 1245 inventory (p. 473). In the words of Sparrow Simpson it was 'of white embroidered in purple, ornamented both in front and behind with stars and crescents; in each star a topaz or an almandine' (p. 446). The *alemandine*, a sort of ruby, is mentioned in the Old French romances of antiquity, figuring in the SATF glossary to Benoit de Ste Maure's *Troie*. The apparent fantasy of romance is the reality of the inventory. What concerns us particularly here is the headband or circle, bejewelled with peridots, because the pierced, triforiated ornaments are gold roundels representing besants: 'In circulo inferiori sunt quasi bisantii triphuriati cum periodotis, similiter thau cum lapidibus.' The Old French examples of *trifoire* never indicate the figures and designs represented. A sign that the wearer has visited the Holy Land, besants are heraldic devices as are also the thau or St. Antony crosses. This is good evidence of a formal decorative element and of a design that is repeated in a series upon the circle round the head, a circle fashioned out of thin gold plate.

Some further evidence along the same lines is supplied by morses or cope clasps. The 1295 inventory lists more than a score of these in detail. The morse was a large ornament 'from five to six inches in breadth'.[12] It was however small enough for the goldsmith's art to be exercised largely upon design. With particular reference to the St. Paul's collection, it is possible to identify the morses through their owners, and then to compare identical objects listed as early as 1245 and again fifty years later. From this comparison the 1295 inventory appears more precise and more informative, the weight of morses, for example, being given. In 1245 the complete account of the morse belonging to Cynthius Romanus reads thus:

> Morsus Cinthii Romani argenteus
> deauratus ad instar lunae semi-
> -plenae, cum ymagine Pauli et duobus
> angelis collateralibis, ornatus
> preciosis lapidibus per circuitum.
>
> (ed. Simpson, p. 481)

In 1295 the opening is expanded as follows:

> Morsus Cynthii Romani argenteus,
> exterius deauratus, cum limbo
> triphoriato de auro ad modum
> lunae. . . .
>
> (Dugdale, p. 310)

The expanded version makes it clear that the ornamented border of gold represents a half-moon in carved and pierced work. Another similar item is William of Ely's clasp. From the expanded entry in Dugdale I select the relevant part:

> Morsus Willielmi de Ely argenteus
> . . . cum multis lapidibus et perlis
> insitis in limbis, et quadraturis
> triphoriatus aureis.
> Cresta ejusdem argentea cum triphorio
> exterius aureo, et lapillis insitis.
>
> (p. 310; cf. Simpson, p. 481)

Perhaps itself square-shaped, the morse is adorned with gold squares in pierced work, while at the top the crest forms a separate and distinctive part. In connection then with triforium-work, the roundel, the crescent and the square, carved in gold, all appear in the thirteenth century

---

[12] D. Rock, *The Church of Our Fathers*, 1903, vol. II, p. 31.

inventories. Suitably decorative, they can set off by their own simplicity any precious stones that accompany them. I have spoken of pierced work, and there is some direct evidence for this in the 1295 inventory. From the expanded description in Dugdale of John of St. Laurent's morse, I quote the opening as follows:

> Morsus Johannis de Sancto Laurentio
> argenteus, deauratus, cum limbo et
> medio circulo aurato triphoriato,
> inserto grossis lapidibus, et camautis
> et perlis; sed deficiunt duo Leunculi,
> et una perla magna. .
>
> (p. 310)

Though the inventory lists gems missing from the jewelled clasps, this is the only item where carved objects, here two representations of small lions, are reported lost. Other types of metal ornament were often solid, like the marguerites in the Limerick mitre, perhaps produced in a series by the process of die-stamping.[13] But if solid, these gold lions would have been secure. The missing animals must have been in gold pierced work which over the years could become worn and broken. From the 1245 list we know that this clasp had been used for more than half a century. I have not been able to reconstruct the complete designs of the St. Paul morses, but we do know however that in 1380 Charles V transformed a fibula into a morse.[14] A typical early thirteenth-century fibula is an open-work brooch, circular, two and three quarter inches broad, with a central cabochon joined by six arms to an outside band of filigree and stones.[15] The 1245 inventory describes the morse of Peter of Bleys as having a red stone in the middle, though this brooch seems to have been square, not circular (p. 481). As we have seen, another morse had stones on the border and in the middle of the circle, as well as gold lions in triforium-work. The fibula type, cited above, is a little smaller than the large gold eagle brooch in open work belonging to the Empress Gisela and dated about

---

[13] H. Wilson *Silverwork and Jewellery*, 2nd ed., 1912, pp. 267–70, discusses this old method first described by Theophilus, chapter LXXV, and here illustrated, in Plate X, by a French thirteenth century chalice with impressed and stamped work.

[14] Texier, *Dictionnaire d'Orfèvrerie*, *Encyclopédie Théologique*, ed. Migne, XXVII (1857), s.v. *fermail*.

[15] K. Hoffmann, *The Year 1200*, New York, 1970, vol. I, pp. 117, 123.

1025 A.D.[16] The eagle is not solid or flat, and has been hammered up
with the background segments cut away. The St. Paul morses may have
been bigger but otherwise somewhat similar to such brooches. With
many morses listed in 1295 it is interesting to observe the qualification
'triforiatus' used of goldsmith's work. Several times the term lends
precision to vague words, 'de auro puro', 'ornatus', about identical
ornaments in 1245. Triforium-work characterizes almost two-thirds of
the twenty-one morses specified in 1295, though twenty-eight
altogether are listed then.

The gold chalices in the inventories tend to be plain, though one is
described as of Greek work, *de Graeco trifurio*.[17] However there are two
gilded cups worthy of remark in the inventory of English royal plate
dated 12 Ed. III.[18] Both have a foot and a cover, both have some
enamel work. One is described as *ovrez de trifforie* and the other as *od
triffarie*. *Trifary* is the form we will see used by Alexander Neckam.
More instructive is a smaller item, ewer with cristal bowl:

> Un eawer dont le ventre de cristal
> od pie et covercle d'argent dorré
> od oeuvre de triffoir.

(item 33, p. 170)

Triforium-work adorns the silver gilt foot and cover. An Anglo-
Norman late twelfth century romance *Horn* describes a pure gold cup
decorated with pierced work:

> A trifuire iert entallé de bon or melekin.

(ed. Pope, l. 937)

An early thirteenth century chalice of silver gilt has its stem and bulb
or knob decorated with open-work roundels which suggests typical
metal-work for a cup.[19]

The Old French examples of *entaillier a trifoire* never happen to
indicate actual goldsmithing designs. It is therefore of outstanding
interest to find Latin examples where this type of metal-work is
mentioned with some hints about design and method. In the 1245
inventory there are at St. Paul's two pairs of silver candlesticks, both

---

[16] O. von Falke, *Der Mainzer Goldschmuck der Kaiserin Gisela 1024*, 1913,
p. 12 ff.

[17] *Archaeologia*, 50 ii, 466. Cf. 442.

[18] *Antient Kalendars and Inventories*, ed. F. Palgrave, 1836, vol. III, pp. 166–7.

[19] K. Hoffmann, *The Year 1200*, New York, 1970, vol. I, p. 103.

decorated with triforium-work. The first have a dragon design, 'pedibus draconibus insculptis triforiatis' which Mr. Oman translates 'with pierced feet chased with dragons'.[20] Described as old (*antiqua*) and portable, these weighed seven pounds together, being certainly heavier than the small dragon type in bronze represented today in the Victoria and Albert Museum and elsewhere.[21] I suggest that our dragons were carved in full relief like the figures on the stem and base of the Gloucester candlestick, though the latter stands 19⅞ inches while the first pair may have been shorter. A gift of Richard de Storteford, chancellor in 1184, the second pair are described as 'opere triforia, operata sunt cum hominibus leones equitantibus' which Oman translates 'of pierced work made with men riding upon lions'.[22] These candlesticks recur in the later inventory since the donor is identical and the weight iiij lb., xiij s. in 1295 is the same except for an extra iiij d. in 1245. But the 1295 list affords us different information, describing the pair as 'opere fusorio, cum animalibus variis in pedibus fabricatis' (ed. Dugdale, 311). In view of this reference to various animals, it is difficult to imagine that the design was that of a single horseman 'Samson on a lion', similar to the small cast bronze candlestick in the Victoria and Albert Museum, numbered M595—1910. R. de Storteford's candlesticks were in cast metal, like the richly gilt Gloucester one in a white alloy cast by the waste-wax process. Like it, men and animals could have been carved in full relief, with the design covering at least the feet and the base.

Like the smaller candlesticks, the medieval censer is comparatively small and often in bronze. Although its function required perforations in the metal cover at least, a censer is only described as having triforium-work where the metal is specifically gilded. This confirms the general observation that, as far as metal-work is concerned, triforium-work is confined to gold or gilded objects. The language and the technique belong to the goldsmith, the gilder in the strict sense. The 1245 inventory (*Archeologia* 50 ii, p. 467) has the following entry:

> Thuribulum deauratum cum
> coopertorio trifuriato opere,
> ponderat liij solid. iij d. cum scutella cupri.

[20] Charles Oman, *English Church Plate 597–1830*, 1937, p. 69.

[21] See the late twelfth century one with dragons as feet and base in K. Hoffmann, vol. I, p. 87.

[22] *English Church Plate*, p. 69.

The copper gilt cover weighed little more than the heaviest cope clasp. An entry from a late medieval inventory at Exeter is comparable:

> 6 thuribula argenti cum cathenis
> argenteis quorum 4 deaurata exterius
> cum triffura subtili.[23]

In a comprehensive, well-illustrated paper, Mr. Tonnochy divides censers into two types, the hemispherical one being an architectural development and the spherical one having only the slightest architectural features.[24] The simpler censers represented in plates iiA and lxB show openwork birds, animals or crosses, and pierced work. Since the representation of simple motifs is in line with the examples of triforium-work so far considered in the present article, it is possible to suppose that similar figures adorned the censer at St. Paul's, and others like it elsewhere.

An object of entirely secular utility is the chessboard which could be a work of art. Palgrave's edition of the royal inventory, dated 12 Edward III, lists as item 64, p. 173:

> Un eschequier de jaspe et de cristal
> garni entour d'argent dorré od
> oevre de triffaire, pris iiii livre.

On p. 201 the item is repeated but with the variant 'ove oevre tryffere'. The pieces of quartz and of crystal are mounted in a silver-gilt frame in pierced work, so that carrying and handling the board must have been facilitated in the way I have suggested for the openwork cresting of reliquaries. A comparison may be made with the silver gilt cover of a gospel-book holder belonging to St. Paul's in 1295:

> Textus lingneus desuper ornatus platis
> argenteis deauratis, cum subtili triphorio
> in superiori limbo. . . .
>
> (ed. Dugdale, p. 314)

Triphorio, here used as a noun, is a fine decoration along the top edge, perhaps serving as a frame or perhaps as a handle to open the case. In the Westminster Abbey inventory of 1540 there is an item given in English, a 'texte Book . . . covered on the forsyd with plait of sylver and gylt garnished at ij corners of the same syd with brances of sylver

---

[23] G. Oliver, *Lives of the Bishops of Exeter*, 1861–87, p. 310.
[24] A. B. Tonnochy, 'A Romanesque censer-cover in the British Museum', *Archeological Journal*, LXXXIX (1932), pp. 2–3 and 9.

and gylt lacking the same at the other ij corners, with a crosse and the ymages of Mary and John gravyd on the same plait. . . .'[25] In *Archaeologia*, vol. 52, p. 235, Legg identified with this a similar gospel-book cover listed in 1388 where the images are engraved 'in triffurato auro et lapidibus ac perlis'. It is possible that the silver-gilt branches are part of a projecting border in pierced work, framing the images.

Littré's example illustrating *trifoire* describes an ivory whip as follows:

> En sa main tint une corgie
> De soie, en un baston d'yvoire
> Ki entaillies ert a trifoire,
> Dont li ouvriers fu en grant paine.

> (*Li Chevaliers as Deus Espees* ed. Foerster, ll. 396–9)

Late medieval inventories mention ivory whips, carved with figures, one of which has three silk cords,[26] but there are no surviving specimens. In the thirteenth century romance the ivory carving seems to be in pierced and open work, well executed, but without gold and gems. Yet, in 1295, the ivory stick or *baculus* owned by H. de Wengham has triforium-work in gold with gems. Really noteworthy is the precentor's staff at St. Paul's:

> Baculus cantoris de peciis eburneis,
> et summitate cristallina, ornata circulis
> argenteis, deauratis, triphoriatus
> lapidibus insertis.

> (ed. Dugdale, p. 316, col. 2)

Instead of the bishop's crook, the summit has a solid cristal knob.[27] The ivory pieces are mounted in silver-gilt rings, and the staff is ornamented with pierced work together with jewelled incrustations.

With greater consistency than Littré, Godefroy chose an example of *trifoire* in Robert Biket's *Lai du Cor*:

> Li corn estoit de iveure
> Entaillez de trifure;
> Peres i out assises
> Qui en l'or furent mises.

> (ed. F. Wulff, Lund, 1888, ll. 41–4)

[25] *Trans. of the London and Middlesex Archeol. Society*, IV (1875), p. 323.

[26] R. Koechlin, *Les Ivoires Gothiques Français*, 1924, vol. I, p. 461, n. 4.

[27] K. Hoffmann, vol. I, p. 153. Cf. Cahier et Martin, *Mél. d'Archéol.* IV (1854), pp. 171–3.

Although this horn may not be based on reality, I suggest that it possessed metallic mountings in gold or gilt. The interest of the passage derives from all the elements of triforium-work being present, carved and pierced ivory, with ornamental strips of worked gold, set at intervals with gems. Yet used in medieval times as reliquaries, surviving ivory horns tend to be plain. When they are carved as at Maestricht, the metallic mountings are modern work.[28]

Finger-rings are not listed in the St. Paul's inventories, with one exception, a ring worn by bishops known as the pontifical. Worn over the glove and in the middle of the third finger, this huge ring is described as being of triforiated gold:

> annulus pontificalis aureus triphoriatus,
> cum topacio magno et aliis multis lapidibus ornatus.
>
> (ed. Dugdale, p. 315)

It is probable that 'triphoriatus' means 'in pierced work' since there are such rings surviving from the Middle Ages. Two rings belonging to the Empress Giselda, dated about 1025 A.D., have piercings upon the shoulders.[29] On an arm reliquary at the Victoria and Albert Museum, numbered M–353–1956, I have seen a finger-ring with small perforations running round its hoop. The pontifical must have carried its large topaz at the head with many stones on the border. It is the gems alone, not the designs, that are described in Old French romances.

The great St. Ethelbert reliquary at St. Paul's contained one hundred and thirty stones while even a small object like the pontifical ring has many stones. In the St. Paul morses, the 1295 list terms any large gem a 'Kamahutus' while the 1245 one specifically names the saphyr, the topaz, the cornaline. For 'Kamahutus' the Old French equivalent is 'camahieu', a word still used in the seventeenth century and even beyond to designate the cameo of antiquity. When not engraved, stones in the Middle Ages were 'tallow cut' or 'en cabochon'. In triforium-work, precious stones are commonly associated with the gold decoration so that it is not surprising to find in 1853 Laborde defining Old French *trifoire* as 'ouvrage incrusté. . . . Se disait principalement des pierres précieuses'. His definition relies on a passage in the *Grandes Chroniques* about sacred vessels 'de fin or esmeré et

---

[28] Bock and Willemson, *Die Mittelalterlichen Kunst- und Reliquienschätze zu Maestricht*, 1872, Fig. 38, 50 and 51.

[29] *Der Mainzer Goldschmuck*, Plate V, rings 8 and 9.

aornés de très riches pierres précieuses, d'oeuvre triphoire'.[30] Here the proximity of gems to gold has deceived Laborde who confines to the incrustation of gems what is a technique of metal-work. In 1857, under *trifoire*, Texier copied Laborde's definition with examples almost verbatim. Even Littré still repeats Laborde, though he expands his definition:

> 'Art de mettre en œuvre les pierres
> précieuses, de les enchâsser.'

Yet, as we have seen, his example from *Li Chevaliers as Deus Espees* does not concern gems at all. Under *triforium* in Cabrol-Didron's *Dictionnaire des Antiquités Chrétiennes*, 1953, Leclercq unites Enlart's definition, which I have already quoted, with Laborde's earlier one. Accordingly *triforium* and *trifoire* become part of an identical definition: 's'appliquait à toute chose percée de jours ou d'arcades, par exemple à la monture des pierres précieuses.' I myself believe that gems are not an essential part of triforium-work. Without any jewelled incrustations, censers, candlesticks and saddlebows can all be described as 'triforiati', or 'a trifoire'. The Ambazac reliquary (*Trésors des Eglises de France*, 1965, p. 191) has a crest of copper gilt in pierced work decorated by enamels and gems. In contrast Hoffmann's catalogue, item 162, describes a bronze reliquary with an openwork gilt crest having 'a series of two arcades, or keyholes alternating with a large quatrefoil'. Despite the absence of cabochons, the second crest is, in my view, 'triforiata' like the first, because censers and candlesticks with triforium-work may also lack jewels.

Braun-Ronsdorf has recently pointed out that in 1295 at St. Paul's one in five fabrics were decorated in precious metals,[31] and yet I have not encountered triforium-work in the vestments listed. I have no recorded uses either of Old French trifoire in this connection, and only three examples of triforium-work in the 1245 Latin inventory (ed. Sparrow Simpson). Firstly the Prior of Achon's white silk cope seems decorated with repeated circular designs, 'opere triforio mirabiliter contexto' (p. 478). Next a stole and maniple are 'trifuriatim intexto auro' (p. 488) where the adverb parallels the phrase 'ad modum triforiae' (ed. Dugdale, p. 329). Then Gilbert of Banaster's green cope has an orphrey of

[30] Laborde L., *Notice des Emaux exposés dans les galeries du Musée du Louvre*, 1853, vol. II, under *trifoire*.
[31] 'Gold and Silver Fabrics from Medieval to Modern Times', *CIBA Review*, (1961–3), p. 10.

triforium-work, being 'addubbata aurifigio trifuriato' (p. 479). In his
historical survey Francisque Michel attempted to distinguish between
woven patterns and ornamental bands 'à façon de trifoire'.[32] His
distinction helps little in the understanding of gold thread weaving or
embroidery.

A well-known passage from the twelfth century *De Utensilibus* by
the Englishman Alexander Neckam (+1217) gives credence to a working in relief whether by an embroiderer's stitches or a goldsmith's
hammer. Neckam writes of small fine needles for suitable raised work,
'ad opus anaglafarium' or, as the French gloss has it, for 'tripharye'.[33]
Elsewhere in the same terms he writes of sculpture upon metal and in
relief. However the French gloss in the manuscript used by Scheler
gives 'burdure' instead of 'tripharye'.[34] By close association with
sculpture in bas relief, the noun 'trifoiree (tripharye)' designating
pierced work has become a synonym in Neckam for 'opus anaglafarium'. In the inventories edges and borders are frequently associated
with triforium-work while in Neckam 'bordure' becomes an alternative gloss for the noun 'trifoiree'.

Most of the Old French examples of *l'uevre Salemon* collected by
Professor West show the phrase in association with carving (*entaillier*)
and with *trifoire*.[35] In my view, *l'uevre Salemon* is inclusive of all kinds
of carving and of triforium-work, whereas *l'uevre trifoire* excludes
other techniques such as engraving ('opus gravatum'). In the field of
metalwork, *l'uevre Salemon* appears as a general term and *l'uevre
trifoire* as a particular one. It seems significant that the term Solomon-
work is not in the inventories. In the field of architecture, Francisque
Michel has given twelfth century Latin examples of Solomon's name
associated with buildings.[36] On the other hand architectural *trifoire* is
confined to a specific part of a building. The fixed phrase must originate
in King Solomon's building the temple as recorded in the Old Testa-
ment book of Kings. In medieval culture such allusions are very easily
made. His name may be used directly about the excellent builder
himself, or indirectly about excellent craftwork and excellent craftsmen.

[32] F. Michel, *Recherches sur le commerce . . . des étoffes de soie, d'or, etc.*, 1854,
vol. II, p. 185.

[33] *A volume of Vocabularies*, ed. T. Wright, 1857, pp. 101 and 118.

[34] *Jahrbuch für Rom. u. Englische Lit.*, VIII (1867), p. 66.

[35] G. D. West, 'L'Uevre Salemon', *Modern Language Review*, XLIX (1954),
pp. 176-82.

[36] F. Michel, vol. II, p. 102, n. 1.

It may be used to praise excellence of workmanship or to serve as an exemplary model for art objects. In *Girart de Roussillon* the phrase is used of architectural carving in marble so that Solomon the builder is dominant:

> Li caire e li estel furent marmoine,
> Bien entaillat a l'obre de Salemoine.
>> (ed. W. M. Hackett, SATF, ll. 131–2)

In the same work Fouchier and his men rob Charles Martel of treasure by carrying off three hundred goblets (hanaps), and here Solomon the art patron is dominant:

> Treis cens enas en portent de taus facos,
> De l'obre que fait faire reis Salemons.   (ll. 3529–30)

The document giving the most precise use of Solomon-work that I know is a collection of laws in British Museum Additional MS. 14252 and compiled in 1216. The regulations in question which govern the conduct of Lorrainers or foreign merchants have been dated about 1130. The ship must wait in the Thames till representatives come to take goods for the king's use for which payment will be made within a fortnight. The first category of goods to be specified are valuable gold and silver plate or, in the actual wording, 'veissele d'or u d'argent del ovre Salemun'.[37] This non-literary use antedates the earliest Old French example in the *Eneas* by some twenty years. There is no reason to suppose the phrase refers to a specific technique since the king seeks the compulsory purchase of valuable imports in general. This legal document strangely underlines the importance of Solomon's memory for precious materials and workmanship in the arts. It was natural that in a great age for Western art his memory should be much alive, for example in the writings of Theophilus and of Suger. Both speak about David's unworthiness, through the shedding of blood, for the task with which Solomon was entrusted, the building of the Lord's house. Writing of the gifts of the spirit (Isaiah XI, 2–3) and the art of the craftsman, Theophilus particularly emphasises the relevance of the spirit of knowledge which traditionally, of course, was represented by Solomon, as is evidenced by the iconography of the Xanten bowl (*Revue de l'Art Chrétien* (1886) 325, 32).

[37] Mary Bateson, 'A London Municipal Collection of the Reign of John,' *English Historical Review*, XVII (1902), p. 499. I owe this reference to the kindness of Professor Brian Woledge.

If my view of Solomon-work, 'l'uevre Solomon', is correct, then it is triforium-work, 'l'uevre trifoire' that presents the lexicographer with the real difficulty. A specific technique long lost even to craftsmen cannot be identified and completely understood without touching and viewing. I therefore offer most tentatively my conclusions on Old French *trifoire* as follows. No doubt formed on the pattern of a word like *trichorium*, the place where there are three apses, *triforium* seems logically to have designated at first a place where there are three openings. It is interesting also that another architectural term *transforia*, 'perforation', is attested in the records of Milan cathedral.[38] I suggest that Old French *trifoire*, derived from *triforia*, designates in metal work that which has several perforations, that which has a series of piercings. The significance, 'a piercing right through', can be deduced from two self-defining passages in Old French poems. There was, of course, in Old French, *tresforer* 'to pierce through', from Latin *transforare*, a verb general in meaning. Attested by the derivative *triforiatus* in the St. Paul inventories, medieval Latin *triforiare* had, in my view, a narrower application than *transforare* and was favoured by goldsmiths because such a term proved necessary to describe a particular decorative technique. After piercing the thin gold plates, discarding the background segments and hammering up the carved designs, the craftsman obtained a continuous decoration not flat but in relief. Such a type of decoration was specifically suited to the borders of an object or, if used elsewhere, the work could find anchorage in a circle at the centre. Through constant association, *opus triforium*, French *nevre trifoire*, became understood as a strip of gold decoration which might run lengthwise along a straight surface, the horizontal crest, or else round a circumference, the circular brooch.

Old French *trifoire* falling into gradual disuse disappears during the Middle French period though the term survives at a late date, for example in locksmithing as recorded in Gay's *Glossaire Archéologique*. Obsolescence may have been due to a superior type of decoration being preferred, along with changing style and taste, for instance as enamelling work grew finer and more sophisticated. Simple and elegant, triforium-work, often on a tiny scale, sometimes relied on rich gems to contrast with the gold design. I found it impossible to formulate a rounded definition from Old French poems alone because these do not expand the term in any meaningful way. On the other hand, in the

---

[38] *Annali difabbrica del duomo di Milano* (1877–85). See Appendici 2, p. 315.

French and Latin inventories, reliquaries, candlesticks, cups, clasps, mitre, chessboard, finger-ring and staff, are all present so that the great variety of objects illuminates the problem. On close examination, I discovered triforium-work represented by gold roundels on a mitre, gold squares or little lions on clasps, dragons on candlesticks. Largely a technique of carving on metal, the designs it assumed were diversified, but it remained unobtrusive and appropriate to its essentially decorative role.

Quatrains and Passages of Eight Lines in Beroul: Some Stylistic and Linguistic Aspects

C. A. ROBSON

Fellow of Merton College, Oxford

I

The existence of monorhymed quatrains in many Norman, and especially Anglo-Norman, octosyllabic couplet poems, was first observed by Paul Meyer. The subject was carried further by two more recent critics: first, by Mario Roques, who drew attention, in 1922, to the grouping of couplets into larger units, then, in 1970, in the long awaited commentary on Beroul of the late Alfred Ewert.[1] The latter observes that the frequency of loosely rhyming couplets justifies us in taking some account of two or more successive couplets linked by the same approximate rhyme or assonance.

The 'two prosodic features' alluded to in the title of Roques' article on the *Vie de Sainte Grégoire* are (i) a series of monorhymed quatrains, placed at the final climax of the story in the longer *A* version (and in two manuscripts contaminated with it, B_2 and B_3); and (ii) the grouping of couplets into sentences of eight lines in the oldest manuscript of the more ancient and briefer *B* version, B_1. This is the important

---

[1] Works frequently cited in this article are: M. Roques, 'Sur deux particularités métriques de la *Vie de Saint Grégoire* en ancien français', *Romania*, XLVIII (1922), pp. 41–61, 'Notes pour l'édition de la *Vie de Saint Grégoire* en ancien français', ibid. LXXVII (1956), pp. 1–25; and *The Romance of Tristran* by Beroul, edited by A. Ewert, Oxford, Blackwell, I (Introduction, Text, Glossary, Index), 1939, II (Introduction, Commentary), 1970. Line-references in Beroul refer to the Text in vol. I, page-references to Ewert refer to vol. II; references to the Introduction are to vol. II, pp. 1–56. The Commentary is referred to, in the textual notes on p. 201 below, by the siglum E; M³ refers to the edition of the same text by E. Muret, *Classiques français du moyen âge*, 3ᵉ édition revue, 1928.

Egerton 612, in the British Museum, an Anglo-Norman manuscript containing Adgar's *Legends of the Virgin*, copied about 1200 A.D.

Roques takes great pains to convince his reader that the eight-line grouping is not a mere subjective fancy of an editor, but a relic of an older form of poetic art. The first 128 lines of B_1 contain fourteen eight-line groups, one six-line and one ten-line group; this part of the text is quoted in full. In the next 180 lines Roques finds twenty-one eight-line groups, and only two six-line groups. After this we lose track of the groupings somewhat; but the proportion of eight-line units in any given portion of the text is never less than 50–70 per cent. The writer points out that these segments are not produced by the placing of an editorial full stop at the requisite points: a segment of eight lines very often makes up 'an indivisible unity, each line of which, right up to the end, is necessary to complete the sense'.[2] He also shows, by printing parallel texts, how the structure of the old poem is obscured by minor additions, expansions and variations in the *A* version.

The theory underlying this demonstration is that, at an early stage in the twelfth century, and in previous times, these poems were meant to be sung or chanted. The scribes who copied the Clermont-Ferrand manuscript, c. 1000 A.D., divided the *Passion* into quatrains, the *Saint-Leger* into sixains (consisting in each case of two or three prosodically distinct couplets), and the musical notation accompanying the first quatrain of the *Passion* points to the reason:

> Strophe et couplet mélodique sont dès lors inséparables: l'une est faite pour l'autre qui lui assure en retour une individualité certaine, en dehors de toute disposition graphique et malgré les confusions que peut créer la succession ininterrompue de rimes plates.[3]

In a lengthy note to a later article on the same subject (1956) Roques shows, nevertheless, how important the *disposition graphique* (or the lack of it) might be in the transmission of these ancient poetic structures. The scribe of the *Passion* wrote most of it continuously like prose, without indentation for the separate quatrains; he used large initials for the initial word of each quatrain, but these are not all equally visible, and could easily have been overlooked by a future copyist unacquainted with the old system.[4] Thus both copyists and *remanieurs*, by expansion, variation and sheer miscopying, succeeded in garbling the ancient form

[2] See pp. 51, 54 of the first article.
[3] Ibid., p. 59.
[4] P. 23, n. 1.

in which the minstrels of the early Old French period recited the Passion and the Lives of the Saints.

In the course of his studies of this text, which extended over more than half a century, the focus of Roques' interest appears to have shifted from the overtly monorhymed quatrains in the A version (and in the two contaminated manuscripts B_2 and B_3) to the hidden eight-line structure of the old B version; and, in his article of 1956, he finally concludes that the quatrains are a late addition of the A version, whereas the eight-line passages must go back to the twelfth century as shown by the date of the oldest manuscript.

In the present article I also shall keep a balance between these two aspects of the old poems; I shall attempt to show that many traces of monorhymed or assonating quatrains survive in the Beroul manuscript. But these, unlike the monorhymed quatrains of the *Vie de Saint Grégoire*, are ancient, and by the second half of the twelfth century they are already being effaced and eliminated in the new eight-line structure by the strophic poet who composed the essential elements of 'Beroul I'.

II

On p. 4 of his recently published Introduction to Beroul, Ewert shows the existence of at least four monorhymed quatrains in the text: 725–8 (in -*ez*), 2703–6 (*lie, jugie, herbergie, couchie*, where the scribal -*ie* stands for -*iee* throughout), 1117–20 (*destruite, luite, merite, vite*), and 1891–4 (*lui, quit, endormi, vi*). To these we can safely add the closely similar quatrain 781–4 (*quit, destruit, merci, soufri*).

The last three cases imply non-standard phonology, dialectal or 'advanced'. But the pronunciation of *ui* as *uí*, rhyming with *i*, is a normal part of the poet's usage in couplet rhyme: *lit: nuit* 655–6, *hardi: lui* 851–2, *endormi: lui* 2017–18, *pris: puis* 4437–8. The effacement of -*t* after *oi, ui* is also found in couplet rhyme, not only in 1891–2 where it is necessary for the first couplet of the quatrain, but also in 123–4 (*quit: lui*); cf. Ewert, Introduction, Consonants § 22, Vowels § 35.

On the other hand, we find in 721–4 a quatrain on the rhymes *quit, nuit, issut, boçut* (MS. *issuz, boçuz*), which presupposes the descending diphthong *úi* and (probably) the analogical hard -*t* in the past participles; cf. Ewert, Vowels § 34. Even allowing for both these features, and introducing the emendation of -*uz* to -*ut* (thus eliminating the 'correct' nominatives of the scribe), we still have only an approximate rhyme which passes over the second element of the diphthong. Here, as often elsewhere, each couplet considered internally has an exact rhyme in the standard language, but the two couplets are linked together by an inexact or dialectal rhyme. There can be little doubt that the quatrain so produced is a genuine part of an ancient prosodic structure, since it forms part of a longer passage in continuous rhyme to which Ewert draws attention on p. 4 (713–18 -*oit*, -*ois*, -*oit*; 725–8 -*ez*). Omitting two intrusive couplets from the extant text, we obtain a passage of sixteen lines on four rhymes:

> 709–10, 713–18: -*oit*, -*oit*, -*ois*, -*oit*
> 721–4: -*uit*, -*ut* (MS. -*uz*)
> 725–8: -*ez*.

The *prima facie* case for the existence of lengthy passages in quatrains is strengthened by an examination of 1673–1746 (the slaying of the hostile baron by Governal). Here we find numerous quatrains (1707–8, 1711–12 -*ait*, 1713–16 -*u*, -*us*; 1729–32 -*i(e)e*, -*ie*, written -*ie* throughout; 1739–42 -*este*, -*estre*) in an episode apparently independent of the Eilhart version of the *estoire*, and curiously barbaric and pre-chivalric in tone.

This type of prosodic investigation is encouraged by Ewert who, on page 4, goes on to observe that, since 'mere assonance' (or, as he calls it on p. 31, 'imperfect rhyme') is occasionally used in couplet rhyme, licences of this sort can reasonably be allowed when we are looking for continuous monorhyme between two or more successive couplets. This is a very welcome suggestion; but the evidence quoted in support is rather meagre, and the argument itself only hesitantly advanced. The real difficulty is that Ewert, even in his treatment of couplet rhyme, does not draw any clear boundary between 'mere assonance' and 'imperfect rhyme'; nor does he distinguish such approximate rhymes from dialectal rhymes and from 'impossible rhymes' which require emendation or the assumption of a lacuna in the text. In his overlapping discussions of these problems on pp. 4, 7–8, 15–16, 31 and elsewhere, he assembles a body of difficult cases under the loose heading of 'tolérances' or 'poetic licences', without establishing any fixed criteria by which to discriminate between rhymes in the poet's own (southwestern) dialect, conventional doublets in the standard language and rhyming licence properly so called.

To introduce some provisional order into the subject, we must begin with axioms and stipulative definitions. It is axiomatic, both in assonance and rhyme, that the tonic accent must be respected: masculines must be associated with masculines and feminines with feminines. There must also be agreement, in all the rhyming or assonating words, of the 'syllabic peak' of the tonic syllables, that is, the most prominent element in the syllable, which may be a vowel, a diphthong, or merely the first element in a descending diphthong.

Mere assonance requires nothing further.[5] Perfect rhyme requires that the final (or 'decrescendo') segment of the word, consisting of sonant, second element in a diphthong, implosive consonants, and post-tonic (or feminine) e where present, should be identical. Between these two extremes, there are a number of intermediate stages. There may be agreement between the rhyming words in respect of a single consonantal *segment*, or a single consonantal *feature*, occurring after the syllabic peak. This rhyming element, which may be regarded as the most sonorous and audible element in the latter part of the syllable, suffices to constitute imperfect or approximate rhyme.

When the tonic vowel is followed by a consonant cluster, one consonant may dominate at the expense of others. Thus, when a *t* or *s* in absolute final position is 'supported' by a sonant (the term 'sonant' being understood in a very broad sense, to include liquids, nasals, the second elements of diphthongs and even the weak pre-consonantal *s* of Old French), the supporting consonant may be passed over, as in the rhymes *rs:s* (ten examples in Beroul), *rt:t* (two examples) and *st:t* (three examples); see Ewert, Consonants §§ 28, 33. There is also an isolated case of pre-consonantal *s* being passed over before a nasal (*meïmes:dimes* 599–600), and another isolated rhyme, explicable on the same general principle (*entre:estre* 3151–2). In so far as the 'sonant' may be thought to be already effaced in the poet's own speech, some of

---

[5] Assonance as defined here is not to be equated with the highly evolved prosodic form of the Digby *Roland* and the later assonating epics, where we find a rigorous distinction between eight simple vowels and three 'monophonematic' diphthongs *ie*, *oe* (*ue*), *ei*, which are treated in every way like simple vowels. On the other hand, the consonants are usually assumed to be random, without even the loose classification into sonants, plosives, nasals, which we find in the prosodies of other languages. Yet there are strong elements of monorhyme as well (a^{nas}, e^{nas}, o^{nas}, all of which may combine with a feminine ending). For my view of this system, which seems to be a late development out of imperfect rhyme, cf. my articles in *Actas do IX Congresso Internacional de Linguistica Romanica* (1959), Lisbon, 1961, II, pp. 11–27, and *Boletín de la Real Academia de Buenas Letras de Barcelona*, XXXI, 1965–6, pp. 251–63 (a paper to the Société Rencesvals conference in 1964).

these are normal rhymes in an 'advanced' or dialectal phonology; but, from another standpoint, they can all be regarded as imperfect rhymes, utilizing a conventional rhyming licence, in the standard language.

A different pronunciation of the final consonant cluster conferred a more sonorous pronunciation on the sonant, at the expense of the absolute final consonant; this was especially marked where the sonant was a nasal. Thus we have the rhymes *nt:nz* (five examples) and *st:s* (two examples); see Ewert, Consonants §§ 32, 35. The isolated rhyme *ator:corz* (4101-2) is explicable on the same principle. On the other hand, where final *t* and *z* are 'unsupported' (that is, occur directly after the tonic vowel), this explanation will not fit, and it seems preferable to emend on the lines suggested by Muret and Ewert: *chiet: couchiét*, MS. *couchiez* 1815-16, *mesfet:vet*, MS. *mesfez* 2171-2, *dit:banit*, MS. *baniz* 3277-8. Here as elsewhere (cf. 723-4 above) we abandon the scribe's 'correct' nominatives to obtain the desired rhyming agreement. Similarly, at 1439-42, where the MS. has *petitet, brachet, berseret, prez*, we should substitute the oblique form *prest* (cf. 796) to obtain a mono-rhyming quatrain (with the licence *st:t* discussed above), rather than operating with the hypothetical *berserez* (not attested in the Beroul MS.) as proposed by Muret.

Yet another type of licence is found in the approximate rhymes *tre:te* and *bre:ble*, where the sonants occurring in the syllabic pattern *plosive + sonant + off-glide* are equated with each other or with zero: *metre:regrete* 1943-4, *voitre:cuite* 3685-6, *chanbre:ensenble* 597-8. This licence is often camouflaged by the scribal variants *magistre:tristre* (for *triste*) 345-6, *destre:celestre* 4161-2. There is an oddly suggestive passage in the manuscript:

> Des estoiles le cors savoit,
> Les set *planestres* devisoit,
> Il savoit bien que ert a *estre*
> Qant il oiet un enfant *nestre* . . .   323-6

where the occurrence of yet another rhyme-doublet, *planestres* for *planetes*, in the body of the line, perhaps points to a lost quatrain:

> Li nain savoit des cors celestres
> Si devisoit les set planestres,
> Il savoit bien que ert a estre
> Qant il oiet un enfant nestre . . .

See Ewert, Consonants §§ 28 and n. 2, 27, and cf. p. 8.

A more peculiar instance of rhyming licence (usually regarded hitherto as a Picard dialectal feature) is the passing over of the second element of the diphthong *ie*, usually before feminine *e*, so that the past participle feminine of the first conjugation, in *-i(e)e*, rhymes with that of the second conjugation, in *-ie*. Only one example of this licence occurs in couplet rhyme in the Beroul manuscript:

> La cortine ot dedenz partie,
> Vit la chanbre, qui fu jonchie   4413-4

—and this is eliminated in the Ewert edition by the adoption of the reading *percie* for *partie* (cf. *Studies . . . presented to M. K. Pope*, Manchester, 1939, p. 93, and the Commentary p. 259, and Vowels § 8; the point is further discussed by Professor Reid in *Modern Language Review*, LX (1965), p. 355 and n. 3). Whatever the case may be in this isolated instance, the rhyme *-ie*:*-i(e)e* is essential for the quatrains—and the point is underlined by the invariable[6] scribal use of *-ie* for *-iee*:

> Tristran se jut a la fullie;
> Chau tens faisoit, si fu jonchie;
> Endormiz est, ne savoit mie
> Que cil eüst perdu la vie . . .   1729-32

> Onques ne fu dit tel maniere
> Tant dolerose ne tant fire
> Qui en savroit tote la pire
> [Ne] seust, por Deu le roi, eslire . . .[7]   1185-8

Here the scribe has *man'e*, *fire*, which stands for the normal rhyme *maniere*:*fiere* in the standard poetic language, but the whole quatrain rhymes in *-ire*. A similar scribal tendency reappears in the unique manuscript (copied c. 1200) of the satirical poem of Etienne de Fougères (bishop of Rennes, 1168-78), *Le Livre des Manières*. The poem is composed in monorhyming quatrains which obey the phonological rules of the standard language—but these are sometimes grouped into

---

[6] Except in *alegiee: meschiee* 3443-4, cf. Ewert, Vowels, § 8. The scribe does not write *i* for *ié* in absolute final position; but on the above definitions the agreement *ié*: *i* (as in 885-8) counts as an imperfect rhyme, not an assonance.

[7] I reject the arbitrary emendation of *en savroit* to *orendroit* (Paris, Muret, Ewert), and suggest [Ne] to make minimal syntactic sense, although this leaves a hypermetric line, unless *seust* is treated as an 'Anglo-Norman' synezesis.

larger units on a continuous assonance or monorhyme. In one case the assonance *i . . . e*, or *ie . . . e*, is continued for five stanzas; here too the scribe invariably writes *ie*, or *i . . . e*, for *iee* or *ie . . . e*. Both poets are connected with the south-western area, and neither manuscript contains any important Picard features; hence it seems more appropriate to attribute these scribal tendencies to an awareness of rhyming licences in the old poetic language, rather than to Picard influence.

Other unusual rhymes are explicable in terms of a common phonetic feature: a nasal, lateral, bilabial plosive or unvoiced plosive element forming the common element in two phonemes, as in *dit*: *bric*, *roïne*: *signe* 3579–82, *vile*: *merville* (MS. *mervelle*) 2455–6, *mervelle*: *selle* 3799–3800, *gabe*: *chape* 2879–80; see Ewert, Consonants §§ 25 n. 3, 27, and cf. p. 31. Taking account, furthermore, of sporadic dialectal or 'advanced' features (*ie*: *e* < A, *s*: *z*, cf. Ewert, Vowels § 7, Consonants § 31), we can perhaps conclude that all couplets in the Beroul text are linked by perfect rhyme, or by imperfect rhyme using the licences defined above, and that residual cases must be eliminated by emendation (*chanbre*: *prenent* 771–2, substitute a phrase with *prendre* as proposed by Ewert), or by assuming a lacuna in the text, or as at 2821–2 the careless work of an interpolator. 'Mere assonance' is thus eliminated altogether from the couplets, although it plays a considerable role in the formation of quatrains.

III

Having cleared the ground by a re-examination of the principles of couplet rhyme in Beroul, we can now cite a number of quatrains linked by monorhyme with the above-defined licences and dialectal features:

> S'or en savoit li rois un mot,
> Mon cors seret desmenbré to[s]t,
> E si seroit a molt grant tort,
> Bien sai qu'il me dorroit la mort.[8]   65–8; cf. 2197–2200

---

[8] Although *mot* elsewhere rhymes with a close *o* (Ewert, Vowels, § 16, n. 1), I suggest that it should have the standard form with open *o* here; *tot* then = *to[s]t*; for the old Western impf. *-o(u)t* rhyming with *-ort* (2197–2200), see Ewert, Conjugation, § 47 and n. 2.

'Seignors' fait il a ces barons
'Tenez vos bien a vos archons;
Mal ait cil fans qui est si mos!
Ostez ces manteaus de vos cox . . .[9]   3813-6

Afaitiez fu, a un dain trait,
Li sans en chiet, li brachet brait,
Li dains navrez s'en fuit le saut,
Husdent li bauz en crie en haut.   1607-10

S'il prent el bois chevrel ne dai[n]s,
Bien l'enbusche, cuevre de rains,
Et s'il enmi lande l'ataint,
Com il s'avient en i prent maint . . .   1629-32

. . . Et eslira l'escouellier
Et l'estovra a nos couchier,
Sire, en leu de tes beaus mengiers
Avra de pieces, de quartiers . . .   1205-8; cf. 873-6 below

Tristran s'esvelle, vit la teste,
Saut esfreez, sor piez s'areste;
A haute voiz crie son mestre:
'Ne vos movez, seürs puez estre . . .   1739-42; cf. 737-40
                                                              below

Mervelles lor fust meschoiet
Se Tristran ses braies n'avoit; (MS. Et T., ravoit)
La roïne avoit en son doi
L'anel d'or des noces le roi . . .   1809-12

Au roi dïent li chevalier:
'Laison a seurre cest traallier,
En tel leu nos porroit mener
Dont gries seroit le retorner'.   1523-6

Salemon dit que droituriers
Que ses amis, c'ert ses levriers,
A vos le poo[n] nos prover,
Vos ne volez de rien goster.   1461-4

---

[9] Here *mos* = *mous*, *cox* = *cous*, hence the sonants passed over are *n* and *u*; alternatively, if the diphthong *ou* is levelled, we have the merging of close *o* with close *o* nasal, common at all stages of the language.

Si l'avoit fait lïer li rois
Par le commandement as trois,
Qu'il li out si les poinz estroiz
Li sanc li est par toz les doiz.   1051-4

Aperçut soi qu'il ert marriz,
Venuz s'en est aeschariz:
'Lasse,' fait ele, 'mes amis
Est trovez, mes sires l'a pris!'   3161-4

De luien puet l'om oïr les huz
De ceus qui solle la paluz,
Cil qui la passe n'est seürs,
Atant es vos le roi Artus.   3699-3702

'Sire, Tristran est eschapez,
Les plains, les bois, les pas, les guez
Set forment bien, et molt est fiers,
Vos estes oncle et il tes niés.   1101-4

De seche busche fait buen feu:
Molt avoient a faire queu!
Il n'avoient ne lait ne sel
A cele foiz a lor ostel.[10]   1295-8

The above can all be explained on the same principles, of rhyming licence or dialect rhyme, as the couplets. But unlike the couplets, many quatrains are formed by an assonating link: 143–6 (-iers:-ié), 275–8 (-ir:-in), 333–6 (-ace:-ales), and, in the passage cited below, 569–72, 583–6, 623–6, 635–8, 675–8, 679–82, 687–90, 705–8, 713–18, 951–4.

[10] This rhyme implies a vocalization of final *l*, generally attributed to the analogy of the pre-cons. *l* in the history of standard French. The three low vowels of 'Vulgar Latin' tend to form triphthongs with -*u*, and pre-cons. *l*, cf. the history of *dieu, pieu, lieu, yeux*; here the reflexes of FOCU, COQUU, SALE, OSPITALE appear to have merged, probably in the form **ëu**. Another phonological feature of the S.-W. appears in the *Livre de Manières*:

> Li un ne volent nomer four
> Mes li deien qui est l'espour
> I conpase tot o avour,
> Segont l'ovre et seron le four.

Here *four* = *fuer* (<FORU) 'price, market', and it rhymes with *avour, espour* = *avoir, espoir* (*qui* = *cui*; *seron* = *segont*). This merging of the reflexes of *ŏ* and *ē* in the free syllable (cf. Walloon *ŏ*) enables us to diagnose a possible assonance in Beroul 887–880 *ois: uel*.

Thus, while the *couplets* of Beroul are mainly in standard rhymes, with a strong minority of 'aberrant', that is, dialectal and/or imperfect, rhymes, but no 'mere assonance', the *quatrains* are composed pretty well equally in 'aberrant' rhymes and assonances, with only two correct standard rhymes (725–8, 2703–6, already cited by Ewert).

IV

We must now deal with a quite different kind of quatrains, those which compose the two complementary halves of the eight-line strophes, and which are not necessarily marked by continuous rhyme or assonance; these are however frequently marked by an initial line or *vers d'intonation* containing special mnemonic formulas. These formulas, when they occur in a *vers d'intonation*, will be printed below in small capitals.

A prima facie case for the existence of such eight-line strophes, as in the B version of the *Vie de Saint Grégoire*, can be made out by an examination of (for example) ll. 573–80, 581–8 (see pp. 190–1 below). One is a meditation on the difficulties of a love affair at court; the other is a narrative passage, and opens the central sequence of episodes of the Tristran story: the hostility of the barons, the recall of the dwarf, his ruse of the flour between the beds, the capture of the lovers and their condemnation to the stake, miraculous escape and flight to the woods (ll. 581–1284).

A large red initial marks the division between these two eight-line passages in the Beroul manuscript; each of them forms (in the words of Mario Roques) 'an indivisible unity, each line of which, right up to the end, is necessary to complete the sense'.[11] Lines 573–80 contain a

---

[11] The need to end the strophes with a full stop, where possible, makes for some alteration in the traditional punctuation, as at 558 (cf. Reid in *Vinaver Misc.*, p. 267), 610, 662, 690, 704, 714, 748, 778, 820, 896, 922, 936. In general, however, both the normal punctuation of the editors and the rubricated initials of the MS. (see note 13 below) confirm the eight-line passages. At 682, 888, where the last line of one strophe announces a speech in the next, I place a colon. Punctuation is bound to vary according as one aims to print (a) the eight-line strophes themselves, (b) the extant text as expanded, with due regard for sense, or (c) the expanded text as interpreted by the rubricator. Thus the added couplet 147–8 is really two separate lines, 147 being an addendum to the strophe 139–46 and 148 an introduction to the strophe 149–56; the syntax is masked by the rubricator who places the large initial at the head of the strophe (149), cf. Reid, *Vinaver Misc.*, pp. 265–6. In general, however, the usage of the rubricator is deserving of the most careful consideration, if not respect.—A peculiar licence by the strophic poet occurs

meditation of the poet on the fate of the lovers, ll. 581–8 describe, in
oratio obliqua, the ultimatum of the barons. If we skip over fourteen
lines of the extant text, we shall come to a series of similar eight-line
passages (603–10, 611–18, 619–26, 627–34, 635–42), which together
with 581–8 constitute a complete section of the narrative: the hostility
of the barons and the recall of the dwarf. We shall find that every such
section, consisting on six eight-line strophes, corresponds to a division
of Eilhard's German version of the same narrative.

Lines 581–8 contain two important formulas, in the opening lines of
the first and second quatrains: *trois barons* (581) and *son nevo* (585).
These belong to the formulaic openings, of which the most important
are the following:

(a) formulas of address: *Sire, Seignor* (pl., 627), *Rois, Roïne* 391,
   Niés 687, *Oncle, chiers sire* 555, *Maistre* 979, *Beau mestre* 1009;

(b) formulas of imprecation and oathtaking: *por (amor) Deu* 93, 217,
   por Deu le roi 5, *Sire, merci* 783, 1221, *Dame, merci* 93 (cf. 106);
   Par Deu, li sire glorios Qui forma ciel et terre et nos 225–6, *Par cel
   seignor qui fist le mont, Totes les choses qui i sont* 889–90;

(c) formulas of asseveration, containing the word *bien*: *Or voi je
   bien* 123, *Qar bien savon* 615, *Bien vit* 737; *Bien sai* 203, 207, *Bien
   set* 333, *Vos savez bien* 935, *Li rois sout bien* 459;

(d) names and designations of the principal characters: *Tristran,
   Yseut, li rois, le roi, la roïne; li nains, le nain, li troi, li troi felon, li
   troi baron; Governal, son mestre* 975, 1263, *Brengain, Dinas li sire
   de Dinan,* 1085, cf. 1125, 1129, 1133, *Ivain(s),* 1190, 1229, 1247;

(e) formulas relating to the uncle-nephew relationship: *Tes nies* 607,
   mon nevo 399, *son nevo* 585, *Se ton nevo* 619, *Di ton nevo* 649, *De
   mon nevo* 269, *Por mon nevo* 507, *O ton nevo* 404; *mon oncle* 139,
   mis oncles chiers 143;

(f) formulas (in ll. 387–805) relating to the royal bedchamber: *A sa
   chanbre* 387, 757, *a la chanbre* 805, *en la chanbre* 551, 701, 771, *de la
   chanbre* 659, *Dedenz la chanbre* 725; *devant ton lit* 655, *Live du lit*
   745, *el lit* 767; *la nuit* 679, 701;

---

at ll. 946–8, where the division between the sentences is displaced, by a kind of
enjambement, so that the formulaic word *Seignors* occurs in the second, not the
first line of the strophe. Such a variation (comparable to a delayed resolution of a
musical cadence) is only effective if it is extremely rare, and is no doubt used to
underline the effect of suspense: Tristran is hurtling to his death out of the chapel
window, and the poet deliberately delays telling us how his life is saved.

(g) formulas containing the emphatic pronouns *il*, *cil* ('the other', 'the hero', 'the opponent'): *Et il* 639, *Et s'il* 663, *Cil* 675;

(h) formulas indicating exit of the speaker, containing parts of the verb *aler*: *Por mon nevo va* 507, *G'irai* 515, *Rois, por li vois* 523.

Chains of four-line or eight-line strophes marked by these formulaic opening lines are frequent in the text, for example: (1)

(1) DAME, POR AMOR DEU, MERCI	93
Ahi! YSEUT, fille de roi	101
DAME, or vos vuel MERCI crier,	105–6
Ne puis ne poi a vos parler	*(interverted in ms.)*
Qar j'ai tel duel c'onques LE ROI	109
DAME, granz. . . .	113
(2) Molt vi MON ONCLE iluec pensis	139
Ne deüst pas MIS ONCLES CHIERS	143
(3) BIEN SAI que molt me het LI ROIS	203
BIEN SAI que j'ai si grant prooise	207
(4) YSEUT, POR DEU, de moi pensez	217
PAR DEU, li sire glorios (etc.)	225
(5) A SA CHANBRE LI ROIS en vient	387
ROÏNE, ainz vien a vos parler	391
SIRE, onques jor ne vos menti	395
DAME, veïs puis MON NEVO	399
O TON NEVO soz cel pin fui,	
Ge·l vi et pus parlai a lui	403–4 *(interverted in ms.)*

The first four of these sequences can easily be linked up, by the omission of a few couplets of the extant text, into a continuous series of eight-line strophes:

> . . . 93–100, 101–8, 109–16 (?118), 119–26
> (Tristran's opening speech)
> 131–8, 139–46, 149–56 (His first appeal to Yseult)
> 163–70, 171–8, 179–86 (Her reply)
> 203–10, 217–24, 225–32 . . .
> (His second appeal and her reply).

13

These eight-line strophes fall into groups of six, as in the passage of Tristran's first appeal to Yseult and her reply, and each group (of $6 \times 8 = 48$ lines) is embedded in the extant text in longer passages, usually of 68–76 (i.e., 72 ± 4) lines, consisting of two segments each of 32–40 (i.e., 36 ± 4) lines:

> *127–130* 4 *lines added at the beginning*
> 131–8, 139–46
> 147–8 2 *lines inserted*
> *149–56
> 157–62 6 *lines inserted*
>
> > 36 lines
>
> *163–70, 171–8, 179–86
> 187–96 10 *lines added at the end*
>
> > 34 lines
>
> *197–
>
> > = 70 lines

This relationship remains constant throughout the first part of 'Beroul I' (ll. 1–1284), which consists of some fourteen or fifteen passages of the type just illustrated; six of them (ll. 511–974) are printed in full below. In a previous analysis[12] I drew attention to the parallel structure of Beroul and Eilhart, each major episode of the latter containing some 500–600 lines, divided into sub-sections (basically eight in number) which average out in the relevant part (ll. 3765–4330) at 64–5 lines each. It can now be shown that each of the groups of six eight-line strophes, expanded to passages of 68–76 lines in the extant text, corresponds to one of the sub-sections in Eilhart, according to the following formula:

Eilhart	8-line groups	Beroul MS.
(average) 64–5 lines	six (=48 lines)	(average) 72 lines

The episode of the 'flour between the beds' and the capture, condemnation and escape of the lovers (ll. 3765–4330 in Eilhart) was previously delimited as ll. 569–1262 in Beroul; I now think the correct delimitation of this episode is 581–1284. This division accords better with the rubrics of the Beroul manuscript, all of which can now be explained

---

[12] See *Studies in Medieval French presented to Alfred Ewert*, Oxford, 1961, pp. 55 sqq.

in terms of the eight-line strophes, the added passages and the longer segments of 2 × 36 ± 4 lines.[13]

V

There appears to be a complicated, three-cornered relationship between the underlying monorhymed or assonating quatrains, the eight-line strophes and the work of the revisor or expander who, in most of the early part of Beroul I, is responsible for the extant text.

The strophic poet used monorhyming or assonating material, but sparingly, and he often sought to camouflage or conceal it or in other ways to minimize its impact on the hearer.[14] Thus in the passage quoted below (511–974), we find only eleven quatrains, composing the

[13] I have marked with an asterisk, in the passage printed below, the lines with rubricated initials in the MS.; it will be seen that all such initials occur either (i) at the head of a segment of 32–40 lines in the extant text, or (ii) at the head of an eight-line strophe, or of the second quatrain of such a strophe, or (iii) at the head of an interpolated passage due to the hand of the revisor. Many of the essential rubrics delimiting the passages of 32–40 lines were noted in my previous analysis; but I failed to perceive the importance of the series *581, *649, *725 . . . in the analysis of the passage printed below. Until the discovery of the eight-line strophic passages and the interpolations, many rubrics remained unintelligible, cf. the comments of Professor Reid, *Vinaver Misc.*, pp. 265–6 and n. 4. As a result of this new orientation, we are now dealing with exact (not approximate) figures; thus in the printed passage below the page-units add up thus

. . . 36 + 34
34 + 34 + 38 + 38 = 144 [i.e., *581–724]
32 + 32 + 40 + 33 + 39 + 40 = 216 [i.e., *725–938; two lines are missing]

The assumption of the two missing lines is confirmed by an examination of ll. 757–86; this passage has only 30 lines, instead of the minimum of 32 found elsewhere, and the strophe occurring after 764 appears to lack the two initial lines (no other reconstruction is possible on the assumption that the revisor did not break up the strophes; the two lines are accidentally omitted from the extant copy). Other passages of fixed length occur throughout 1–1284 (e.g., *163–96, *197–232, *233–64, *265–304, *1045–82, 1083–118, *1119–54, *1155–). The figures can only be made to check on two assumptions: (a) the author of the 44–54-line passages (*Ewert Studies*, p. 63) has made important additions to the Queen's speeches (9–60, 339–84 and 407–32, 437–58) at the beginning of Beroul I; and (b) there is a lacuna (of 14 lines) after 1164, as suggested in M3.

[14] Cf. the passage 323–6 discussed on p. 176 above; and the sequence of rhymes *asise, bise*, . . . *asise* . . ., *falise, alise* (accepting Muret's correction) at ll. 917–22, cf. *glise, iglise* 957–8.

first or second half of a strophe, marked by continuous rhyme or assonance: 623–6 *ir:i*; 635–8 *in:is*; 675–8 *or:on*; 679–82 *ié:ier*; 687–90 *ez:er*; 721–4 *uit:ut*; 725–8 *ez*; 737–40 *enble:endre*; 873–6 *or:ort*; 885–8 *ié:i*; 951–4 *as:an*. But all save the last three occur in the relatively short episode of the dwarf and the 'flour between the beds' (623–740); and when the dwarf disappears from the scene the monorhyming and assonating material becomes much scarcer. This suggests that in this episode, as in the 'slaying of the hostile baron' (1673–1746), poets had access to abundant earlier material.

The considerable remains of monorhyme and assonance in the extant text are also due in part to the work of subsequent revisors and expanders of 'Beroul I', and to the author of 'Beroul II'. The first revisor, who expanded the 48-line strophic passages to sections averaging 72 lines, showed great respect for his inherited material; he never breaks up an eight-line strophe, but contents himself as a rule with short interpolations between the strophes and longer ones at the beginning or end of a section (cf. 187–202, 787–804, 897–914). In a few cases, however, he breaks the section into two by a massive interpolation in the middle (cf. 749–64, 821–65). Many of his brief additions are of a pseudo-naïve kind, either clumsily forestalling the action of the poem (cf. 531–4, 693–6), or drawing attention to its subtleties of characterization ('What a clever rogue Brengain is!' 519–22; 'Did you ever hear of such a wicked villain?' 643–8), or insisting sententiously on the working of divine providence in the plot (909–14). This naïveté is most marked in the slightly clownish observations on and additions to the horrific episode of the 'flour between the beds' ('what a pity the Queen did not change the sheets and save her honour!'; Tristran tries to cover up by pretending to be asleep and snoring) (749–64). But he also writes long speeches for the characters (cf. 787–804, which expresses in *oratio recta* the train of thought worked out in a close-knit strophic passage, 805–20), and is responsible for the wholly admirable addition of the 'chorus' of the Cornish people (especially 827–59).

The twelfth-century couplet romances of Tristran and Yseult have not survived in their original French form; what we possess are German derivatives (Eilhart and Gottfried) and fragments, mainly of a later date. When the Beroul manuscript was written out fair from a jongleur's performing copy, after 1250, the spirit and message of the old couplet poems was largely lost. Even the square-cut style of composition, obeying the *loi du couplet*, and building up quatrains and eight-line strophes, was being abandoned; thus, in the chorus of the

Cornish people, a section often begins with the second line of a couplet, forming a counterpoint with the prosodic pattern:

> Ha! nains, ç'a fait ta devinalle!
> Ja ne voie Deu en la face,
> Qui trovera le nain en place,
> Qi nu ferra d'un glaive el cors!   843
>
> Ahi! Tristran, si grant dolors
> Sera de vos, beaus chiers amis,
> Qant si seroiz a destroit mis! (MS. ceseroit)
> Ha! las, quel duel de vostre mort!   847
>
> Qant le Morhout prist ja ci port,
>   etc.

The revisor of the mid-thirteenth century appreciated the dramatic contrasts of the old poem, the atmosphere of romantic love and knightly daring, but not the subtle web of guilt involving Marc, his sister's son and his Irish bride; and his interventions can be deplorably heavy handed. It is understandable that he should have re-emphasized the element of continuous rhyme and assonance, which fitted well enough with his archaizing and 'naïve' approach to the *matière*.

We are thus easily misled if we pay too much attention to the rhyming and assonating quatrains in the reconstruction of the eight-line strophes. Even in the episode of the dwarf and the flour (623–740) which contains no less than eight such quatrains (listed above), not all the rhyming and assonating elements are part of the strophic poem. Thus I was at first tempted to reconstruct 701–20 thus:

> LI NAINS LA NUIT EN LA CHANBRE ert,
> Oiez comment cele nuit sert:
> Entre deus liez la flor respant,
> Que li pas allent paraisant;   704
>
> Se l'un a l'autre LA NUIT vient,
> La flor la forme des pas tient;
> Tristran vit le nain besuchier,
> Et la farine esparpellier.   708
>
> Porpensa soi que ce devoit,
> Qar si servir pas ne devoit,
> Pus dist: Se l'un a l'autre iroit   711–713
> Qui iroit or, que fous feroit: 714

BIEN VERRA mais, se or i vois.'
Le jor devant, Tristran, el bois,
En la janbe nafrez estoit
D'un grant sengler, molt se doloit: 718

La plaie molt avoit saignié,
Deslïez ert, par son pechié.   720

This reconstruction maximizes the element of monorhyme and assonance in the quatrains composing the eight-line strophe, and gives us an entire strophe on 'similar' rhymes (Ewert p. 4). But, as things stand, 721–24 has to be combined in a single strophe with 725–8 and placed in the next section, thus ignoring the important division of the extant text marked by a rubricated initial at 725. Further investigation shows that the revisor does not break up a strophe (as by the interpolation of 711–12). Two important steps in the plot: (i) Tristran notices the dwarf strewing flour (707), and (ii) he has been previously wounded in the leg (717), are given too little prominence. Moreover, 693–700 would have to form an eight-line strophe, and 693–6 are suspect (since they forestall a situation which only arises after Tristran has noticed the dwarf's machination). A reconsideration of the strophic poet's style finally raises doubts as to whether he would have composed an entire strophe on the rhymes -*oit*, -*ois*, -*oit*—and a new reconstruction has to be devised, which satisfies most of the above-mentioned criteria (see p. 194 below). The implications are that the incidence of continuous rhyme or assonance in 705–18 are largely due to the revisor.

The use of rhyming or assonating quatrains was carried on by the author of Beroul II, who may have been a contemporary of, or even identical with, the expander of Beroul I: passages such as 3415–26 and 3539–46 point to a highly self-conscious use of the device by a thirteenth-century poet.

THE TEXT OF BEROUL, ll. 511–974

[Cf. EILHART, section *g*, (viii)]

[Brengain is sent by Marc to recall Tristran to the court]

  I. BRENGAIN li dit: 'SIRE, IL me het,
     Si est a grant tort, Dex le set,
     Dit par moi est meslez o vos,
     La mort me veut tot a estros: 514
     G'IRAI, por vos le laisera
     Bien tost que ne me tochera:
     Sire, por Deu, acordez m'i,
     Quant il sera venu ici.'   518

     Oiez que dit la tricherresse!
     Molt fist que bone lecherresse:
     Lores gaboit a essïent
     Et se plaignoit de maltalent.   522

  II. 'ROIS, POR LI VOIS,' ce dist BRENGAIN,
     Acordez m'i, si ferez bien.'
     Li rois respont: 'G'i metrai paine,
     Va tost poroc et ça l'amaine.'   526
     YSEUT s'en rist, et LI ROIS plus,
     Brengain s'en ist les sauz par l'us,
     Tristran estoit a la paroi,
     Bien les oiet parler au roi.   530

     Brengain a par les braz saisie,
     Acole la, Deu en mercie
     • • • • • •
     D'estre o Yseut a son plaisir.   534

 III. BRENGAIN mist TRISTRAN a raison
     'Sire, laienz en sa maison
     A li rois grant raison tenue
     De toi et de ta chiere drue: 538
     Pardoné t'a son mautalent,
     Or het ceus que te vont meslant,
     Proïe m'a que vienge a toi,
     Ge ai dit que ire as vers moi.   542

 IV. Fai grant senblant de toi proier,
     N'i venir mie de legier,
     Se li rois fait de moi proiere,
     Fai par senblant mauvese chiere.'   546

[Tristran returns and is reconciled to King Marc]

TRISTRAN l'acole, si la beise,
Liez est que ore ra son esse,
A la chanbre painte s'en vont,
La ou li rois et Yseut sont.   550

V. *TRISTRAN EST EN LA CHANBRE entrez:
'Niés,' fait li rois, 'avant venez,
Ton mautalent quite a Brengain,
Et je te pardorrai le mien.'   554
'ONCLE, CHIERS SIRE, or m'entendez:
Legirement vos defendez
Vers moi, qui ce m'avez mis sure,
Dont li mien cor el ventre pleure.   558

    Si grant desroi, tel felonie!
    Dannez seroie et el honie!

VI. Ainz nu pensames, Dex le set,
Or savez bien que cil vos het
Qui te fait croire tel mervelle,
D'or en avant meux te conselle: 564
Ne porte irë a LA ROÏNE,
N'a moi, qui sui de vostre orine.'
'Non ferai je, beaus niés, par foi.'
Acordez est Tristran au roi.   568

    *Li rois li a doné congié
    D'estre a la chanbre; es le vos lié!
    Tristran vait a la chanbre et vient,
    Nule cure li rois n'en tient.   572

[Interlude: the poet muses on the difficulties of concealing a love affair]

Ha! Dex, qui puet amor tenir
Un an ou deus sanz descovrir?
Car amors ne se puet celer,
Sovent cline l'un vers sa per,   576
Sovent vienent a parlement,
Et a celé et voiant gent,
Par tot ne püent aise atendre,
Maint parlement lor estuet prendre.   580

[Cf. EILHART, section *h*, (i)]

[The three barons demand that Tristran be banished from court]

I. *A la cort avoit TROIS BARONS,
   Ainz ne veïstes plus felons,
   Par soirement s'estoient pris
   Que se li rois de son païs   584
   N'en faisot SON NEVO partir,
   Il nu voudroient mais soufrir,
   A lor chasteaus sus s'en trairoient
   Et au roi Marc gerre feroient.   588

   Qar, en un gardin, soz une ente,
   Virent l'autrier Yseut la gente
   Ovoc Tristran en tel endroit
   Que nus hon consentir ne doit,
   Et plusors foiz les ont veüz
   El lit roi Marc gesir toz nus;   594

   Quar, quant li rois en vet el bois,
   Et Tristran dit 'Sire, g'en vois',
   Puis se remaint, entre en la chanbre,
   Iluec grant piece sont ensenble: 598

   'Nos li diromes nos meïmes,
   Alon au ro et si li dimes,
   Ou il nos aint ou il nos hast,
   Nos volon son nevo en chast.'   602

II. Tuit ensenble ont ce cons[el pr]is,
   Li roi Marc ont a raison mis,
   A une part ont le roi trait:
   'Sire,' font il, 'malement vet: 606
   TES NIÉS s'entraiment ET YSEUT,
   Savoir le puet qui c'onques veut,
   Et nos nu volon mais sofrir:'
   Li rois l'entent, fist un sospir.   610

III. Son chief abesse vers la terre,
   Ne set qu'il die, sovent erre:
   'Rois,' ce dïent li troi felon,
   Par foi, mais nu consentiron: 614

[Marc agrees that the dwarf be brought back to court]

QUAR BIEN SAVON de verité
Que tu consenz lor cruauté,
Et tu sez bien ceste mervelle:
Q'en feras tu? Or t'en conselle!   618

IV. SE TON NEVO n'ostes de cort
Si que [il] jamais ne retort,
Ne nos tenron a vos jamez,
Si ne vos tendron nule pez: 622

De nos voisins feron partir
De cort, que ne·l poon soufrir,
Or t'aron tost cest geu parti:
Tote ta volenté nos di.'   626

V. *'SEIGNOR, vos estes mi fael:
Si m'aït Dex, molt me mervel
Que mes niés ma vergonde ait quise,
Mais servi m'a d'estrange guise: 630
Conseliez m'en, ge·l vos requier,
Vos me devez bien consellier,
Que servise perdre ne vuel,
Vos savez bien, n'ai son d'orguel.'   634

VI. 'SIRE, or mandez LE NAIN devin
Certes, il set de maint latin,
Si en soit ja li consel pris,
Mandez le nain, puis soit asis.'   638

ET IL i est molt tost venuz:
Dehez ait il conme boçuz!
Li un des barons l'en acole,
Au roi en mostre sa parole.   642

Ha! or oiez qel traïson
Et confaite seducion,
A dit au roi cil nain Frocin!
Dehé aient tuit cil devin!
Qui porpensa tel felonie
Con fist cist nain, qui Dex maudie?   648

[Cf. EILHART, section *h*, (ii)]

[The dwarf's plan: Tristran is sent with a message to Arthur's court]

I. *'DI TON NEVO q'au roi Artur,
   A Carduel, qui est clos de mur,
   Covienge qu'il aut par matin,
   Un brief escrit an parchemin   652
   Port a Artur toz les galoz,
   Bien seelé, a cire aclox: 654

Ia. ROIS, TRISTRAN gist devant TON LIT
    Anevoies, en ceste nuit,
    Sai que voudra a lui parler,
    Por Deu, que devra la aler;   658
    ROIS, DE LA CHANBRE is a prinsome,
    Deu te jur et la loi de Rome,
    Se Tristran l'aime folement,
    A lui vendra a parlement.   662

Ib. ET S'IL n'i vient, et ge nu·l sai,
    Se tu nu voiz, si me desfai,
    Et tuit ti homë autrement,
    Prové seront sanz soirement;   666
    ROIS, or m'en laise covenir
    Et a ma volenté sortir,
    Et se li çole l'envoier
    Desi qu'a l'ore du cochier.   670

Li rois respont: 'Amis, c'ert fait.'
Departent soi, chascun s'en vait.   672

Molt fu li nain de grant voidie,
Molt par fist rede felonie.

II. CIL en entra chiés un pestor,
    Quatre derees prist de flor,
    Puis la lia a son gueron:
    Qui pensast mais tel traïson?   678

*LA NUIT, quant ot LI ROIS mengié,
Par la sale furent couchié,
Tristran ala le roi couchier:
'Beaus niés,' fait il 'je vos requier: 682

III. Ma volenté faites, ge·l vuel,
     Au roi Artus, jusqu'a Carduel,
     Vos covendra a chevauchier,
     Cel brief li faites desploier: 686

[The flour between the beds]

NIÉS, de ma part le salüez,
O lui c'un jor ne sejornez,'
Du mesage ot Tristran parler,
Au roi respont de lui porter.   690

'Rois, ge irai bien par matin.'
'O vos, ainz que la nuit ait fin.'
Tristran fu mis en grant esfroi
Entre son lit et cel au roi
Avoit bien le lonc d'une lance;
Trop out Tristran fole atenance: 696

IV. En son cuer dist qu'il parleret
A la roïne, s'il pooit (var. A l'ajorner se il)
Qant ses oncles ert endormiz:
Dex! quel pechié! trop ert hardiz: 700
*LI NAINS LA NUIT EN LA CHANBRE ert,
Oiez conment cele nuit sert:
Entre deus liez la flor respant,
Que li pas allent paraisant.   704

Se l'un a l'autre la nuit vient
La flor la forme des pas tient.

V. TRISTRAN vit LE NAIN besuchier,
Et la farine esparpellier,
Porpensa soi que ce devoit,
Qar si servir pas ne soloit,   710
Pus dist: 'Bien tost a ceste place
Espandroit flor por nostre trace,
Veer se l'un a l'autre iroit:
Qui iroit or, que fous feroit.   714
Bien verra mais se or i vois.'
Le jor devant, Tristran, el bois

VI. En la janbe nafrez estoit
D'un grant sengler, molt se doloit;
La plaie molt avoit saignié,
Deslïez ert, par son pechié: 720

TRISTRAN ne dormoit pas, ce quit,
Et li rois live a mie nuit,
Fors de la chanbre en est issut,
O lui ala li nain boçut.   724

[Cf. EILHART, section *h*, (iii)]

[Tristran leaps into the bed and back; his wound bleeds on the flour]

I. *DEDENZ LA CHANBRE n'out clartez,
   Cirge ne lanpë alumez,
   Tristran se fu sus piez levez:
   Dex! porqoi fist? Or escoutez!   728

   Les piez a joinz, esme, si saut,
   El lit le roi chaï de haut,
   Sa plaie escrive, forment saine,
   Le sanc qui·n ist les dras ensaigne.   732

II. La plaie saigne, ne la sent,
   Qar trop a son delit entent,
   En plusors leus li sanc aüne,
   Li nains defors est a la lune: 736

   BIEN VIT josté erent ensenble
   Li dui amant; de joie en trenble,
   Et dist au roi: 'Se ne·s puez prendre
   Ensenble, va, si me fai pendre.'   740

III. *Iluec furent LI TROI FELON
   Par qui fu ceste traïson,
   Porpensee priveement;
   Li rois s'en vient, Tristran l'entent: 744
   Live DU LIT, tot esfroïz,
   Errant s'en rest molt tost salliz,
   Au tresallir que Tristran fait,
   Li sans decent (malement vait!)   748

   De la plaie sor la farine;
   Ha! Dex, qel duel que la roïne
   N'avot les dras du lit ostez,
   Ne fust la nuit nus d'eus provez;   752
   Se ele s'en fust apensee,
   Molt eüst bien s'anor tensee;
   Molt grant miracle Deus i out,
   Qui·s garanti, si con li plot.   756

[The king, the dwarf and the three barons surprise the lovers]

> *Li ros a sa chanbre revient,*
> *Li nain, que la chandele tient,*
> *Vient avoc lui. Tristran faisoit*
> *Senblant conme se il dormoit,*   760
> *Quar il ronfloit forment du nes,*
> *Seus en la chanbre fu remés,*
> *Fors tant que a ses pies gesoit*
> *Pirinis, qui ne s'esmovoit.*   764

IV.   .   .   .   .   .   .
            .   .   .   .   .   .

> Et la roïne a son lit jut,
> Sor la flor, chauz, li sanc parut;   766
> LI ROIS choisi EL LIT le sanc,
> Vermel en fure[n]t li drap blanc,
> Et sor la flor en pert la trace,
> Du saut li rois Tristran menace.   770

V. LI TROI BARON SONT EN LA CHANBRE
> Tristran pensent a son lit prendre,
> Cuelli l'orent cil en haïne,
> Por sa prooise, et la roïne;   774
> Laidisent la, molt la menacent,
> Ne lairont justise n'en facent,
> Voient la janbe qui li saine:
> 'Trop par a ci veraie enseigne!'   778

VI. 'Provez estes,' ce dist LI ROIS,
> Vostre escondit n'i vaut un pois,
> Certes, Tristran, demain, ce quit,
> Soiez certains d'estre destruit:'   782
> IL li crie: 'SIRE, MERCI!
> Por Deu, qui pasion soufri;
> Sire, de nos pitié vos prenge!'
> Li fel dient: 'Sire, or te venge.'   786

[Cf. EILHART, section *h*, (iv)]

[Tristran and Yseult are made captive; he offers no resistance, relying on the trial by combat]

'Beaus oncles, de moi ne me chaut,
Bien sai, venuz sui a mon saut,
Ne fust por vos acorocier
Cist plez fust ja venduz molt chier,
Ja, por lor eulz, ne le pensasent
Que ja de lor mains m'atochasent: 792

Mais envers vos n'en ai je rien,
Or, tort a mal ou tort a bien,
De moi ferez vostre plesir,
Et je sui prest de vos soufrir: 796

Sire, por Deu, de la roïne
Aiez pitié'—Tristran l'encline—
'Qar il n'a home en ta meson,
Se disoit ceste traïson   800
Que pris eüse drüerie
O la roïne par folie,
Ne m'en trovast en chanp, armé:
Sire, merci de li, por Dé!'   804

I. LI TROI qui A LA CHANBRE sont
    Tristran ont pris et lïé l'ont,
    Et lïee ront la roïne,
    Molt est torné a grant haïne: 808
    Ja, se TRISTRAN ice seüst
    Que escondire nu·l leüst,
    Mex se laisast vif depecier
    Que lui ne lïé soufrist lïer.   812

II. Mais en Deu tant fort se fiot
    Que bien savoit et bien quidoit,
    S'a escondit peüst venir
    Nus n'en osast armes saisir   816
    Encontre lui, lever ne prendre,
    Bien se cuidoit par chanp defendre:
    Por ce ne se vout vers le roi
    Mesfaire soi por nul desroi.   820

    Qar, s'il seüst ce que en fut
    Et ce qui avenir lor dut,
    Il les eüst tüez toz trois,
    Ja ne les en gardast li rois:
    Ha! Dex, po[r]qoi ne les ocist?
    A mellor plait asez venist.   826

[The king resolves to burn them alive without trial]

      Live la noisë et li bruit,   860
      Tuit en corent droit au palés;
      Li rois fu molt fel et engrés,
      N'i ot baron tant fort ne fier
      Qui ost le roi mot araisnier
      Qu'i[l] li pardonast cel mesfait.   865

III. Or vient li jor, la nuit s'en vait   866
        ·   ·   ·   ·   ·

      Li rois conmande espines querre
      Et une fosse faire en terre;   868
      LI ROIS, tranchanz de main tenant,
      Par tot fait querre les sarmenz,
      Et assenbler o les espines
      Aubes et noires o racines.   872

IV. Ja estoit bien prime de jor,
      Li banz crierent par l'enor,
      Que tuit en allent a la cort,
      Cil qui plus puet plus tost acort: 876

      Asenblé sont Corneualeis,
      Grant fu la noise et li tabois,
      N'i a celui ne face duel,
      Fors que li nains de Tintajol.   880

V. *LI ROIS lor a dit et monstré
      Qu'il veut faire dedenz un ré
      Ardoir son nevo et sa feme;
      Tuit s'escrient la gent du reigne: 884

      'ROIS, trop ferïez lai pechié
      S'il n'estoient primes jugié,
      Puis les destrui, sire, merci!'
      Li rois par ire respondi: 888

VI. 'PAR CEL SEIGNOR qui fist le mont,
      Totes les choses qui i sont,
      Por estre moi desherité
      Ne lairoie ne·s arde en ré,   892
      Se j'en sui araisnié jamais,
      Laisiez m'en tot ester en pais.'
      Le feu conmande a alumer,
      Et son nevo a amener.   896

      Ardoir le veut premierement,
      Or vont por lui, li rois l'atent.   898

[Cf. EILHART, section *h*, (v)]
[Tristran is led to execution; he asks to enter a chapel to pray for God's mercy]

*Lors l'en ameinent par les mains,
Par Deu, trop firent que vilains!
Tant ploroit, mais rien ne li monte,
Fors l'en ameinent a grant honte.   902

Yseut plore, par poi n'enrage,
'Tristran,' fait ele, 'quel damage
Qu'a si grant honte estes lïez!
Qui m'oceïst, si garisiez,
Ce fust grant joie, beaus amis,
Encor en fust vengement pris.'   908

*Oez, seignors, de Damledé,
Conment il est plains de pité:
Ne vieat pas mort de pecheor,
Receü out le cri, le plor
Que faisoient la povre gent
Por ceus qui eirent a torment.   914

  I. Sor la voie par ont il vont
    Une chapele sor un mont   916
    U coin d'une roche est asise,
    Sor mer ert faite, devers bise;
    La part que l'en claime chancel
    Fu asise sor un moncel,   920
    Outre n'out rien fors la falise,
    Cil mont ert plain de pierre alise.

 II. S'uns escureus de lui sausist,
    Si fust il mort, ja n'en garist,   924
    En la dube out une verrine,
    Que un sainz i fist, porperine;
    TRISTRAN ses meneors apele:
    'Seignors, vez ci une chapele;   928
    Por Deu, quar m'i laisiez entrer,
    Pres est mes termes de finer.

III. Preerai Deu qu'il merci ait
    De moi, quar trop li ai forfait;   932
    Seignors, n'i a que ceste entree,
    A chascun voi tenir s'espee,
    VOS SAVEZ BIEN, ne pus issir,
    Par vos m'en estuet revertir,   936
    Et quant je Dé proié avrai,
    A vos eisinc lors revendrai.'

[He leaps from the chapel window on to the shore, and Governal also escapes]

IV. *Or l'a l'un d'eus dit a son per:
    'Bien le poon laisier aler';   940
    Les lians sachent, il entre enz,
    Tristran ne vait pas conme lenz,
    Triés l'autel vi[n]t a la fenestre,
    A soi l'en traist a sa main destre,   944
    Par l'overture s'en saut hors,
    Mex veut sallir que ja ses cors

V. Soit ars, voiant tel aünee.
   SEIGNORS, une grant pierre lee   948
   Out u mileu de cel rochier,
   Tristran i saut molt de legier:

   Li vens le fiert entre les dras,
   Qui·l defent qu'il ne chie a tas,   952
   Encor claiment Corneualan
   Cele pierre le Saut Tristran.

   *La chapele ert plaine de pueple
   Tristan saut sus, l'araine ert moble.

VI. Toz a genoz est en la glise (var.: sont en l'iglise)
    Cil l'atendent defors l'iglise,
    Mais por noient; Tristran s'en vet,
    Bele merci Dex li a fait!   960
    La riviere granz sauz s'en fuit,
    Molt par ot bien le feu qui bruit;
    N'a corage que il retort,
    Ne puet plus corre que il cort.   964

    * Mais or oiez de Governal:
    Espee, çainte, sor cheval,
    De la cité s'en est issuz,
    Bien set, se il fust conseüz,
    Li rois l'arsist por son seignor,
    Fuiant s'en vet por la poor;   970

    Molt ot li mestre Tristran chier,
    Qant il son brant ne vout laisier,
    Ançois le prist la ou estoit,
    Avoc le suen l'en aportoit.   974

555 Onche (?)
610 fus
621 Nos nos
624 nes
629 meuergonderoit, *corr. by scribe to* meuergonde ait
642 Li rois li m.
645 frociz
651 alle
652 .I. deus escrit
663 sil i uient, *cf. Eilhard 3842*
665 si home (*I take 664–5 thus:* 'If you do not see it, slay me, [you] and all your men, [if it be] otherwise
687 saluer
688 seiorner
697–8 *expanded to three lines in MS., cf. Ewert ad loc., and Reid in Vinaver Misc.* p. 275
716 Le roi deuant
723 issuz
724 bocuz
732 qui ennist
736 *M³, E punctuate after* defors est; *I think that the poet implies that the dwarf is standing outside in the moonlight, not that he saw the lovers by the light of the moon*
756 Qui es
763 gegoit
770 *M³, E punctuate after* Du saut; *I take the line to mean* 'The king threatens Tristran because of his leap'
772 T. par ire a son lit prenent, *an impossible rhyme, corr. Ewert ad loc., cf. II 31, 130*
778 *M³, E attribute this line to the king; the eight-line structure suggests rather that it sums up the verdict of the witnesses (cf. 777); the king's judgement and sentence follow in 779–82*
819–20 *Cf. Reid in Vinaver Misc., p. 277—For the section 827–59 (not printed here) see pp. 186–7 above*
867 querre] quiert
878 tibois
888 par ice
892 nel
894 Laisiē
921–2 faloise, aaise, *corr. M³, cf.* 917–18 asise, bise, *and n. 14 above*
957 Toz a genoz sont en ligliglise; *the couplet in the strophic poem meant* 'He falls on his knees on the soft earth'; *but with* sont *for* est, *taking* toz *as nom. pl. instead of nom. sing., it means* 'they are all on their knees in the church.' *The expanded form allows for both meanings.*

Rectus Vindicatus?

WILLIAM ROTHWELL

Professor of French Language, University of Manchester

Many years ago, when the recipient of this present volume was working in the Manchester Department of French Studies—which had already been distinguished by the linguistic work of John Orr and M. K. Pope—there appeared the famous *tour de force* entitled 'On Homonymics', written by John Orr for a similar volume presented to Miss Pope. Republished in *Words and Sounds in English and French*[1] and provided with a set of explanatory notes, this brilliant dialogue between the all-wise and forward-looking linguistician, Orthos, and the benighted philologist, Rectus, is still widely read and enjoyed and, if one is to judge by recent references to it, would seem to be still regarded by many as authoritative. Leaving aside the dazzling rhetoric which whirls the reader along together with the hapless Rectus, 'On Homonymics' is, in essence, an assertion that since the vocabulary of medieval French was afflicted with numerous instances of phonetic development having brought together inside the same phonetic shell words of different meaning, and since this situation was intolerable from the point of view of intelligibility, French speakers throughout the centuries have been obliged to alter or eliminate at least one element in the clashes or confusions so as to restore comprehensibility. Had Rectus not been restricted, however, to the role of what I think is known in America as the 'fall guy', he could have found numerous examples to prove quite incontrovertibly[2] that in the Middle Ages at least, whatever may be said about later centuries, French was supremely indifferent to what we now see as confusion and was probably less concerned than Orthos would have us believe to purge itself of homophones. Indeed, medieval writers give every appearance of

---

[1] Oxford, 1953.
[2] See my 'Homonymics and Medieval French', *Archivum Linguisticum*, 14, pp. 35–48 and Orr's waspish rejoinder ibid., 17, pp. 77–90.

rejoicing in this phenomenon, often using homophones as a 'clever' stylistic device to show off a versifier's literary dexterity:

> Quant Frere Jacobin vindrent premier el monde,
> S'estoient par semblant et pur et net et monde
>
> Tant ont eu deniers et de clers et de lais,
> Et d'execucions, d'aumosnes et de lais
>
> La beasse qu'est torte lor a fet molt grant tort;
> Encore est coreciee se fromages estort.
> A l'apostole alerent li droit contre le tort,
> Li droiz n'ot point de droit ne la torte n'ot tort.[3]

Only when the grammarians turned their attention to a methodical study of the French language from the second half of the sixteenth century onwards do we find emerging the modern attitude and the recognition of a need for clarity.

The whole question of the toleration of confusion in medieval French is, however, wider than the discussion between Orthos and Rectus would indicate. It affects not only the lexical but also the syntactical organization of the language. This is seen clearly when one looks at even one aspect: the way in which verbal prefixes are used. Most students of Old French have probably noticed in passing the occasional instance of an unexpected prefix, but even such eminent authorities as Nyrop and Pope, when dealing with prefixation, do not appear to have seen the full extent and significance of the hesitations they mention. In his third volume of the *Grammaire historique*[4] (p. 216) Nyrop deals briefly with the question and puts it firmly in the domain of word formation:

> Ce phénomène (*sc.* changement de préfixe) est bien moins fréquent que le changement de suffixe . . . 1° Dans quelques mots, on trouve en français, et déjà dans la vieille langue, un autre préfixe qu'en latin classique; le changement doit donc avoir eu lieu déjà en latin vulgaire. Exemples: *absconsus*—v.fr. *escons*, *concordare*—*acorder*, . . . 4° Au moyen âge il y avait souvent hésitation entre deux

---

[3] Rutebuef 'Les Jacobins' ll. 17–18, 25–6; 'Les Cordeliers' ll. 53–6 ed. Faral/ Bastin (Paris, 1959–60). It is difficult to see how the question of holograph affects the issue here (see Orr, *Arch. Ling.*, 17, p. 84). Either the forms are *intentionally* made alike or they just happen to turn out that way—a very unlikely happening).

[4] *Grammaire historique de la Langue française* (Copenhagen, 1899–1930).

préfixes. On trouve *acoragier—encoragier, adamagier—endamagier, aragier—enragier,* . . .

According to Nyrop, then, a few spasmodic changes of verbal prefix were made in the period between Classical Latin and the beginnings of written French—apparently without any kind of pattern—and there was a later period in which medieval usage fluctuated in the case of certain prefixes and in certain verbs, but again without any discernible pattern. The question of the overall transfer of verbal prefixes from Latin to French could, however, easily provide material for an entire monograph and would be found to be more complicated and perhaps more systematic than Nyrop would allow. For Miss Pope, on the other hand, the question presents itself in terms not of word formation but of sounds (p. 439, para. 1138). Her brief comment: 'Prefixes were often interchanged, e.g. *amaier, affraier* for *e(s)maier, e(s)fraier*' is placed under the general heading of 'Anglo-Norman Vowel-Sounds', as are both her paragraphs 1152 and 1177 to which she further refers. As in the case of Nyrop, there is no indication that the changes mentioned might be anything other than spasmodic.

The first point to emerge from a comparison of Nyrop with Pope is, then, that whilst the former thinks in terms of a semantic confusion between *a-* and *en-*, the latter gives examples of *a-* being confused with *es-*. The question is, therefore, more complex and more interesting than Nyrop's evidence alone might lead one to believe. If the exchange of prefixes were confined to *a-* and *en-*, it could be argued that this was simply part and parcel of the general hesitation in the use of the prepositions *ad* and *in* beginning in Latin and stretching right up into the French of the late fifteenth and even early sixteenth centuries.[5] Miss Pope's examples, however, linking *a-* and *es-* introduce another, quite different element. The confusion here can hardly be semantic in origin, since, far from lying close together in meaning, these two prefixes from the etymological point of view are diametrically opposed (Latin *ad* and *ex*). The confusion here must be either phonetic or syntactic, or both. That is to say that, whilst a speaker or writer might prefix a verb with *a-* instead of with *en-* (e.g. *avironner/environner*) because he is aware that in his linguistic system the prepositions *a* and *en* often have the same meaning, he will use *a-* instead of *es-* only if

---

[5] See C. Fahlin, *Etude sur l'Emploi des Prépositions en, à, dans, au Sens local* (Uppsala, 1942), also my 'Contribution à la Syntaxe de la Préposition en moyen français' in *Revue de Linguistique romane* Tome 35, 1971, pp. 156-166.

they sound alike (in certain combinations with following consonants—see Pope para. 1177/ii), or if for him the prefixes a-, en-, es-, are roughly interchangeable as syntactical tools, not having each a precise meaning of its own.[6] The fact of phonetic similarity under certain conditions would, of course, contribute to this latter state of affairs.

To postulate this 'explanation by syntax' is to question the whole idea of the linear transmission of prefixes from Latin into French, or, in this instance, into Anglo-Norman. In a study on similar lines in the more conservative domain of Provençal, I have already attempted to show that the *langue d'oc* had a system of prefixation which owed far less to Latin than is generally supposed.[7] Perhaps there is need for a fresh look at the *langue d'oïl* also, but an exhaustive study of verbal prefixation in the whole domain of northern French, even if limited to *a-*, *en-*, *es-*, would require space far beyond the scope of this article. All that will be attempted here is an examination of some of the material gathered for the forthcoming Anglo-Norman Dictionary, and any conclusions drawn must be understood to apply only to Anglo-Norman and not necessarily to be capable of uncritical transference to the whole of continental French.

Looking at this question very generally, one point which casts doubt on the adequacy of the opinions of both Nyrop and Pope as quoted above is the existence in the Middle Ages in both Anglo-Norman and continental French of numerous verbs with a cumulative prefix, e.g. *enes-*. In cases such as *enesbahir* and *enesjoir*, for example, phonetic considerations simply do not apply, and the semantic content of the double prefix *enes-* is no greater than that of the single prefix *en-* or *es-*: from the point of view of meaning neither *enesbahir* nor *enesjoir* can be distinguished from the more usual *esbahir* or *esjoir*. In addition, in both England and France the use of a prefix quite often makes no perceptible change in the meaning of a verb. One finds pairs of verbs such as *creire/encreire, dire/endire, ferir/enferir, hair/enhair, peiner/apainer*—merely a few examples, not a comprehensive list—where the choice of one or other of the pair would seem to be dictated less by semantic considerations than by the necessities of metre or by simple personal

---

[6] This 'confusion' may well not be limited to this particular group of prefixes. A comparison of the *Cambridge Psalter's quer atriblé e humilié* with the *Oxford Psalter's quer contriblet e humilitet* (Ps. 50.18) gives at least a hint of this possibility.

[7] See 'Some Aspects of Verbal Prefixation in Old Provençal', in *The French Language, Studies presented to L. C. Harmer* (London, 1970), pp. 26–36.

preference.[8] This would seem to indicate that the value of a medieval French prefix is relative and that the links between medieval prefixation and the Latin system are more apparent than real, more morphological than semantic.

Returning to Anglo-Norman: in many cases the alternation of prefixes which is widely found in all manner of medieval texts both early and late is of no more than academic interest. The existence side by side of *aracer/esracer*, *assaier/essaier* or even of *aveiller/enveiller/esveiller* need not be in any way an obstacle to the immediate comprehension of the texts in which they are found, the radical being determinant, not the prefix. The author of a Life of St. Edward shows rather neatly the lack of real etymological meaning attaching to prefixes when he uses *es-* and *en-* forms in consecutive lines:

> Il unt de l'esguarder (i.e. seeing God) poer
> Et de l'enguard naist lur voler   (ll. 38–9)

Putting on one side, then, a very large number of verbs—they are far more numerous than is generally realized and could easily fill page after page—in which the fluctuation of prefix does not bring difficulties of a semantic order, it will be possible to concentrate attention on a number of cases where this fluctuation may well give rise to problems of interpretation and may at the same time throw interesting sidelights on the way in which Anglo-Norman worked in actual practice.

To take a very simple case to begin with. Given the fact that *avigurer* means 'to strengthen' as below:

> après un poi de temps qe ele estoit bien avigouré de bones viaundes
> . . . ele reprist sa beauté.   (*Trivet* p. 206.2)

one might expect *esvigurer*, by virtue of its ablative prefix, to mean 'to weaken', 'to debilitate'. It can indeed have this meaning, as shown by the *Chanson de Guillaume*:

> Ore unt Franceis l'estur esviguré (i.e. 'put an end to')
> K'il ne trovent Sarazin ne Escler
>
> (ll. 3343–4)

---

[8] There is no need to labour the obvious parallel with the prepositions *vers*, *envers*, *devers*, *par devers*, etc.

Yet this is not always so:

> Quant ce oi le frere, si fu esviguré
> De ce que par sun angle l'ot Deu recunforté
>
> *(Vitas Patrum* ll. 1575-6)

Esvigurer is here carrying the same meaning exactly as *avigurer* and the opposite meaning to *esvigurer* in the *Chanson de Guillaume*: the semantic value of the verbal prefix is nil.

Moving to a slightly more involved case we find in Anglo-Norman the group *accuser/encuser/escuser*. From the point of view of etymology the distinction between these three is clear enough: for the proponents of the theory of homonymic clash it is essential that they should be kept apart: from the phonetic point of view there is no obvious reason why they should ever be confused. Yet clash they do and confused they are. That *encuser* should occur as a common variant of *accuser* may occasion but little surprise:

> Nul hom ne deit en confession encuser fors sei meismes.
>
> *(Ancren Riule*[1] p. 243.32)

Yet this same form *encuser* is also a variant form of *escuser*. When the humility of St. Modwenna and St. Bride keeps both of them from claiming any credit for a wondrous happening, the writer puts it like this:

> Mais Modewenne, la Deu amie,
> Ke vers humblesce tuz jurz se plie,
> La vertu, qe fu furnie,
> Sur sei ne l'ad pas acuillie.
>
> . . . .
>
> Mais Bride s'est bien encusee
> Kar ele ne fud pas ja si osee
> Que ele fust neis purpensee
> De la vertu, que est ovree
>
> *(St. Modwenna* ll. 3933-44)

There can be no doubt from the context that St. Bride is *ex*cusing herself, not *ac*cusing herself. Context, not etymology, is the determining factor here. On the other hand, the noun made from *escuser—escusour—* can be found with the meaning 'accuser':

> Par le mentir de un escusour
> Si avera il perdu de enfaunce
> Sun servise e sun labour
>
> *(Political Songs* 16. ll. 25-7)

Another case in point is that of *enspirer/espirer*. If those using Anglo-Norman had had a strong sense of the clear values of these prefixes, one would expect to find the first of these words used in the sense of 'to inspire', 'breathe in', etc., and the second to have the meaning 'to breathe out, exhale, expire'. Sometimes this does happen, as in the following case:

> Par travail espira il tut hors
> *(St. Richard* l. 1270)

Yet very often writers seem to make no distinction in their use of these forms:

> Saint Espirt ou voelt espirt (='blows')
> *(Dialogues* f. 50va)

> Par ount [un] home espire e vit (='breathes')
> *(Chevaler Dé* l. 712)

> Seint Richard ki espiré fu del seint esperit (='inspired')
> *(St. Richard* l. 517)

> Les vestementz de Aaron . . . enspirount les celestiens
>   sacramentz (='exhaled')
> *(St. Jerome* f. 2vb)

Indeed, the *Lumere as lais* uses *espirer* for 'to breathe', 'to breathe into' and 'to inspire', all in the same few folios:

> Kar par ices (*sc.* winds) puet espirer Humme e beste e alener
>   (f. 39r22)

> Ly seynt esperit espire vie E beauté dune   (f. 22v30)

> E pur quey est nomé seynt esperiz
> Pur ceo ke del un e del autre (*sc.* God and Christ) ensement
> Espirez est pardurablement   (f. 22v24)

More complicated is the case of *apprendre/enprendre/esprendre*. These ought to mean 'to learn', 'to undertake', 'to set fire to' or 'catch fire' respectively. Often they do in fact have these meanings and can be usefully opposed:

> Li apostle . . .
> Del seint Espirit n'ierent espris,
> Ne de preechier uncore apris   *(St. Clement* l. 724)

Yet cases such as the following abound:

le moine ke cest overane aprent (='undertakes')

(*Disticha* f. 123 ra)

un frere demanda a l'abbé M.,
Car il voleit amprendre de lui aukon sen (='learn')

(*Vitas Patrum* (H) l. 1884)

Gent ke esteint par li espris de Deu (='taught')

(*Miracles* 58 l. 33)

Femme enprent enfant sur livere (='teaches')

(*Nominale* l. 145)

Li un ke fu enpris de la medicine Jesu Crist, ceo fu seint Poel
(='learned') (*Ancren Riule*² p. 130.19)

De ces deus fuz (=pieces of wood) deussez vus enprendre
(='set alight') e enbraser le feu (*ib.* p. 151.4)

Orthos would argue that these confusions were intolerable and have therefore ultimately produced (or helped to produce) the modern French solution where only *apprendre* remains as a fully active, everyday verb. But this reasoning fails to answer the root question as to why they should ever have been morphologically confused in the first place if those who used them were alive to the semantic value attaching to the prefixes and were even vaguely aware of a problem arising from their indiscriminate use.

Or take the case of *estraire*. Given the fact that there are two verbs *estraire* in Anglo-Norman, when one of these gets mixed up with *atraire* the result can be rather disconcerting for anyone who would try to determine meaning by appeal to the Latin etymon:

(1) Grant pechié est leisser estraire
Le poeple Deu senz sucurs faire (*St. Clement* l. 13369)

(2) Surse de science lur duneit,
Des quels les philosophes unt estreit
Lur philosophie pleinement (*Secré des Secrez* l. 1395)

(3) . . . . ces
Ki mal funt e ne poent mes
Pur destinee kis i estreit (*St. Clement* l. 10617)

. . . .

(4) (When a man and woman love each other)
le curage de humme. . . .
Astreit est de amer folement,
Dunt volunté unt de fere folie   (*Lumere as lais* f. 62r14)

(5) Trop i a long demuere faite
Ke aucun raison n'ai estraite
Por quei la femme ne conceit   (*Medica* f. 21va)

(6) Se ce est fleume, vous le devés atraire par
oximel donier   (*Romania* 32 p. 83)

(7) Chascun atreit vers sun ostel   (*St. Gilles* l. 1566)

In the first example *estraire* means 'to stray, go astray'; the *estreit* of (2) is the normal 'derived, drawn'; in (3) however, the same word has virtually the opposite sense, meaning 'drives, impels'; (4) gives the same sense, but this time with *atraire*; in (5) it is 'adduced, put forward'; the *atraire* of (6) would seem to call for the prefix *es-* rather than *a-*, the sense being to 'draw out, extract'; finally, the *atreit* of (7) means 'retires, goes off', and so would appear again to have a totally 'wrong' prefix, if we are to judge by normative standards. As if this were not enough, Frère Angier twice uses *entraire* in the *Dialogues* with the meaning 'to extract, pull out':

De l'aeve laquele il entreist de la roche   (f. 4vb)

Q'il ot de l'aeve entraeit l'enfant   (f. 41va)[9]

Finally, when we see this same verb being used to mean 'to press upon, in, down' we must surely reflect on the assumptions underlying the theory of the homonymic clash:

Si aucun os est remis emplaié
Et vous ne trovés ki l'entraie
Ou fer ou fust qui dedens seit   (*Medica* f. 10ra)

(The medical problem here is to find what is pressing on the bone.) What one must not forget is that these are not cases where phonetic development or dialectal peculiarities have chanced to bring together

---

[9] It would be unkind to seek to befog the reader by asking him to reflect on lines from Angier's *Vie de St. Grégoire:* Mais q'en ciel onc estrast paien Ne vos puet nus oem affermer (ll. 2716-17). Let us put this down to a slip of the pen— *estrast* for *entrast*—and pass on with perhaps just a hint of a qualm.

words which originally differed from one another in form; these are cases where writers have *chosen* to use forms which to us appear ambiguous, even though there was no linguistic necessity to do so. Since their intention was in all cases to communicate, not to obfuscate, one can only assume that they knew that their choice of form would not be detrimental to their intelligibility and that they felt no concern about creating a 'homonymic clash', since the context rendered their meaning clear.

Lest it might be thought that *estraire* is an isolated example, let us look for a moment at some of the forms taken by the *at(t)endre/entendre* group. In many cases, admittedly, the *at(t)endre* forms have the sense of 'to (a)wait, remain', etc., whilst the *entendre* ones have the meaning 'to strive, be intent upon, understand', so that no difficulty need arise:

> Ici atent le juise   (*St. Brendan* l. 1561)

> Ly bacheler ne attendi plus,
> A grant haste leve sus
> (*Dialogue de St. Julien* l. 1166)

> Mult esteit de male vie
> E mult entendant a folie   (*Miracles* 21 l. 6, etc)

Yet often this pattern is not adhered to:

> par vivre issi
> E par tels eises aver ci,
> Pur nient atendrez joie aillurs (='expect')   (*St. Jean* l. 2473)

> a l'amur de cest mund vei plusurs atendanz (='striving after')
> (*Beauliu* l. 15)

> E quel pru est oir le ren
> Ke l'em ne put atendre bien (='understand')
> (*Philosophie* (R) l. 2422)

> Li rays . . . par oydire atent
> Coment . . . (='hears')   (Langtoft, *Chronique* ii p. 310)

> Car 'quer' en seinte escripture est atendu par 'teste'
> (='signified, betokened')   (*Ancren Riule*[2] p. 153.1)

All the examples above ought logically to fall into the *entendre* group, yet all have the *atendre* form. If this were simply a case of one-way movement, with *at(t)endre* steadily usurping the role of *entendre*, it would be relatively easy to deal with: unfortunately, the converse is also found, where *entendre* takes the place of *at(t)endre*:

> ly covenist issi entendre
> Ke li fiz Dieu venist en terre   (*Dialogue de St. Julien* l. 218)
>
> Mes il entendent geskes al dereyn jur   (*Lumere as lais* f. 67v)
>
> et tous ceulx de la dite nef seront entendantz au maistre
> (*Black Book* (V) p. 54)

The sense in the first two cases is clearly 'to wait' and in the last example that the sailors will 'attend upon, wait upon' the master of the vessel. So far context has been a sure guide, but occasionally even when context has been fully considered there can remain some hesitation. In John of Howden's *Rossignol* we find the following puzzling passage:

> Si tu veloies, amor tendre,
> A toun gree le (*sc.* poet's soul) prendre,
> Cest soun reclaim no poet atendre
> Que ne se aille tantost rendre   (ll. 4681–4)

My own feeling is that *atendre* here means 'to hear', the poet's soul flying off like some water-fowl at the sound of the lure, but the sense 'to wait for' cannot be ruled out.[10]

Even all these examples, however, do not give a complete picture of the complexity of the situation: an additional complication is that the verb *atteindre*—in both its common and its legal sense—also takes on occasion the form *at(t)endre*:

> et s'il puisse prover et attendre l'achatour . . .
> (*Liber Albus* p. 262)
>
> Si vous consaile que vous hantiez la science quelle vous
> mielz profitera en estat a quelle vous taillerez attendre
> (*Sampson* p. 374)

---

[10] A close study of Provençal might well show a similar confusion of the two verbs that cannot be explained in purely phonetic terms. A version of St. Benedict's *Rule*, written in Avignon, has this passage:

En las festas de totz los sanhs . . . atendut que .l psalm e las antiphenas . . . sian dig que partenon al jorn (MS. Avignon 707 f. 35v).

The meaning is clearly 'see to it that'. . . . .

(Simon Magus) Tant avreit parlé avant main
Que mun travail serreit tut vein,
Quant par ses arz tant feit avreit
Que ma parole poi attendreit.   (*St. Clement* l. 4482)

Le geant li oi, si ly ala fraper.
De sa masue li quida ben sener,
Mes il faili de ly, si atent le destrer,
Si ke il li fet a terre trebucher.   (*Boeve* l. 1311)

In the first of these examples the legal flavour of the text is a good
indication of the fact that we are dealing with the meaning 'to attaint,
convict', but the other examples are, perhaps, less immediately obvious.
In the *Sampson* quotation *attendre* has the meaning 'to strive for' and in
the *St. Clement* 'to achieve'. In the last quotation it has been necessary
to make a slight alteration to the punctuation, because it is clear from
the punctuation of the printed edition and from the editor's 'erwarten'
in his glossary that he has failed to see that *attendre* here means 'to hit'
and not 'to await'.[11]

This kind of pitfall sometimes catches the modern editor too. A
passage from the recent *ANTS* edition of *The Life of St. Catherine*[12]
provides a neat illustration of the way in which an awareness of
change of prefix can solve a problem.

O chier cumpaignum, que fesum
Puis que nus el bon Deu creum,
Qui nus ad fait si grant honur,
Que guerpi avun nostre errur,
Si nus mustre la dreite vie
E par martyre nus envie?   (ll. 1123–8)

The glossary translates *envie* in l. 1128 as 'invite', and although the
variant MSS. W and P give *enveie* and *envoie* respectively, the editor's
note to the line gives no hint of the possibility of *envie* being no more
than the present tense of *envier* for the more usual *avier* or *avoier* 'to
guide, set on the road', etc.

In this case, and in all the examples of the *at(t)endre/entendre* group
discussed above, had the writers felt any need to avoid confusion they

---

[11] See also ll. 545, 631, 1185, 1810, 3492 where 'erwarten' is nonsensical.
Stimming hedges his bets for ll. 545 and 631, putting them under both *ateindre*
and *atendre* in his glossary.
[12] Ed. W. McBain (Oxford, 1964).

could have done so without the slightest difficulty. That they did not choose to do so and that sometimes, even in the same text, they used different prefixes with the same verb without any change of meaning must be seen as a strong indication that they saw no reason to differentiate. This point is illustrated by the use of *abraser* and *esbraser* 'to set fire to' in the *St. Modwenna*:

Si abrasez cel abbeie   (l. 1218)

Qui unt poer et peine mis
De l'abeie esbraser   (ll. 1472–3)

Other texts further confuse *enbraser* 'to clasp', etc., and *enbraser* 'to set alight, kindle' as in the following examples, thus producing an *abraser/enbracer/esbraser* complex:

Le forte escu enbrace e prist le branc asseré
(*Boeve* l. 1707)

Ki feseit un furne enbracer
(Bozon, *Vie de St. Catherine* l. 117)

Similarly, when *esloigner*, the more usual word, is found as *alungner/aluigner* in the life of St. Modwenna it is liable to confusion with *aluigner* 'to prolong':

Que li esperit tant benuré . . .
De nus ne seient aluigné
Par folie e par peché   (ll. 5281–4)

Mes ne s'est weres alungnee
De l'abbeie . . .   (ll. 3412–13)

'Frere', fet ele, 'n'en parlez mie
D'aluigner mais ci ma vie   (ll. 6697–8)

This confusion is not limited to the one text. In the *Pseudo-Turpin* we find:

fust aloyné icel jour en l'espace de troys joures   (l. 1255)

and it is only in the light of the context and general sense of the passage that we can understand *aloyné* to mean 'stretched, extended'. The *Statutes of the Realm* provide an even clearer example of the confusion by using *esloigner* itself to mean 'to prolong, extend':

Purceo qe multz des prisons devienent appellours pur lour vies
esloigner   (vol. I p. 165 xxxiv)

15

Doubts about the importance of the homonymic clash as a significant factor influencing word-change in medieval French are further
strengthened by the frequent occurrence of cases where a word is made
to mean not only two quite different things, but even two completely
opposite things. Whilst for the writer of the *Vitas Patrum acumuniement*
means, as one would expect, 'communion':

E com il vindrent al seint acumuniement   (l. 3763)

for Trivet it means 'excommunication', no less!:

sour peine de acomyngement   (p. 346.10)

The same applies also in reverse, with *escomunier* (and variants) usually
meaning 'to excommunicate':

Si fut por iceste acheison
Par nom del pape escumungié (*St. Grégoire* 2411)

but being capable on occasion of carrying precisely the opposite sense.
When, in one of the Mary legends, the son of a Jew takes communion,
the father is most upset: here is how Adgar puts it:

De la dolur, ke il ad entendu,
Ke sun enfant escuminé fu,
Reschine de dens cume resue   (24 ll. 151–3)

The value of the prefix, or rather its lack of value in Anglo-Norman,
is clearly brought out by the fact that on occasion it can be simply
omitted without any loss of meaning. Whilst the *Apocalypse* uses the
full form *escumenge* for 'excommunication':

mettre hors Seinte Iglise Par escumenge   (ll. 1904–5)

the *Statutes of the Realm* use simply *comenge*:

Par sentence de comenge   (vol. I p. 187)

It is easy to dismiss this as no more than one example among many of
the well-attested Anglo-Norman use of aphetic forms, but this contributes not at all to the understanding of how the language was able
to function without any apparent loss of intelligibility in spite of these
lost prefixes.

To return to the question of one word having two quite contradictory senses: both *ap(p)orter* and its noun *ap(p)ort* are in this situation, as will be seen from a comparison of the following examples:

puske ceo noveles me aportés   (*Boeve* l. 98)

cf.   Endementers les apport
La tempeste qe fust fort
(*Geanz* (L) ll. 231-2)

Si l'aporta od lui larecinusement
(*Vitas Patrum* l. 2969)

The adverb *larecinusement* provides the key to the meaning 'carried off' in this last example, the verbal prefix contributing nothing to the sense. Similarly, *ap(p)ort* can mean both 'income, proceeds' and 'export':

De terre aveient environ
Dunt pussent vivre a fuison,
Estre l'aport de lur autel   (*St. Osith* ll. 1463-5)

des apportz de monoie hors de son Roialme par les collectours de Pape   (*Statutes* II p. 41)

Precisely the same possibility of contradictory meaning is offered by the closely related verb *amener*. Again, this often means what it 'ought' to mean, i.e. 'to bring':

N'amaine pas grant gent od sei   (*St. Gilles* l. 1707)

but it is quite capable of meaning the exact opposite:

marchandises, lesqueus sount defenduz d'amener hors de la terre
(Rough *Register* p. 140)

avantdites nefs sont amenez et retraiz
(*Black Book* p. 64)

It will be noticed here again that the writers put into their sentences one word which removes any ambiguity: in the one case it is the useful little *hors*; in the other the same effect is achieved by the use of the synonym *retraiz*. In other words the context makes the position clear.

The use of contradictory meanings is seen yet again in *emporter* which can mean in the very same text both 'to take away' and 'to bring forward, advance':

> Quecunquez chose que tu averas emportee en despenses del toen
> *(St. Jerome* f. 5ra)

> meux voillaunt aprendre choses estranges vergoignousement que emporter ses choses nyent sagement (Latin: quam sua aliis impudenter ingerere). *(ib.* f. 1ra)

In the case of the prefix *en-* it is sometimes tempting to attribute the confusion of meaning brought about by its non-etymological use to the fact that two main senses attached to the Latin *-in*: on the one hand it had negative, privative force; on the other hand it had the positive meanings of interiority or increase. For example, the Anglo-Norman *enfuir* can mean either (1) 'to flee' or (2) 'to bury':

> ele se enfut de li et se musce
> *(Ancren Riule*[1] p. 154.17)

> Il fud dunc mort . . .,
> E a [Paggle] fud enfuid   *(Estoire* l. 1374)

In this case the two meanings are sufficiently far apart for the differentiation to be easy. This applies also to the two meanings of *enfermeté* (1) 'illness', (2) 'fortress':

> Les enfermetez e les granz maladies
> *(Apocalypse* l. 3412)

> Lu covenable ad encerché
> Ou il put fere enfermeté   *(Merlin* l. 74)

With the verb *enfermer*, however, there is perhaps another problem. In the following truncated example it would be perfectly possible to interpret the verb as 'to lock up, shut away':

> la reine ert enfermee   *(Estoire* l. 87)

It is only when the rest of the sentence is added that the meaning is clearly seen to be 'to fall ill':

> la reine ert enfermee
> Ne mes oit jorz nen ad duree

A similar situation exists with regard to *enfamer*: in continental French this is found with precisely opposite meanings in virtually the same semantic field:

de boine fame enfamés (= 'famed, renowned')
Vostre alme volez enfamer por lui en cest siecle engresser (= 'to defame, dishonour')   (God. III, 138)

In Anglo-Norman so far only the latter sense of 'to dishonour' has been recorded, e.g.:

Tant le fet le mounde enfamer
(*Chevaler Dé* l. 781)

It will be noticed that in this example the immediate context alone is not sufficient to show that *enfamer* means 'to dishonour' rather than to 'honour'. It is necessary to turn to the whole picture before the sense becomes clear. The writer is dealing with the power of the attractions of the flesh and of the world to deflect the true knight from his godly aims:

Tant le fet le mounde enfamer,
Sa char(e) norir et tascuner
Que trestot tourne a son desir
Les armes dount d[e]it Deu servir

This again emphasizes the fact that total context almost always provides a key which is adequate for the elimination of semantic confusion.

Similarly, although *enclore* and *esclore* ought logically to be kept apart as here:

moy e mes compaignons enclosames la launde de haut mur
(*Fouke* p. 5.27)

Mes esclos est par sun peché,
Cum lepruz des seinz engeté   (*Manuel des Pecchez* l. 9777)

there is always the odd example such as the following to provide disconcerting evidence to the contrary:

E esclos en une bele cité   (*ib.* l. 9738)

Similar considerations apply, naturally enough, when dealing with certain verbs prefixed by *a-*. Anglo-Norman speakers and writers were apparently not put out in any way by the ambivalence of *aprester*, for instance:

> Cil aprestet tuz lur busunz   (*St. Brendan* l. 1635)

> Ceux qe avoient apresté al roy lour biens
> (*Anonimalle Chron.* p. 22.2)

In the first of these cases *aprester* means 'to prepare, make ready' and in the second 'to lend'.

This verb calls to mind another related fact. Whilst *aprester* means 'to lend', as one would expect, its antonym *emprenter* (also found as *aprom(p)ter*, *apprompter*) has both this meaning and the opposite one of 'to borrow', so that once again only context can make clear whether a thing is being borrowed or lent. If Anglo-Norman writers were willing to tolerate flexibility even in a sphere which touched their pocket, they must have been supremely indifferent to what the modern linguistician sees as the homonymic clash:

> Barlaam li ad trestut cunté
> Cument ces dras out emprenté   (*Josaphaz* l. 844)

> moi pleise apprompter un noble
> (*Sampson* (MS. Longleat 37 f. 75r)

Insufficient attention has been paid to the whole question of 'confusion' in medieval French, and it has been too readily assumed that the medieval mind reacted linguistically in a similar way to the modern mind. Even in the up-to-date, authoritative and widely read *Introduction to Theoretical Linguistics* of Professor J. Lyons[13] uncritical reference is made both in the text (p. 90) and in the notes (p. 484) to the works of Gilliéron, Orr and their followers. But there is no indication that for many years past there has existed a body of work which would cast doubt on the validity of at least some of their theories.[14]

It would be both churlish and foolish to deny the contribution of Gilliéron to French linguistics, for he was instrumental in adding a whole new dimension to the subject, and the linguistic geographers have paid just tribute to his pioneering work by building on his original *ALF* a network of regional atlases of remarkable accuracy and

---

[13] Cambridge University Press, 1968.

[14] A. Tobler in *Sitzungsberichte der königlichen Akad. der Wissenschaften* 1904. Clédat in *Revue de Philologie française* 34, 1922. G. Millardet *Linguistique et Dialectologie romanes* (Paris, 1923).

refinement. Medievalists might well similarly acknowledge the penetration and insight of an inspired innovator by making a close, detailed study of the way in which forms fuse and blend in medieval French, apparently without serious loss of intelligibility. But it is not enough to attempt to graft Gilliéron's ideas on to medieval French with insufficient evidence in support.

One day a medievalist may, perhaps, follow Gilliéron's lead and pass on from his *Faillite de l'Etymologie phonétique* to write a *Faillite de la Morphologie étymologique*, for Orr was undoubtedly right when he wrote jestingly: 'Those ignorant medieval scribes, whose Old French is so shaky, do mix up the forms most reprehensibly' ('Homonymics', p. 99). Perhaps the Anglo-Norman scribes were even more guilty in this respect than their continental counterparts, for many of them were, after all, using someone else's language, not their own native tongue. But when all due allowance is made for the Anglo-Norman character of the evidence adduced in the present study, it may serve to show that perhaps Rectus was right to be sceptical of Orthos's rhetoric and would have been justified in twisting one of the latter's famous quips to bring it nearer the truth: 'You can't get very far in philology—as distinct from linguistics—if you hold to the dogma of uniformity of speech' (put the other way round in 'Homonymics' p. 110). The morpho-syntactical history of medieval French has yet to be written: it will only be satisfactorily written when the language is regarded neither as a corruption of Latin nor as a crude and unsophisticated precursor of Classical French, but is considered as a valid system of communication in its own right, with its own inner necessities.

LIST OF TEXTS QUOTED

Adgar: Adgars Marienlegenden, ed. C. Neuhaus (Altfr. Bibl. 9).

Ancren Riule[1]: *The French Text of the Ancrene Riwle*, ed. J. A. Herbert (EETS 219).

Ancren Riule[2]: *The French Text of the Ancrene Riwle*, ed. W. H. Trethewey (EETS 240).

Anonimalle Chronicle, ed. V. H. Galbraith (Manchester, 1927).

Apocalypse: Anglo-Norman Rhymed Apocalypse, ed. O. Rhys (ANTS 6).

Beauliu: Le Sermon de Guischart de Beauliu, ed. A. Gabrielson, Skrifter . . . Vetenskafassamfundet i Uppsala 1909.

Black Book: Black Book of the Admiralty, ed. T. Twiss (Rolls Series 1).

Boeve: Der anglonormannische Boeve de Haumtone, ed. A. Stimmung (Bibl. norm. 7).

Bozon, Vie de St. Christine in *Seven More Poems by Nicholas Bozon*, ed. Sister Amelia Klenke (New York, 1951).

Chanson de Guillaume, ed D. McMillan, SATF 1949–51.

Chevaler Dé, Traitee del Chevaler Dé, ed. K. Urwin, RLR 68, 1937.

Dialogue de St. Julien, Dialogue de St. Julien et son Disciple, ed. A. Bonjour (ANTS 8).

Dialogues, Dialogues of St. Gregory, BN MS. f.fr. 24766.

Disticha, Everart le Moine's translation of the *Disticha Catonis* in Lambeth Palace MS. 371.

Estoire, Gaimar, *Estoire des Engleis*, ed. A. Bell (ANTS 13).

Fouke, Fouke Fitzwarin, ed. L. Brandin (CFMA 1930).

Geanz, Des Grantz Geanz, ed. G. E. Brereton (Oxford, 1937).

Josaphaz, ed. J. Koch (Altfr. Bibl. 1).

Langtoft's *Chronique*, ed. T. Wright (Rolls Series, 1886).

Liber Albus, ed. H. T. Riley (Rolls Series, 1859).

Lumere as lais, in York Minster MS. 16.K.7.

Manuel des Pecchez, ed. F. J. Furnivall (EETS 119).

Medica, Trinity College, Cambridge MS. 0.1.20.

Merlin, Les Prophecies Merlin, ed. J. Koch, ZRP 54.

Miracles, La deuxième collection anglo-normande des Miracles de la sainte Vierge, ed. H. Kjellman (Paris, 1922).

Nominale, ed. W. Skeat, *Transactions of the Philological Society*, 1906.

Philosophie, La Petite Philosophie, ed. W. H. Trethewey (ANTS 1).

Political Songs, Anglo-Norman Political Songs, ed. I.S.T. Aspin (ANTS 11).

Pseudo-Turpin, The Anglo-Norman Pseudo-Turpin, ed. I. R. Short (Diss. London, 1966).

Rough, Register of Daniel Rough, ed. K.M.E. Murray (Canterbury, 1945).

St. Brendan, The Anglo-Norman Voyage of St. Brendan, ed. E. G. R. Waters (Oxford, 1928).

St. Clement, Vie de St. Clément, ed. N. K. Willson (Diss. Cambridge, 1952).

St. Edward, La Vie de St. Edouard le Confesseur, ed. Ö. Södergård (Uppsala, 1948).

St. Gilles, La Vie de St. Gilles, ed. G. Paris & A. Bos (SATF 1881).

St. Grégoire, La Vie de St. Grégoire, ed. P. Meyer, *Romania* 12.

St. Jean, The Life of St. John the Almoner, ed. C. S. Caffrey (Diss. Cambridge, 1953).

St. Jerome, L'Epistle de Jerom a Paulinum, BM MS. Royal 1.C. III.

St. Modwenna, ed. A. T. Baker & A. Bell (ANTS 7).

St Osith, The Anglo-French Life of St. Osith, ed. A. T. Baker, MLR 6.

St. Richard, La Vie de St. Richard, ed. A. T. Baker, RLR 53.

Sampson, H. G. Richardson 'Letters of the Oxford Dictatores' in *Oxford Historical Society, New Series*, 5.

Secré, Le Secré de Secrez, ed. O. A. Beckerlegge (ANTS 5).

Statutes, Statutes of the Realm, Record Commission (London, 1810).

Trivet, The Anglo-Norman Chronicle of Nicholas Trivet, ed. A. Rutherford (Diss. London, 1932).

Vitas, Henri d'Arci's 'Vitas Patrum', ed. B. A. O'Connor (Washington, 1949).

The Writer and his Tools: Proust's Views on Language and on Style in his Letters to Some Critics

STEPHEN ULLMANN

Professor of the Romance Languages in the University of Oxford

All readers of *À la recherche du temps perdu* will have been struck by Proust's intense interest in things linguistic: by the precise and detailed portrayal of various characters through their speech, by the innumerable comments on the most diverse aspects of language, by the long dissertations on etymology and on the magic of proper names. Interest in language is a very common attitude among French writers, but a recent critic was no doubt right when he concluded an article on 'Proust linguiste' with the claim: 'aucun autre écrivain, semble-t-il, n'a accordé tant d'importance aux phénomènes linguistiques'.[1] Nor is this absorbing interest confined to the *Recherche*: it is very much in evidence in *Jean Santeuil*, in *Contre Sainte-Beuve*, in his critical essays and other writings, in his pastiches and even in his letters.[2] In a previous article[3] I have examined from this point of view his correspondence

---

[1] G. Matoré, 'Proust linguiste', in *Festschrift Walther von Wartburg zum 80. Geburtstag*, vol. I, Tübingen, 1968, pp. 279–92: p. 292.

[2] On Proust's linguistic ideas, see recently K. D. Uitti, '*Le Temps retrouvé*: sens, composition et langue', *Romanische Forschungen*, LXXV (1963), pp. 332–61; R. de Chantal, *Marcel Proust critique littéraire*, vol. I, Montreal, 1967, Part II, Ch. 5: 'Qu'est-ce que le style?'; J. Milly, 'Les Pastiches de Proust: Structure et correspondances', *Le Français Moderne*, XXXV (1967), pp. 33–52 and 125–41, and his book, *Proust et le style*, Paris, 1970; Matoré, loc. cit.; J. Mouton, *Le Style de Marcel Proust*, 2nd ed., Paris, 1968, Ch. 1: 'Les Idées de Marcel Proust sur le style'. Cf. also my articles, 'Les Idées linguistiques de Proust dans *Jean Santeuil*', *Revue de Linguistique Romane*, XXXI (1967), pp. 134–46, and 'L'Esthétique de l'image dans *Contre Sainte-Beuve* de Marcel Proust', in *Festschrift W. v. Wartburg*, pp. 267–78.

[3] 'Proust's Ideas on Language and Style as Reflected in his Correspondence', in *The French Language. Studies Presented to Lewis Charles Harmer*, London, 1970, pp. 211–34.

with three friends who played an important part in his life: Montesquiou, Madame de Noailles and Madame Straus. The present study will deal with the letters printed in the third volume of the *Correspondance générale*: these are addressed to several literary critics as well as to two other friends.[4]

Among the general topics of linguistic interest discussed in these letters, the role of grammatical correctness in style is of particular importance. As early as 1908, Proust had boldly asserted, in a letter to Madame Straus: 'Chaque écrivain est obligé de faire sa langue, comme chaque violoniste est obligé de faire son *"son"* . . . La correction, la perfection du style existe, mais au delà de l'originalité, . . . non en deçà'.[5] Eleven years later,[6] he returned to the same problem in a letter to Jacques-Émile Blanche. Having noticed some mistakes and obscurities of syntax in an article by Blanche in *Le Figaro*, Proust hastens to reassure his friend: 'Je vous dirais que, certes, des lapsus grammaticaux n'ont jamais terni un beau style, mais que tout de même il vaut mieux les éviter. . . . Pour ma part je ne tiens aucun compte de ces choses-là dans l'appréciation d'un style, c'est à mon avis par une incompréhension absolue de ce qu'est le style qu'on croit que pureté de style a un rapport quelconque avec absence de fautes. L'absence de fautes est une qualité purement subalterne, nullement esthétique. Néanmoins il me semble plus élégant d'effacer ces taches insignifiantes' (p. 168).

A few months after this letter, Proust published in the *Nouvelle Revue Française* his famous article on the style of Flaubert,[7] where he reiterated the same ideas: 'Laissons de côté, je ne dis même pas les simples inadvertances, mais la correction grammaticale; c'est une qualité utile mais négative.' A subsequent letter to Jacques Boulenger provides an interesting gloss to this essay. In an article in *L'Opinion*, Boulenger had completely misunderstood Proust's attitude, and the latter now finds it necessary to explain his position: 'Chose archisignifiante, vous me faites dire pour Flaubert exactement le contraire de

---

[4] See Jacques-Émile Blanche's preface to vol. III of the *Correspondance générale*, Paris, 1932. On the precise dating of some of the letters contained in this volume, cf. P. Kolb, *La Correspondance de Marcel Proust. Chronologie et commentaire critique*, Urbana, Illinois, 1949, pp. 91–116.

[5] *Correspondance générale*, vol. VI, pp. 92 ff. Cf. R. de Chantal, op. cit., pp. 351 ff.

[6] This letter is dated from 1920 in the *Correspondance générale*; according to Kolb (op. cit., pp. 109 f.), however, it must have been written towards the end of September 1919.

[7] 'À propos du "style" de Flaubert', *Nouvelle Revue Française*, xiv, 1 (1920), pp. 72–90. Cf. R. de Chantal, op. cit., vol. I, p. 355.

ce que j'ai dit. J'ai dit que la beauté grammaticale n'avait aucun rapport avec la correction. Jacques Boulenger me fait dire le contraire' (p. 211).

In several passages, Proust criticizes his own style and in particular his inordinately long sentences. In a letter to Paul Souday, written in June 1921, he recognizes that a sentence criticized by Souday in *Le Côté de Guermantes* is completely unintelligible, and mentions as an extenuating circumstance the deplorable conditions in which his novel is being published: 'si je corrige déjà très mal mes épreuves, quand un livre comme celui-ci paraît imprimé directement d'après mes in-déchiffrables brouillons, mes éditeurs ont beau avoir la gentillesse de surveiller de leur mieux cette impression, elle est terriblement fautive.' This does not, however, completely exonerate him: 'Je ne cherche pas à m'absoudre ainsi du reproche fort justifié de faire souvent des phrases trop longues, trop sinueusement attachées aux méandres de ma pensée. J'ai ri de bon cœur à votre: "C'est limpide." Mais je vous ai trouvé trop bienveillant de prétendre qu'à la troisième lecture cela devient clair, car, pour ma part, je n'y comprends rien' (pp. 93 f.). In an earlier letter to the same critic, Proust complains that the reader may be discouraged when he is told in a review that the book is 'rebutant à lire par l'aspect matériel, par la longueur des phrases (je reviens toujours à "phrases à la Patin")' (p. 74). He is also critical of superfluous sentences in his own writings and those of others; he tells Jacques Boulenger: 'Moi qui aurais été un bon professeur de seconde, je vois dans certains (viz. articles) la phrase qu'il faudrait couper, comme un câble, pour que le merveilleux ballon captif s'envolât vraiment. J'ai lu de vos articles tordants, qui eussent "fait date" si une phrase de trop n'eût scellé sur eux une pierre étouffante. D'ailleurs je fais exactement de même. Mais ce n'est pas une raison' (p. 211). Self-criticism becomes a form of courtesy and wit when he thanks Souday in these terms for a gift of chocolates: 'Ma prose n'a pas, hélas! la saveur de vos chocolats; elle n'en a pas le "coulant" non plus, le merveilleux fondu' (p. 90). Similarly, two references to the style of his early work, *Les Plaisirs et les jours*, need not perhaps be taken too seriously: he wants to send Boulenger a copy of the book 'pour vous montrer que je peux écrire purement' (p. 229), and in a later letter to the same friend he says that *Les Plaisirs et les jours* are much better written than *Swann* (p. 253).

In spite of his theories about grammar and style, Proust was very anxious to observe the rules of correct usage and was therefore most sensitive to criticism in these matters. He was particularly hurt by a review of *Du Côté de chez Swann* which Paul Souday had published in

Le Temps on 10 December 1913, and in which the critic had blamed him for a number of misprints as if they were genuine grammatical mistakes. In a letter written the day after the publication of the review, he protests: 'Mon livre peut ne révéler aucun talent; il présuppose du moins, il implique assez de culture pour qu'il n'y ait pas invraisemblance morale à ce que je commette des fautes aussi grossières que celles que vous signalez.' He then deftly turns the tables on his critic: 'Quand, dans votre article, j'ai lu: "M. Marcel Proust fait preuve d'*une* sens très aiguisé," etc., je n'ai pas pensé: "M. Souday ignore que le mot *sens* est du masculin."' In the same way he assumes that Souday will not attribute to the author's ignorance the more obvious misprints in the book. But, he goes on, 'il serait . . . aussi extraordinaire que j'ignorasse les règles de l'accord des temps. Je vous assure que si le "vieil universitaire" que vous proposez d'adjoindre aux maisons d'édition n'avait à corriger que mes fautes de français, il aurait beaucoup de loisirs'. The indignant letter ends with another reference to the difficult conditions under which the proofs of the book had to be corrected (pp. 62 f.).

The same subject is mentioned from time to time in later letters to the same correspondent: 'sachez bien que les fautes ne sont pas de moi. Je n'aurais jamais écrit quelque chose d'aussi idiot que "rafraîchie de souffles tièdes"' (p. 78); 'l'article sur Flaubert . . . vous prouvera que je ne suis pas aussi indifférent que vous le croyez aux questions de grammaire' (p. 75). He also notes that 'les fautes de Flaubert (qui ne diminuent en rien mon admiration pour lui) sont bien fréquentes' (p. 80).

In several letters, Proust apologizes for the poor quality of what he had just written: 'excusez ce style, je n'ai pas eu la force de signer même une dédicace depuis longtemps' (p. 69); 'excusez le style fautif d'un homme qui a 40 degrés de fièvre' (p. 172); 'excusez je ne dirai pas seulement les défauts de style, mais les fautes de grammaire de cette lettre de plus de dix pages' (pp. 304 f.). Even when writing about his own grave state of health he remains sensitive to stylistic nuances; in the middle of the sentence: 'Je suis depuis sept mois alité avec des crises d'urémie alternant avec des troubles différents et aussi graves,' he inserts the parenthesis: 'pardon des deux "avec"' (p. 301; cf. also p. 205).

The correspondence also contains a number of references to the disorders of speech from which Proust suffered for some time (pp. 45, 82, 87, 157 f., 268, 312). It is obvious from the frequency of these passages that Proust was very worried about this condition. At one point he actually consulted a well known neurologist about the possibility of a trepanotomy.[8] Characteristically, he used even these painful experiences as raw material for his novel, by making Bergotte suffer from some of the same symptoms.[9]

In the correspondence under discussion, Proust comments not only on his own style but also on the language of some of the characters in his novel. Particularly significant in this respect is a letter to Souday in which he contrasts Saint-Simon's references to the 'esprit de Mortemart' with his own, far more detailed technique in describing the 'esprit de Guermantes'. He speaks of his disappointment 'en voyant Saint-Simon nous parler toujours de "l'esprit de Mortemart", du "tour si particulier" à M. de Montespan, à M. de Thianges, à l'abbesse de Fontevrault, de ne pas trouver un seul mot, la plus légère indication qui permît de savoir en quoi consistait cette singularité de langage propre aux Mortemart'. It was this dissatisfaction which made him 'écrire comme un pensum tant de répliques de la duchesse de Guermantes et . . . rendre cohérent, toujours identique, l'esprit des *Guermantes* . . . Hélas! je n'ai pas le génie de Saint-Simon. Mais, du moins, ceux qui me liront sauront ce qu'est "l'esprit des Guermantes", ce qui était tout de même plus difficile à faire que de dire: "cet esprit particulier" sans en donner la plus légère idée' (p. 95). An earlier letter to the same critic identifies Proust's model for the language of the Duchess: 'agacé de voir Saint-Simon parler toujours du langage si particulier aux Mortemart sans jamais nous dire en quoi il consistait, j'ai voulu tenir le coup et essayer de faire un "esprit de Guermantes". Or, je n'ai pu trouver mon modèle que chez une femme non "née", Mme Straus, la veuve de Bizet. Non seulement les mots cités sont d'elle (elle n'a pas voulu que je dise son nom dans le livre), mais j'ai pastiché sa conversation' (p. 85).[10] In another letter, there is a concrete example of the 'esprit de Guermantes' in the form of a pun originally applied by the Duchess to her brother-in-law, Charlus: 'je vous ai constitué dans ma tête comme l'assemblage 1° d'un homme du cœur le plus délicat

[8] See G. D. Painter, *Marcel Proust. A Biography*, vol. II, London, 1965, p. 279.

[9] Cf. *À la recherche du temps perdu*, Pléiade ed., vol. II, p. 326 (*Le Côté de Guermantes*). See also Painter, op. cit., vol. II, p. 321.

[10] Cf. on 'l'esprit des Guermantes' and 'l'esprit des Mortemart', *À la recherche du temps perdu*, vol. II, p. 438 (*Le Côté de Guermantes*). On the linguistic components of the 'esprit des Guermantes', see Matoré, loc. cit., pp. 284 ff., and Mouton, op. cit., pp. 187 ff.

. . . et 2° d'un taquin (Taquin le Superbe, dirait, justement cette fois, Mme de Guermantes' (p. 279).[11]

Several other passages in the correspondence show how full Proust's mind was of the characters of his novel and of their linguistic idiosyncrasies. In a letter to Blanche he quotes a favourite expression of Dr. Cottard, and then apologizes for doing so: 'Je comprends donc qu'on vous ait accusé de "police" quand j'avais écrit de "malice" et *tutti quanti* comme dirait un personnage de Swann qui s'appelle (je n'oserais jamais me citer ainsi mais depuis que Bakst et le comte de Marigny . . . mais c'est trop long de vous dire les louanges exagérées de ces deux lecteurs) le docteur Cottard' (pp. 144 f.).[12] The doctor also appears in a letter to Boulenger: 'Et une fois les funestes sorties passées, je vous "ferai appel", comme disait M. Cottard' (p. 206), and a characteristic feature of the style of his wife is mentioned in an interesting remark on the *mot juste*: 'En principe je suis pour appeler les choses par leur nom et pour ne pas faire consister l'originalité et l'innovation dans l'altération de ce nom. Par exemple Reboux a fait des pastiches. Il a appelé cela: "*À la manière de*" (titre qui je le reconnais a fait fortune). J'ai fait aussi et souvent des *Pastiches*, et je les ai appelés tout simplement: *Pastiches*. Vous verrez que si c'est ma "manière", ce n'est pas celle de Mme Cottard, ou du moins vous le verrez si vous avez la bonté de lire, à supposer qu'ils paraissent jamais, les volumes suivants de Swann' (p. 148).[13]

In his correspondence with foreigners, Proust makes one or two references to his own lack of competence in other languages. In a letter to Mrs. Sydney Schiff he confesses: 'je lis l'anglais très difficilement' (p. 13). To Ernst Robert Curtius he writes: 'En voyant la magnifique connaissance que vous avez des lettres françaises et la façon si ingénieuse dont vous me citez en français, j'aurais voulu vous répondre en allemand. Hélas j'ai craint une trop grande disproportion entre votre français et mon allemand. J'ai une grande admiration pour la littérature et la philosophie allemandes mais votre langue ne m'est pas si familière (bien que je la mette à côté du grec parmi les langues les plus riches)' (p. 311).

Some of the letters contain penetrating remarks on the style of Proust's friends and other people. There is a particularly interesting comment on the syntax of Louis Martin-Chauffier, in connection with

[11] Cf. *À la recherche du temps perdu*, vol. II, p. 465 (*Le Côté de Guermantes*).
[12] Cf. ibid., vol. II, p. 881 (*Sodome et Gomorrhe*).
[13] Cf. ibid., vol. I, p. 256 (*Du Côté de chez Swann*).

an article which the latter had published in the *Nouvelle Revue Française*: 'votre style, style de vos lettres surtout et même de vos articles, me semblait courir, à force d'archaïsme et de préciosité abstraite, le risque de se dessécher, de se refroidir. Voilà mes craintes bien dissipées! Il n'y a pas une phrase qui ne vive, rendue nécessaire par une idée neuve et profonde. La phrase pousse, elle fleurit, et elle a, comme vous dites si bien, . . . "les voiles des pétales et des feuilles".' In a postscript, Proust also makes some specific suggestions: 'songez à éviter l'écueil des phrases trop longues (si drôles dans le pastiche que vous aviez fait de moi) si elles sont abstraites. Évitez la formule dix-septième siècle, ne gardez de cette admirable époque que sa réalité, le fond plein de vie, d'impressions senties et que l'apparente solennité ne doit jamais nous cacher' (pp. 307 f.).

Other remarks, though sometimes expressed in excessively flattering terms, also contain some valuable ideas. Commenting on an article by Boulenger, Proust writes: 'On a un peu honte d'avoir écrit de si gros volumes, comme j'ai fait, quand on voit quelqu'un en deux pages de revue . . ., tout en dessinant le portrait du modèle (moi), faire, grâce aux tons choisis, aux accents inconnus, son propre portrait' (pp. 203 f.). Boulenger's style also suggests an analogy which Proust had already used in his novel:[14] 'Vous avez un style comme les téléphones prédits qui montreront en même temps le visage de la personne' (p. 211). The style of Jacques-Émile Blanche is neatly summed up by another image from science: 'Votre style a une tendance au centrifuge, un[15] sujet précis, roman ou portrait de peintre, le ramène à son centre' (p. 173). Even when Proust receives an angry letter from Montesquiou, he comments on the quality of the writing: 'dans sa folie . . . je crois qu'elle vous amusera, qu'elle vous paraîtra bien et pittoresquement écrite' (p. 260).

Proust can even admire certain types of silence. Speaking of Mme de Pourtalès, he writes to Louis Gautier-Vignal: 'Je n'ai jamais causé avec elle. Mais ai écouté quelques silences très intelligents, ce qui est encore plus symptomatique et plus rare qu'une parole spirituelle' (pp. 318 f.). In another letter to the same correspondent he says: 'Sans vous écrire je pensais à vous, mais perçoit-on à distance l'amical appel

---

[14] 'Sa voix était comme celle que réalisera, dit-on, le photo-téléphone de l'avenir: dans le son se découpait nettement l'image visuelle' (ibid., vol. I, p. 930— *À l'ombre des jeunes filles en fleurs*).

[15] The text has *au*, which is an obvious misprint.

quotidien dont certains silences sont faits, plus qu'on ne perçoit l'harmonie des sphères?' (p. 320).

Among the various elements of style, imagery, and in particular metaphor, had always occupied a central position in Proust's aesthetics. In *Jean Santeuil* there are already a number of remarks on this problem[16], and in *Contre Sainte-Beuve* the outlines of a coherent theory of imagery begin to emerge.[17] In the *Recherche* and in various other writings, Proust returned time and again to these matters. Towards the end of his life, his views on metaphor found their definitive expression in three well known statements:

'Je crois que la métaphore seule peut donner une sorte d'éternité au style'.[18]

'Tous les à peu près d'images ne comptent pas. L'eau (dans des conditions données) bout à 100 degrés. À 98, à 99, le phénomène ne se produit pas. Alors mieux vaut pas d'images'.[19]

'La vérité ne commencera qu'au moment où l'écrivain prendra deux objets différents, posera leur rapport, analogue dans le monde de l'art à celui qu'est le rapport unique de la loi causale dans le monde de la science, et les enfermera dans les anneaux nécessaires d'un beau style; même, ainsi que la vie, quand, en rapprochant une qualité commune à deux sensations, il dégagera leur essence commune en les réunissant l'une et l'autre pour les soustraire aux contingences du temps, dans une métaphore'.[20]

This last passage, from *Le Temps retrouvé*, shows that there is, in Proust's opinion, a fundamental affinity between metaphor and the rediscovery of the past through the process of involuntary memory. It is therefore not altogether surprising that, in an earlier part of the cycle, he should speak of the 'sacred use' for which certain images are reserved.[21]

[16] Cf. my article, 'Images of Time and Memory in *Jean Santeuil*', in *Currents of Thought in French Literature. Essays in Memory of G. T. Clapton*, Oxford, 1966, pp. 209–26, and the paper mentioned in n. 2 above. On imagery in *Jean Santeuil*, see Elfi Zeblewski's unpublished thesis, *Prousts Bildersprache in 'Jean Santeuil'*, Marburg, 1957, summarized in her article, 'Zur Bildersprache in Marcel Prousts *Jean Santeuil*', *Die Neueren Sprachen*, NF, VII (1958), pp. 324–37.
[17] Cf. my article on *Contre Sainte-Beuve*, referred to in n. 2 above.
[18] In the article on the style of Flaubert, mentioned in n. 7 above.
[19] In his preface to Paul Morand's *Tendres Stocks*, 7th ed., Paris, 1923, p. 35.
[20] *À la recherche du temps perdu*, vol. III, p. 889 (*Le Temps retrouvé*). For a variant version of this crucial passage, see the note on pp. 1135 f.
[21] 'Des images si écrites et qui me semblaient réservées pour un autre usage plus sacré et que j'ignorais encore' (ibid., vol. III, p. 129—*La Prisonnière*).

In the correspondence we are concerned with, there are two passages of crucial importance on the problem of imagery. The first occurs in a letter to Jacques-Émile Blanche, written in May or June 1915:[22] 'je trouve les images nées d'une impression supérieures à celles qui servent seulement à illustrer un raisonnement . . . il y a un endroit où vous parlez . . . des cocardes qu'on s'épingle quand on a les pieds dans le sang. Je ne méprise pas ces images dont Taine faisait aussi un grand usage, mais j'aime mieux celles où, que vous parliez des hommes ou de la nature, vous délivrez de la vérité et de la poésie' (p. 109).

The same idea recurs in a letter from 1922 to Camille Vettard: 'Quant au style, je me suis efforcé de rejeter tout ce que dicte l'intelligence pure, tout ce qui est rhétorique, enjolivement et à peu près, images voulues et cherchées (ces images que j'ai dénoncées dans la préface de Morand) pour exprimer mes impressions profondes et authentiques et respecter la marche naturelle de ma pensée' (p. 195).

There are also a number of incidental remarks on imagery or on specific images. Louis Martin-Chauffier having written a pastiche of Proust, the latter congratulates him on some aspects of it: 'Vous avez distingué avec une justesse, parodié avec une drôlerie infinies, quelques particularités de syntaxe que je pense connues de nous deux seulement. Vous vous moquez de mes comparaisons d'une façon délicieuse' (p. 297). To Blanche he gives this advice: 'Un grand nombre de critiques ne s'occupent qu'à relever les fausses métaphores de ce genre. Il est inutile de leur prêter "le flanc" ' (p. 107). Elsewhere he comments on certain similes and metaphors which he had used himself. In the letter to Vettard which has just been mentioned, there is a striking passage comparing Proust's novel to a telescope trained on time. While developing the analogy, he inserts several brief asides commenting on the image itself: 'vous me comprendrez (vous trouverez certainement mieux vous-même) si je vous dis que l'image (très imparfaite) qui me paraît la meilleure[23] pour faire comprendre ce qu'est ce sens spécial c'est peut-être celle d'un télescope qui serait braqué sur le temps, car le télescope fait apparaître des étoiles qui sont invisibles à l'œil nu, et j'ai tâché (je ne tiens pas d'ailleurs du tout à mon image) de faire apparaître à la conscience des phénomènes inconscients qui, complètement oubliés, sont quelquefois situés très loin dans le passé' (pp. 194 f.). To Gautier-Vignal he writes: 'Je me rappelle

---

[22] On the dating of this letter, see Kolb, op. cit., pp. 101 f.
[23] Here Proust has added by pen, on the margin of the typewritten letter: 'Du moins actuellement' (p. 194, n. 2).

même vous avoir dit cette comparaison stupide: C'est comme pour les lettres de souverains qu'il est plus convenable de ne livrer à la publicité que quand le destinataire les a reçues' (p. 321); and to Boulenger: 'Quel "coup droit" (mais les métaphores d'escrimeur doivent vous paraître grotesques' (pp. 256 f.)).

The magic power of proper names, which is another recurrent theme in Proust and which found its supreme expression in the famous Balbec train—'le beau train généreux d'une heure vingt-deux, . . . magnifiquement surchargé de noms'[24]—is touched upon in a letter to Martin-Chauffier: 'par la logique naturelle après avoir affronté à la poésie du nom de lieu Balbec la banalité du pays Balbec, il me fallait procéder de même pour le nom de personne de Guermantes' (pp. 305 f.). In a letter to Boulenger, he comments on the name Martin-Chauffier itself, describing it as a 'nom boylesvien' (p. 258).

Etymology had been one of Proust's hobbies ever since *Jean Santeuil* where there is already a character interested in 'le sens qu'avait autrefois un mot, l'usage d'où ce mot dérivait, les raisons de fait pour lesquelles on ne pouvait croire que ce fût dans tel sens que l'eût entendu tel écrivain'.[25] This interest, which led in the *Recherche* to the long etymological digressions of the vicar of Combray and Professor Brichot, is reflected in several letters which show how seriously Proust took this side of his work. Only a few months before his death,[26] he wrote to Martin-Chauffier: 'Soyez rassuré pour les terribles étymologies que je devais vous demander. Je m'en suis tiré tout seul de mon mieux, ou plutôt fort mal. On mettra ce qu'elles ont de fantaisiste ou d'erroné sur le compte de mes ignorants personnages. Il y a pourtant plus d'un an que je dois écrire à François de P[27] . . . pour lui demander celles des Guermantes[28] et Cambremer' (p. 304). A few years earlier,[29] he

[24] *À la recherche du temps perdu*, vol. I, pp. 385 f. (*Du Côté de chez Swann*). On the Proustian cult of proper names, see e.g. J. Vendryes, 'Marcel Proust et les noms propres', in *Choix d'études linguistiques et celtiques*, Paris, 1953, pp 80–8; J. Pommier, *La Mystique de Marcel Proust*, Paris, 1939; V. E. Graham, 'Proust's Alchemy', *Modern Language Review*, LX (1965), pp. 197–206, and the same author's recent book, *The Imagery of Proust*, Oxford, 1966, pp. 32 f. and *passim*.

[25] *Jean Santeuil*, Paris, 1952, vol. II, p. 14.

[26] See Kolb, op. cit., p. 114, who dates this letter from about March 1922.

[27] The Marquis François de Pâris: see Painter, op. cit., vol. II, p. 357. Cf. also ibid., pp. 86 f.

[28] On the etymology of *Guermantes*, see Graham, *The Imagery of Proust*, pp. 70 and 244 f.

[29] This letter is dated by Kolb, op. cit., p. 113, as 'peu après le 10 décembre 1919'.

had been in touch with some experts on place-names: 'J'avais demandé [un conseil pour les étymologies] à M. Dimier (que je ne connais d'ailleurs pas), lequel m'avait gentiment répondu en m'offrant de me mettre en rapport avec M. Longnon. Du reste, je ne manque pas de gens pouvant m'apprendre toutes les étymologies' (p. 298). He also mentions such consultations elsewhere in the correspondence (pp. 266 and 279).

Apart from Madame de Guermantes's pun on *taquin* and *Tarquin le Superbe*, which has already been mentioned, there are one or two other examples of word-play in the correspondence. One is a clever pun on the name of Sydney Schiff: 'Je pensais à vous tout le temps et à force de dire Schiff, Schiff, ma plainte prenait un peu de celle de Tristan attendant la Nef' (p. 26). In a letter about a book by Jacques-Émile Blanche, Proust criticizes titles based on a pun. Speaking of the suggested title *Impressions et réimpressions*, he comments: 'Le titre est spirituel et joli mais . . . je ne suis pas très partisan de ce genre de titre car sur une couverture, une allitération, une gracieuse plaisanterie fait comme ces photographies plaisantes où un monsieur a pour toujours une mine spirituelle qui eût pu être agréable, fugace' (p. 122).

In a correspondence where Proust replies to various criticisms and also makes suggestions for improving the style of his friends, there are inevitably many observations on particular points of linguistic interest. They cover the whole field of language: phonetics, spelling, vocabulary, grammar, though it is especially the last two which are discussed in some detail. How sensitive Proust was to sound effects can be seen from a letter where he is referring to a preface he wrote to a book by Blanche[30]: 'à cause de sonorités peu euphoniques, j'ai perpétuellement remplacé le mot être, par exister, ou des choses de ce genre' (p. 152). Elsewhere he criticizes Boulenger for violating the rules of elision which he must have learnt at school (p. 245).

Even minute details of punctuation and spelling did not escape Proust's notice, such as for example the absence of quotation marks in a dialogue (p. 162). To Jacques Boulenger he writes: 'depuis huit jours, dès que je m'endors, je cherche l'orthographe que vous donnez dans un de vos premiers livres au mot jockey' (p. 208).

Some of Proust's remarks on words and idioms are concerned with the usage of earlier periods or writers; they show once again how attentive he was to such details. He ends a letter to Boulenger by

[30] See ibid., p. 109, dating the letter from January 1919.

assuring him: 'je suis à votre entière disposition pour Rivière, Martin-Chauffier, Boylesve, Bergson, tout l'univers comme on disait au dix-septième siècle' (p. 251). In a letter to Souday, he states: 'M. de Charlus . . . est une vieille Tante (je peux dire le mot puisqu'il est dans Balzac)' (p. 76). In another letter to the same critic, Proust amuses himself with writing a pastiche of an article by Souday, which includes the following passage: 'Une moitié de la dernière colonne prend la défense des gens du monde que M. Proust fait parler d'une façon trop grossière, mais plus vivante, on l'avouera, que M. de Goncourt quand il fait dire au cimetière à l'aristocratique Mme de Varandeuil: "O Paris! fichue cochonne de grande ville qui n'as pas de terre pour tes morts sans le sou" ' (pp. 100 f.). Commenting, in April 1915,[31] on a series of letters which Blanche had published in the *Revue de Paris*, Proust points out a small but significant anachronism: 'Dans la lettre du 14 août, vous dites que votre ami Cacan croit le 9 août qu'il relèvera de vos amis dans les *tranchées*. Il n'a été question de tranchées qu'après la bataille de la Marne, en septembre. Il se peut donc que ce soit prophétique . . . Mais alors pour une prophétie ce n'est pas assez appuyé'. And Proust goes on to discuss the implications of the mistake: 'Avec ou sans tranchées, les gens diront certainement que ce sont de fausses lettres, écrites après coup . . . Or "tranchées" leur fournira un argument merveilleux, tranchées laissera "passer le bout de l'oreille". Mais même si le genre épistolaire était ici un simple artifice de composition (et fort légitime), alors il serait encore plus nécessaire de supprimer tranchées, de respecter, dans une œuvre toute littéraire et composée, la vérité de l'époque, ne pas faire tenir à un Français d'avant la Marne le langage . . . d'un Français d'après' (pp. 105 f.). It would seem that Blanche was impressed by these arguments since he replaced *tranchées* by *fosses* when the letter was republished as part of a book.[32]

Some of the passages in which Proust objects to certain words and expressions show how strongly he felt on these matters: 'recevoir le livre avant sa "parution" comme on dit affreusement' (p. 157); 'l'affreux et vulgaire mot "crasse" ' (p. 189). He warns Blanche: 'Il y a encore des mots dont je trouve que vous abusez: "hurler", "tocsin" ' (p. 116). Elsewhere he cavils at this sentence in *Le Figaro*: 'avait donné

[31] Cf. ibid., pp. 100 f.

[32] Ibid., p. 101. The word *tranchée* itself is very old (Bloch-Wartburg's *Dictionnaire étymologique*, 5th ed., 1968, dates it from the XIIIth century); '*guerre de tranchées* (*opposé à* guerre de mouvement) s'est dit *spécialement* de la guerre de 1914–18, après la bataille de la Marne' (*Le Petit Robert*).

un *thé* en l'honneur du shah de Perse et un *goûter* en l'honneur du prince de Grèce'. Proust comments: 'J'ai inutilement rêvé à la différence qu'il y avait entre un thé et un goûter. Faut-il penser qu'il y a eu un petit four au thé . . ., ou qu'au goûter on ne peut pas avoir de thé?' (p. 55). He is critical of certain adjectives: 'Je n'aime pas beaucoup *sale typhoïde*' (p. 110); 'je n'ai pas compris votre adjectif "*évitante*"' (p. 24); on the other hand he notes that it is symptomatic of his relations with Montesquiou that 'je ne finis jamais une lettre à lui sans l'adjectif "respectueux" que je ne mettrais pas à quelqu'un ayant la même différence d'âge, mais que j'aurais connu plus tard, et non, comme lui, quand il venait chez mes parents' (p. 254). His interest in idioms, which play such an important part in the linguistic portrait of Dr. Cottard, is shown in this passage from a letter to Boulenger: 'je ne peux pas dire un mot sans que vous ayez l'épée toute prête (je tâche d'éviter les fausses locutions mettre en garde, etc.)' (p. 248).

In the letters to Boulenger, there are also one or two examples of amusing neologisms: 'l'état de ma moribonderie' (p. 239); 'il sera absent ces jours-ci, mais dans quelques jours re-libre' (p. 246); 'Rivière partait le jour même en re-vacances' (p. 264); 'j'aime les deux frères (pas charlusiennement!)' (p. 262).

Observations on various aspects of grammar occur in a number of letters; some deal with particular points whereas others raise wider issues. Thus, a letter to Jacques-Émile Blanche contains some perceptive comments on the stylistic value of verbless sentences: 'Votre habitude excellente puisque personnelle et caractéristique, de faire perpétuellement des phrases sans verbe (ce que grammaticalement je ne conseillerais pas d'imiter mais que j'aime chez vous) vous induit plus que tout à cette tentation de notation pour la notation. C'est presque la forme grammaticale où la pure notation se loge naturellement (et à bon droit du reste puisque qui se borne à constater n'a que faire de verbes). Mais surtout cela abrège tant, qu'un détail insignifiant . . . que vous hésiteriez peut-être à rapporter dans une phrase plus construite vous semble acceptable sous cette forme rapide, comme ces objets peu nécessaires qu'on hésitait à mettre dans sa malle mais qu'on finit par emporter parce qu'ils ne tiennent pas grande place' (p. 113). In the pastiche of an article by Souday, which was mentioned above, there is a reference to Proust's own essay on the style of Flaubert, with some sensitive remarks on the syntax of that writer. Proust starts with a quotation from Flaubert: 'Les modes, les temps des verbes, tout cela, ce sont des blagues, on peut écrire ce qu'on veut, du moment que c'est bien'. Though Proust refuses to go as far as Flaubert, he points out: 'c'est précisément M. Proust qui a montré que Flaubert, en violant les lois de concordance, a produit ses plus beaux effets non de littérale correction, mais de vivante beauté grammaticale'. He goes on to quote this sentence from Flaubert: 'Ils habitaient maintenant en Bretagne un jardin et montaient tous les jours sur une colline d'où l'on *découvre* la mer.' The unexpectedness of the present tense is here, Proust argues, of great expressive value: 'Comme le présent de l'indicatif quand on attendait l'imparfait . . ., n'éclaire-t-il pas d'un rayon la pérennité de cette colline "d'où l'on découvre la mer" en contraste avec la fugitive existence de ceux qui la gravissaient? Montesquieu, La Fontaine, sont pleins de ces sauts brusques qui, grâce à l'inobservance d'une loi grammaticale, donnent au tour une variété délicieuse' (pp. 99 f.).

Another passage in the same pastiche discusses some aspects of negation in French. In his review of *Sodome et Gomorrhe II*, Souday had criticized Proust's comments on some words spoken by the lift-boy of the Balbec hotel: 'J'ai pas pour bien longtemps, disait le lift qui, poussant à l'extrême la règle édictée par Bélise d'éviter la récidive du *pas* avec le *ne*, se contentait toujours d'une seule négative'.[33] 'Bélise s'est gardée d'édicter une règle si fausse,' Souday had objected, 'et à Martine disant: *Ne servent pas de rien*, ce n'est pas le *ne* qu'elle déconseille:

> De "pas" mis avec "rien" tu fais la récidive,
> Et c'est, comme on t'a dit, trop d'une négative'.[34]

Proust first of all points out that he had stated that the lift-boy had gone beyond the 'Bélise rule'. He then makes four further points, three of which are interesting. Firstly, he feels that the rule had been badly formulated by Molière. 'L'analyse logique et la grammaticale voudraient la révision entière, la refonte de ces deux vers incorrects. Ils ne sont pas moins merveilleux, et dans la verve de l'ensemble qui s'arrêterait à la gaucherie du tour? Preuve qu'il ne faut pas être trop grammairien quand on juge.' Secondly, he wonders whether *rien*, derived from the Latin *res*, is really negative here. Thirdly, he argues that 'le liftier du roman n'est pas plus fautif qu'Assuérus: "Que craignez-vous, Esther? Suis-je pas votre frère?" Et le dix-septième siècle parlait souvent ainsi "sans licence poétique". M. Benda, qui se

---

[33] *À la recherche du temps perdu*, vol. II, p. 793 (*Sodome et Gomorrhe*).
[34] *Correspondance générale*, vol. III, p. 98, n. 1.

pique d'en écrire, quand il lui plaît, la langue, imprime couramment, dans les articles de journaux: "A-t-on pas vu l'Europe?", etc. "Est-il pas étrange que?", etc.' (pp. 98 f.).

In another letter to Souday, Proust protests against the vogue of certain elliptical constructions: 'je ne peux trouver les derniers "luxe" (puisqu'on emploie maintenant, même pour les livres, cette manière abrégée et barbare de parler qui fait dire un verre de champagne ou un pneu, et qui est plus offensante étendue aux choses littéraires)' (p. 90). *Pneu* is also mentioned in a letter to Boulenger: 'ce qu'on appelle un "pneu" (hélas!)' (p. 222). Elsewhere he comments briefly on a characteristic feature of the style of the same friend: 'j'ai compris que le côté brusque, le "Voyons", le "Bonne santé" était plus Jacques Boulenger, je veux dire plus une particularité de style, qu'une marque de sécheresse' (p. 207).

When pointing out specific mistakes Proust sometimes apologizes for being so pedantic in matters of grammar. 'J'ai oublié de vous signaler', he writes to Blanche, '(ce qui est du reste de ma part purisme un peu exagéré) un "en" qui n'est peut-être pas tout à fait correct' (p. 126). In another letter to the same correspondent, he discusses at length the syntax of the noun *souvenir*, adding: 'surtout pardonnez-moi de faire ainsi le pion de sixième. . . . Et je vous supplie de ne pas vous méprendre sur ma pensée quand je fais des objections à "souvenir", elles sont purement de grammaire, de logique, de symétrie, de clarté' (p. 149). This does not, however, prevent him from going into minor details of phrasing, such as the ambiguity of a sentence (p. 106), the use of *lamenter* without a reflexive pronoun (p. 168), or a clumsy construction 'où deux "dont" se "commandent"' (p. 121).

In a lighter vein, Proust repeatedly refers, in two letters to Schiff, to the passage from *vous* to *tu* in their relationship. Like Voltaire who had written a poem on 'Les *Vous* et les *Tu*',[35] Proust is intrigued by the problem of *tutoiement*; pretending that he is not sure of his ground, he combines the two forms of address: 'J'ose à peine vous (ou t')écrire . . . la diffusion de vos (ou tes) livres', etc. (p. 48). He also notes some hesitation on this point in the letters of his friend, and reminds him of Mallarmé's lines:

> J'ai souvent rêvé d'être, ô duchesse, l'Hébé
> Qui vit sur *votre* tasse du baiser de *tes* lèvres   (p. 54)

---

[35] Cf. on this poem (*Épître XXXIII*) L. Spitzer, *A Method of Interpreting Literature*, Northampton, Mass., 1949, Ch. 2.

The correspondence examined in this article brings Proust's linguistic ideas into particularly sharp focus since it contains so many comments, general as well as detailed, on his own style and that of his friends. It shows once again his keen interest in these problems, his extraordinary powers of observation, his encyclopaedic knowledge, his sensitivity to stylistic nuances. He was fascinated by every aspect of language: he was equally interested in it as a means of communication, as a source of expressive and aesthetic effects, as a storehouse of philological curiosities, as a vital part of French tradition and culture. No less important to him were what we would now call the psycholinguistic and sociolinguistic aspects of the problem: the role of language, both as a symptom and as an active force, in human behaviour, individual as well as social. As a recent article on Proust's linguistic theories has put it, he regarded the study of language as 'un procédé opératoire destiné à expliciter des conduites individuelles et des comportements sociaux'.[36] This view of language is also reflected in his approach to style, which is essentially psycholinguistic. Flaubert had defined style as 'une manière absolue de voir les choses'. Proust developed this idea in a crucial passage of *Le Temps retrouvé*: 'le style pour l'écrivain, aussi bien que la couleur pour le peintre, est une question non de technique mais de vision. Il est la révélation, qui serait impossible par des moyens directs et conscients, de la différence qualitative qu'il y a dans la façon dont nous apparaît le monde, différence qui, s'il n'y avait pas l'art, resterait le secret éternel de chacun'.[37]

[36] Matoré, loc. cit., p. 292.

[37] *À la recherche du temps perdu*, vol. III, p. 895. There is one passage in the correspondence which seemingly contradicts this conception and the organic unity of matter and manner which it implies. In a letter to Jacques-Émile Blanche, Proust says: 'J'ai . . . quelques éloges à ajouter sur votre forme dont je n'ai pas assez parlé. J'ai tellement pris l'habitude de distinguer chez un écrivain "le fond et la forme" ' (pp. 139 f.). J. Mouton comments on this passage: 'C'est ici simple politesse à l'égard de son correspondant dont il se reproche de n'avoir pas assez loué la "forme". En fait, toutes les idées de Proust sur le style écartent ce dédoublement qui, en tant que méthode d'analyse, aide souvent à une meilleure compréhension des textes, mais demeure absolument inintelligible au créateur' (op. cit., p. 35).

Sur un Vers de Racine

EUGÈNE VINAVER

Emeritus Professor of French Language and Literature in the
University of Manchester

(*Phèdre*, Acte IV, scène 6; vers 1270)

Criminelle à ses yeux, reconnaissant l'horreur de ses désirs, Phèdre
s'écrie:

> Mes crimes désormais ont comblé la mesure,
> Je respire à la fois l'inceste et l'imposture.
>
> (ll. 1269–70)

Que faut-il entendre par *je respire*? Le plus illustre des traducteurs de
Racine et un des plus avertis, Schiller, reproduit le deuxième vers mot
à mot:

> Blutschande athm'ich und Betrug zugleich.

Faut-il assimiler ici *athmen* à *respirer*, tel par exemple que l'emploie
Hippolyte en s'adressant à Aricie:

> Arrachez-vous d'un lieu funeste et profané
> Où la vertu *respire* un air empoisonné?   (ll. 1359–60)

Ce serait méconnaître le fait que Phèdre se considère comme la source
du mal, que c'est en elle et non ailleurs qu'elle situe tout ce qu'elle
connaît d'impur: l'imposture et l'inceste. Aussi a-t-on voulu voir dans
je respire l'image singulièrement hardie d'une criminelle qui 'exhale' le
crime. C'est ainsi que l'interprète entre autres une récente traduction
anglaise:

> Henceforth the measure of my crimes is full.
> I reek with foulest incest and deceit.[1]

---

[1] John Cairncross, '*Phaedra' by Racine*, Genève et Paris (Droz), 1958, p. 92.

To reek with veut dire au figuré 'exhaler'; *to reek with crime*, 'suer le crime'. Traduction conforme à l'avis de la plupart des commentateurs, et notamment à celui de Lanson qui dit dans une note de son édition du *Théâtre choisi* de Racine qu'il s'agit là de quelque chose qui est 'comme le parfum de l'âme'.[2] Il ne fait d'ailleurs que suivre Littré qui cite le vers en question comme exemple de l'emploi métaphorique de *respirer* au sens d' "exhaler comme un parfum". Personne à ma connaissance ne s'est demandé jusqu'ici pourquoi Littré ne cite aucun autre cas de cet emploi. Sait-on si de tels cas existent? En classant comme il le fait le *je respire* de Phèdre le grand lexicographe ne s'est-il pas tout simplement mépris sur sa signification?

Notons tout d'abord ce fait qu'au 17e et au 18e siècle, l'éventail sémantique de *respirer* se divisait, comme aujourd'hui d'ailleurs, en deux secteurs, l'un qui avait pour point de départ le *mécanisme* de la respiration, l'autre sa *valeur de signe ou de symptôme*. La respiration est tout d'abord *signe de vie*, et à ce titre elle confère au français *respirer* comme au latin *spirare* le sens de *vivre*. *Clodius spirans*, dans *pro Milone*, veut dire 'du vivant de Clodius', comme *vous ne respirez qu'autant que je vous aime*, dans *Bajazet*, signifie 'vous ne vivez qu'aussi longtemps que je vous aime'. Une substitution métonymique parallèle à celle-ci, mais qui part de l'idée qu'on respire profondément en prenant quelque relâche, aboutit à l'emploi de *respirer* au sens de 'cesser de travailler':

> Hercule, respirant sur le bruit de vos coups,
> Déjà de son travail se reposait sur vous   (*Phèdre*, l. 943)

Quant au *mécanisme* de la respiration, il comporte, on le sait, deux mouvements: *l'inspiration*, qui fait entrer l'air dans la cage thoracique, et le mouvement qui l'en rejette, autrement dit *l'expiration*. C'est à ce deuxième mouvement que le verbe *respirer* doit la plupart de ses acceptions métaphoriques, analogues à celles du latin *spirare*: d'une part, 'exprimer', 'annoncer', 'proclamer', 'témoigner vivement' (passage du concret à l'abstrait), comme dans *Tout respire en Esther l'innocence et la paix*,[3] et d'autre part 'exhaler' au sens concret:

> La Provence odorante et de Zéphyre aimée,
> Respire sur les mers une haleine embaumée
>   (André Chénier, *Hymne à la Justice*, 17–18)

---

[2] *Théâtre choisi de Racine*, Paris (Hachette), 1901, p. 841.
[3] *Esther*, vers 672.

Qu'un sein voluptueux, des lèvres demi-closes
Respirent près de nous leur haleine de roses
                              (André Chénier, *Animé par l'amour*)

L'inspiration, elle, donne lieu à deux autres développements: à une métaphore qui fait prendre à *respirer* la valeur de 'faire pénétrer dans l'âme', (c'est bien ce qu'Hippolyte entend par 'respirer un air empoisonné') et à une métonymie analogue à celle qui infléchit le sens du verbe *aspirer*.[4] Dans ce dernier cas l'action d'inspirer est conçue comme un geste qui caractérise ou accompagne un désir particulièrement fort. C'est ainsi que s'expliquent cette remarque de Madame de Sévigné: 'les pauvres ne respirent que moi' (lettre du 2 novembre 1673),[5] ce vers des *Plaideurs*:

La fille le veut bien; son amant le respire   (l. 851)

et ces deux vers de *Mithridate*:

Et toujours avec vous son cœur d'intelligence
N'a semblé respirer que guerre et que vengeance (ll. 500–1).

Ce même sens de 'désirer, souhaiter ardemment' reparaît au début de l'acte III de *Phèdre*:

Ciel, comme il m'écoutait! Par combien de détours
L'insensible a longtemps éludé mes discours!
Comme il ne respirait qu'une retraite prompte!
                                               (ll. 743–5)

ainsi que dans la première scène de l'acte V d'*Athalie*:

Pour les rompre, elle attend les fatales machines
Et ne respire enfin que sang et que ruines.
                                               (ll. 1539–40)

---

[4] Ce verbe, construit, au sens de 'porter son désir vers', avec la préposition *à*, conserve par là le souvenir du datif qu'appelle la même acception du latin *spirare*. Properce dit bien: *Cynthia spirat nobis*.

[5] Cette même expression se retrouve dix ans plus tard, sous la plume de Boileau, dans le sixième chant du *Lutrin* (vers 23): 'Chacun, plein de mon nom, ne respirait que moi.'

Tout ce qui précède pourrait se résumer par le graphique suivant:

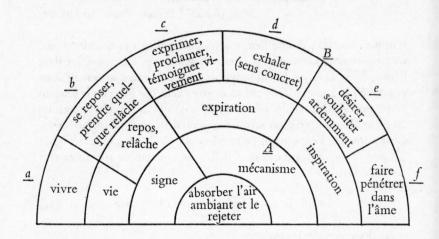

L'interprétation traditionnelle du vers 1270 de *Phèdre* suppose qu'on peut dire en français—ou du moins qu'on *pouvait* dire dans la langue de Racine—*je respire* au sens *c* ou *d* comme au sens *e*: que Phèdre pouvait affirmer qu'elle respirait l'inceste et l'imposture comme Esther l'innocence et la paix. Or il se trouve que la frontière qui, dans notre graphique, sépare le domaine *d* du domaine *e*—la ligne *AB*—ne traduit pas seulement un fait de sémantique historique déterminé par le mécanisme même de la respiration: cette frontière répond à un fait de syntaxe. Il n'y a pas, en effet, d'exemple de *respirer* au sens *c* ou *d* construit, comme il l'est d'habitude au sens *e* et *f*, avec un nom de personne ou un pronom personnel; jamais Racine n'a dit: 'Esther respire l'innocence et la paix' au sens de *Tout respire en Esther l'innocence et la paix*, ni 'je respire' au sens de 'je proclame', 'je témoigne vivement' ou 'j'exhale'. C'est ce que fait observer dans une note R. C. Knight qui seul parmi les éditeurs de *Phèdre*, s'inscrit en faux contre l'explication proposée par Lanson. Son témoignage est formel: 'No example has been quoted in French of the verb in this sense after a personal subject'.[6]

S'agirait-il donc d'un cas isolé? Il suffit de relire les *Remarques* de Littré lui-même pour comprendre combien une telle hypothèse serait

[6] Racine, *Phèdre*, edited by R. C. Knight, Manchester ('French Classics'), 1943.

gratuite.[7] D'Olivet avait prétendu qu'au sens de 'souhaiter' *respirer* ne se disait qu'avec la négative. 'Fausse remarque, déclare Littré, comme le prouvent les exemples suivants.' Et il en cite deux de Corneille,[8] un de Racine—le vers 851 des *Plaideurs*—un de Voltaire et un de Chateaubriand. 'Respirer, dit-il encore, marque un désir plus ardent, une passion plus violente que ne fait *soupirer après*'. Pourquoi alors refuser ce sens—le sens *e*—à un vers qui ne saurait sans invraisemblance grammaticale s'accommoder d'aucune autre explication?

Lorsqu'on replace ce vers dans le mouvement du texte on comprend mieux encore la nécessité de s'en tenir aux données de l'usage:

> Que fais-je? Où ma raison se va-t-elle égarer?
> Moi jalouse? Et Thésée est celui que j'implore?
> Mon époux est vivant et moi, je brûle encore?
> Pour qui? Quel est le cœur où prétendent mes vœux?

Faisant éclater aux yeux de Phèdre l''affreuse vérité', ces vers lui accordent la lucidité du regard qui l'accule à son sort. Qui mieux qu'elle pourrait définir la nature de ses crimes? Crimes d'intention, qui appellent d'abord ce mot si pâle, si neutre—presque une litote— *prétendre*. Mais ce n'est là que le début d'un mouvement ascendant:

> Chaque mot sur mon front fait dresser mes cheveux.
> Mes crimes désormais ont comblé la mesure,
> Je respire à la fois l'inceste et l'imposture,
> Mes homicides mains, promptes à me venger,
> Dans le sang innocent brûlent de se plonger.

Prétendre—respirer—brûler: ardent triangle dont *brûler* forme le sommet, reprise en triptyque de l''ardeur dans mes veines cachée'.

'C'est, nous dit Jean Pommier,[9] vers le milieu de l'acte IV que Racine déclenche le ressort de la jalousie. Là et non plus tôt. J'insiste, parce qu'on s'y est parfois trompé. Phèdre autorise la calomnie vers la

---

[7] Les a-t-il relues lui-même attentivement avant de classer le vers 1270 de *Phèdre* sous la rubrique qui, dans notre graphique, correspond au sens *d*? Il est permis d'en douter; mais il est surtout regrettable que les commentateurs et traducteurs du texte n'aient pas poussé la curiosité jusque-là.

[8] 'Ta bouche la demande (*la vengeance*) et ton cœur la respire' (*Horace*, vers 1272); 'On m'en veut plus qu'à vous: c'est ma mort qu'ils respirent' (*Pompée*, vers 1429). Le *Dictionnaire de l'Académie* de 1694 fait état de cette acception sans en limiter l'emploi aux propositions négatives: 'Sign. encore fig. Souhaiter ardemment'.

[9] Jean Pommier, *Aspects de Racine*, Paris (Nizet), 1954, p. 197.

fin de l'acte III; elle devient jalouse *un acte plus tard*. Ceci ne saurait
expliquer cela'. Jean Pommier répond ainsi à Etienne Gros qui pré-
tendait que la calomnie était la conséquence de la jalousie de Phèdre.[10]
La jalousie est là, mais elle n'est là que pour ajouter au supplice de
Phèdre une *douleur non encore éprouvée*, pour livrer à ses *homicides mains*
une victime de plus. Mains innocentes pourtant, et qui ne deviennent
coupables que par la pensée du crime, qui seule condamne Phèdre à
une horreur démesurée. Thierry Maulnier expliquera cette horreur,
cette agonie de l'âme en disant que Phèdre, 'assoiffée de fraîcheur
angélique', ne peut 'contempler son miroir, y lire la marque d'un
amour ténébreux et illégitime, sans se savoir infiniment plus coupable,
victime d'une innombrable et mortelle dégradation de son être,
[. . .] la seule tache à l'innocence de l'univers [. . .] Délire justicier
aussi violent que le délire de l'amour'.[11] Délire qui se retourne contre
l'impureté du cœur plus violemment qu'il n'aurait fait contre la
souillure de l'acte. Le monde ne saura retrouver sa pureté qu'au moment
déjà proche où Phèdre cessera d'être le récitant d'un crime dont elle a
osé enfin dire le nom.

[10] Etienne Gros, *Philippe Quinault, sa vie et son œuvre*, Paris (Champion), 1926,
p. 322. Cf. Winifred Newton, *Le thème de Phèdre et d'Hippolyte dans la littérature
française*, Paris (Droz), 1939, p. 103: 'Racine [. . .] dédaigne comme une banalité
dramatique [. . .] la jalousie ressort de l'action'.

[11] Thierry Maulnier, *Lecture de Phèdre*, Paris (Gallimard), 1943, pp. 98-9.

Les Sens du substantif français 'Côté'. (essai de classement)

R. L. WAGNER

Directeur d'études à l'École des Hautes Études, Paris

Pour un lexicologue, certains faits d'absence ont autant d'importance que de nombreuses occurrences. Le mot *côté* n'apparaît pas dans l'index qui accompagne *L'Espace Humain* de M. G. Matoré.[1] De fait, l'auteur, s'il l'emploie, n'en traite pas explicitement. Cette absence, dans un ouvrage dont le titre comporte le terme d'*espace*, m'a incité à rouvrir quelques dictionnaires du français moderne afin de vérifier ce qu'ils disent de ce signe.[2] Leur lecture m'a enseigné qu'en dépit des apparences (fréquence modeste, caractère usuel et presque banal), le mot *côté* révèle par certains de ses emplois une activité et une ingéniosité fort curieuses de l'esprit. Si je vous livre, un peu en vrac, mes réflexions à ce sujet, vous en devinez le motif. Des raisons pressantes me dictent le devoir très agréable de m'associer à ceux qui, par le présent hommage, vous expriment à la fois reconnaissance, estime et amitié. Mais, comme vous le verrez, un calcul quelque peu égoïste ternit la pureté de ces sentiments. J'ai la conviction en effet qu'un médiéviste tel que vous, grand lecteur, lecteur expérimenté et attentif aux faits de vocabulaire, saura répondre aux questions que ces dictionnaires m'ont

[1] Paris, la Colombe, Éditions du Vieux Colombier, 1962, vol. 1, p. 299. (Collection: Sciences et techniques humaines, 2.) L'objet de cette intéressante étude est indiqué par le sous-titre: *L'Expression de l'espace dans la vie, la pensée et l'art contemporains.*

[2] Du dictionnaire de Littré à celui de Larousse (*Dictionnaire du français contemporain* publié sous la direction de M. J. Dubois) en passant par le D.A.A.L.F. de M. P. Robert et le *Petit Robert*, la structure d'ailleurs raisonnable des articles réservés à notre mot ne varie guère. Un examen des divergences qu'on observe aura sa place dans une étude—en préparation—sur un ensemble plus vaste de dictionnaires français monolingues. On y critiquera leurs façons d'articuler, de définir *côté* ainsi que d'autres termes sémantiquement apparentés à celui-ci.

posées. Je vous les soumets donc, *in fine*, avec la certitude que vous y apporterez tôt ou tard une réponse.

Tandis que *côte*, issu presque sans accident du latin *cŏstam*, occupe un rang honorable dans la couche noble du lexique français, *côté* est d'une origine moins relevée. Sa finale le signale comme prolongeant un dérivé; ses valeurs d'emploi, ainsi que celles de ses congénères romans postulent un *costātum*, de sens collectif, différent de l'adjectif *costātus* utilisé par Varron. C'est ce qu'enseigne le F.E.W. à la fin de l'article *costa* (II, 1245 sqq.). Le sémantisme actuel de *côte* est à la mesure de sa naissance. En français commun le mot fait partie du vocabulaire des morphologistes (anatomistes, vétérinaires et bouchers, botanistes); par métaphore il symbolise les pourtours d'un littoral et les pentes, aussi, qui créent des saillies sur une surface plane (de même que les côtes en font de légères sur une poitrine maigre). Ce terme mérite, certes, une étude mais celle-ci ne révélerait rien, au fond, qui ne fût prévisible une fois établi le sens étymologique de *costa*. *Costa* n'a pas subi l'offensive d'un mot étranger apte à le déloger.[3] N'oublions pas non plus que dans les traductions de la *Genèse* il figure pour désigner la pièce du squelette d'Adam dont Dieu se servit pour former Ève. Tout mot français promu au rôle de servir à l'intelligence du texte sacré en tire un éclat durable.

[3] On sait que la nomenclature latine des parties du corps a tenu bon en français, à quelques exceptions près, assez mystérieuses d'ailleurs. M. W. V. Wartburg a attiré depuis longtemps l'attention sur l'insertion de *hanche*, qui est devenu un signe commun en français. Mais les dialectes du Nord et du Nord-Est (picard, rouchi, wallon) ont possédé et possèdent encore des termes d'origine germanique dont l'occurrence demeure encore inexpliquée. Les faits de peuplement, le bilinguisme créent des circonstances favorables aux emprunts, mais cela n'éclaire pas le caractère toujours limité, singulier des emprunts. Pourquoi, dans ces régions, sont-ce le nombril et la nuque, par exemple, qui portent des noms étrangers plutôt que le genou ou le nez? Mystérieuse est l'origine de la base *Bod* (le dictionnaire étymologique de M. E. Gamillscheg avance un gallo-roman *boddēna* alors que R.E.W. (3ᵉ éd.) et le F.E.W. s'en tiennent à *Bod*) à laquelle se rattachent *boudine*, *boudène*. Cette dernière forme était encore vivante dans la région du Hainaut au début de ce siècle (cf. Anne-Marie Fossoul-Risselin, *Le Vocabulaire de la vie familiale à Saint-Vaast* (1890–1914), Liège, Impr. George Michiels, 1969, vol. I, p. 184. (Mémoires de la Commission Royale de toponymie et de dialectologie, section wallonne, 12.) pour désigner le nombril. Depuis *Romania Germanica* (I, II—102, p. 207) de M. E. Gamillscheg et la note antérieure de J. Haust (*Romania*, XLV (1918–19), p. 180) rien, à ma connaissance, n'a précisé ni renouvelé les problèmes que pose *haterel* désignant la nuque. Le F.E.W., t.XVI, 136, renvoie, sous *Halter*, à la notice de J. Haust.

Mais les bâtards et les parvenus ont parfois une destinée plus intéressante que les enfants racés de la main droite. À preuve, les places que le mot *côté* a successivement conquises et qu'il tient encore en français aujourd'hui: ce signifiant y est devenu le symbole d'un réseau bien ordonné de notions directrices. Nous les passerons d'abord en revue, sans nous soucier de chronologie, en essayant d'éclaircir leur apparentement.

(1) À la différence de *côte*, *côté* n'a pas de place dans la nomenclature médicale actuelle. Les définitions convergentes du D.L.F., du D.A.A.L.F., du P.R. et du D.F.C. lui font désigner la partie latérale du corps comprise entre l'aisselle et la hanche. Mais elles enregistrent simplement une valeur d'emploi usuelle en effet, familière, qu'on retrouve dans la locution populaire *un point de côté*. Les spécialistes appelleraient, eux, ce que nous dénommons le *côté* du corps, au moyen de 'face latérale du thorax'; encore cette zone superficielle n'a-t-elle à leurs yeux aucune unité: les anatomistes la décomposent en plusieurs régions secondaires.

D'autres valeurs du terme découlent du fait que *côté*, loin de dénoter comme *côte* une pièce du squelette, en est venu assez tôt à signifier une ligne de démarcation concrète ou idéale. En français courant, *côté* s'applique, bien au-delà de la portion du corps indiquée par les lexicographes, à toutes celles qui de la tête aux pieds circonscrivent les zones latérales de notre corps. *Les côtés* entrent ainsi en relation avec *le devant*—*la poitrine* et *le dos* qui se rapportent, eux, aux surfaces antérieure et postérieure du volume constitué par l'ensemble de l'individu. L'avant et l'arrière étant déterminés par rapport à la direction de la vue.

(2) Le corps humain sert de modèle. C'est à lui qu'on rapporte un peu partout, instinctivement, les surfaces et les volumes dont la figure est analogue à la sienne. Quelques-uns des termes qui en désignent les parties constitutives prennent du même coup une valeur métaphorique. Mais le squelette allongé des quadrupèdes comme la structure linéaire des vers fournissent d'autres références. Un arbre, de stature verticale, a une tête, un tronc, un pied. Une procession, un défilé s'étendent entre une tête et une queue. Il est donc normal que *côté*, pourvu ou non d'un adjectif tel que *droit* ou *gauche*, ait été retenu par les géomètres pour désigner les lignes latérales d'un rectangle ou les faces latérales longues d'un parallélipipède. Un emballage porte ainsi l'inscription *côté à ouvrir*. Le même signe dénote en français les deux bords d'un chemin, les parties latérales d'une église bordant la nef (cf. *les bas-côtés*), celles d'un autel et d'une scène de théâtre (cf. *côté cour—jardin*).

Lisière, lui, s'appliquant aux extrémités d'une étoffe ainsi qu'aux frontières d'un terrain ou d'une région.

(3) Mais en géométrie le sème/latéral, allongé/ encore très sensible quand on parle des côtés du corps, d'une route, d'un rectangle ou d'un parallélipipède, n'est déjà plus pertinent puisque *côté* s'applique aux quatre lignes *égales* d'un carré (*faces* dénotant les quatre surfaces égales d'un cube). Dans cet emploi le sème majeur de *côté* est devenu celui de/ limite/.

Cette notion de limite, les ethnologues la tiennent à bon droit pour fondamentale. Une clôture définit l'ensemble qu'elle circonscrit, prélevé sur un ensemble plus vaste. Le *līmes* signifiait, en latin, le chemin qui bordait un domaine. Le *līmen*, dans cette langue, dénotait une portion essentielle de l'ensemble plus restreint que constitue une demeure. Il semble qu'en latin postclassique ces deux termes soient entrés en contact. Au second correspond en français *seuil* (a. fr. *suel* < *solum*), opposé à *linteau* (a. fr. *lintel*) qui, lui, prolonge pour le sens le latin *līmen*(*superum*). Le *seuil* marque le point privilégié qu'est l'entrée d'un domaine ou d'une maison. En bien des endroits, il comporte un signe symbolique avertisseur du passage en quelque sorte rituel que l'on effectue pour pénétrer dans la demeure. Il arrive, par exemple, qu'avant de la franchir, on doive ôter des pieds sandales ou souliers empreints des impuretés du dehors.

L'ensemble défini par des limites est comme soustrait de son environnement et comme protégé contre lui. Pour ceux qui l'occupent, il devient le lieu de leur existence, ce que l'ancien français exprimait au moyen de l'adverbe *ci*. À *là* était dévolu le rôle de symboliser l'environnement général, c'est-à-dire tous les lieux extérieurs au *ci*. La langue exprime encore cette relation par des faits de vocabulaire auxquels nous ne prêtons plus attention tant ils sont communs et semblent évidents. Le passage du *ci* au *là*, du *enz* au *fors*, quand il s'effectue à travers des limites visibles ou idéales, n'est pas neutre. On *sort* (a. fr. *ist*) de l'ensemble qui constitue le *ci* et on y *entre*; on ne sort pas de l'environnement où on était allé se promener pas plus qu'on y entre. '*Là, je sors de mon bien*' me disait une fois un paysan avec qui je traversais un vaste guéret. Ses yeux, plus vifs que les miens, avaient matérialisé la ligne idéale rejoignant deux pierres lointaines qui divisait en deux cette pièce de terre.

Le lieu du *ci*, quand il est clos, se divise en sections autour d'un point remarquable. Le nom abstrait de *centre* que porte celui-ci se prête à des valeurs métaphoriques. De même celui des sections ou *côtés* que l'on détermine par rapport à lui. C'est dans l'une d'elles, protégée, que les habitants du lieu accumulent leurs provisions, dissimulent des objets précieux. Suivant les contextes, la locution *mettre de côté* signifie 'ranger', 'mettre en sûreté', 'épargner'. Une autre partie recèle les déchets et les vieilleries devenues inutiles qu'on *rebute*. *Écarter*, enfin, évoque l'acte de ménager une *distance* entre le lieu du *ci* et son environnement. Au moyen des déverbaux *écart*, *rebut* la même base verbale engendre des locutions parallèles *mettre à l'écart*, *mettre au rebut*. *Écart* et *distance*, eux, entrent en collocation avec *tenir*. Si je le rappelle, c'est qu'il serait temps de se demander quels sont les verbes, en français, aptes à former des locutions verbales et des locutions idiomatiques. Les relevés que nous avons fait faire d'après des textes prouvent que *mettre* et *tenir* se situent assez haut dans la liste sans avoir pourtant la fécondité d'*avoir*, de *faire* ou de *prendre*. Ces verbes appartiennent au fonds du lexique gallo-roman. Chacun d'eux fait partie d'un ensemble et en constitue le terme neutre (cf. *prendre* par rapport à *saisir* en a. fr., *mettre* par rapport à *tirer*, *jeter*, *envoyer*, etc.). Ils symbolisent un certain nombre de relations fondamentales—possession, appropriation, création, disposition—entre l'être qui en est le sujet et quelque chose. Une étude détaillée de leurs emplois, des collocations qu'ils admettent, révélerait peut-être la place qu'ils occupent dans les structures lexicales profondes. Elle devrait naturellement porter sur l'ensemble du domaine roman.

(4) L'environnement lui-même des ensembles ainsi délimités n'est ni vague ni indéfini. Le trajet du soleil le sillonne d'est en ouest, il a ses régions chaudes ou tempérées ou froides. Chaque paroi de la demeure fait obstacle à des vents dont la nature et les pouvoirs diffèrent. Une grande partie des activités de l'homme s'exercent en dehors du lieu où il réside. On observe dès lors sans surprise que le mot de *côté*, en français, se réfère aux sections ou régions de l'environnement autant qu'à celles qui sont incluses dans l'ensemble du *ci*. Des locutions telles que *du côté de chez Swann*, *les à-côté d'une chose*, *aller chacun de son côté*, *venez donc de mon côté* en sont la preuve.

D'où, par rapport à E et en référence à des critères utilitaires (tirés de l'ensoleillement, de la pluie, du vent), des expressions telles que *le bon côté*, *le mauvais côté* d'une demeure. Ici intervient en français le mot *part* dont les relations avec *côté* (sensibles dans *de part et d'autre*, *d'un côté et de l'autre*, *prendre une chose en bonne part* ~ *la prendre du bon côté*) mériteraient d'être étudiées de près.

Dans cette même valeur, *côté* en vient alors à symboliser non plus les limites latérales d'un rectangle ou d'un chemin mais les *surfaces situées de part et d'autre d'une ligne concrète ou idéale qui partage un vaste espace*. Au pied des versants d'une chaîne de montagnes s'étendent des régions étrangères l'une à l'autre. On réside ainsi *d'un côté* ou de l'autre des Alpes, des Pyrénées. Dans la mesure où le mot *lé* désigne encore la

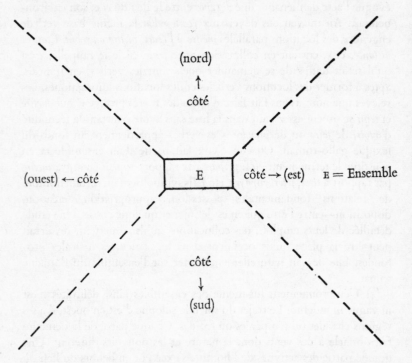

largeur d'un fleuve ou d'un canal, voire leurs deux rives, les régions que sépare cette voie deviennent ses côtés.

Dernier point à considérer. La limite de l'ensemble se confond avec celle de l'environnement. Celui-ci et celui-là sont en situation de *proximité*. La proximité, dans beaucoup de langues, est figurée par des expressions centrées autour d'un nom désignant une pièce soit latérale, soit antérieure, soit postérieure du corps. En ancien, français, *coste* entrait dans cette série;[4] il en reste une trace dans la locution figée

4 Cf. a.fr. *encoste, a coste, de coste* dans l'article *coste* de l'*Altfranz. Wörterbuch* de Tobler—Lommatzsch. Mais sous sa forme substantive *coste* évoquait aussi en a.fr. cette notion, comme l'atteste l'exemple relevé par Tobler: *Très de delé, sa coste l'a assis moult prochain* où, du fait de *lātus* présent dans *delés, sa coste* joue, à

côte-à-côte, mais celle-ci appartient plutôt aux énoncés informatifs. Les énoncés narratifs recourent de préférence à *(tout) à côté de*.[5]

En adoptant le point de vue empirique de L. Bloomfield, on peut dire que ces significations de *côté* sont 'premières' parce qu'elles correspondent à des situations typiques. Elles ne se différencient que par un changement de repère. Dans un cas *côté* se réfère à l'ensemble délimité dans l'espace environnant. Dans l'autre, il fonctionne comme si, cette fois, c'était l'environnement qui était divisé ou sectionné par l'ensemble construit.

(5) Avec d'autres valeurs de *côté*, on s'écarte de cette situation typique. Les entourages de ce terme le prouvent. Jusqu'ici *côté* s'accommode de collocations prévisibles. Il peut être déterminé en (1) par deux adjectifs seulement: a. fr. *destre* ou *senestre*, fr. mod. *droit* ou *gauche*. En (2), des critères utilitaires rendent compte de la présence d'adjectifs variés (*ensoleillé, chaud, froid, exposé, protégé, venteux, pluvieux*, etc.). A *bon* et à *mauvais* est dévolu le rôle de synthétiser les jugements qu'on porte sur ces avantages et sur ces inconvénients. Par ailleurs apparaît aussi en (3) et en (4) une détermination syntagmatique du type *de* N: *du côté du nord* ~ *sud, du côté de l'Espagne, du côté de chez Swann, à côté de*.

Des collocations plus étendues et d'un tout autre caractère prouvent que, pour une valeur liée cette fois à une situation atypique (mais sentie analogue aux premières métaphoriquement), le sème de/direction/ s'associe à un autre sème plus difficile à définir. Il comporte bien un jugement de valeur, comme dans le cas où on parle du *bon* ~ *mauvais côté* d'une demeure; mais le jugement a, cette fois, pour objet *une ou*

---

peu près comme *son cors*, le rôle d'un substitut du pronom *lui*. Dans cette valeur, *lez* concurrençait *coste* en ancien français. Cf. *lez a lez* dans *Altfranz. Wörterbuch*, V, 388.

[5] Les distributions de *côte-à-côte* et de *à côté de* sont semblables en ceci que les deux adverbes s'associent à la fois à la notion de station (ex. *se tenir*) et à celle de mouvement (ex. *marcher, avancer*). Elles ne diffèrent ici que par un point: le nombre (singulier, pluriel) et la relation des agents. *Côte-à-côte*, comme a. fr. *andui* ou *entre*, est presque un morphème de duel. Mais la nature des sujets a aussi une valeur démarcative. En français commun *côte-à-côte*, comme il est prévisible, s'emploie par référence à des sujets de la classe *Animé*. On ne dirait pas que deux bâtiments sont construits ou s'élèvent côte-à-côte; ou si on le fait c'est en vertu d'une métaphore anthropomorphique (ex. *Nos deux maisons s'élevaient côte-à-côte*). *Maison, chalet* symbolisent alors le *ci* des possesseurs et se substituent à eux en quelque sorte.

plusieurs propriétés profondes, essentielles de l'ensemble à l'exclusion de son environnement.

Par 'ensemble' il convient alors d'entendre non plus la figure concrète du corps, d'un parallélogramme ou d'un carré, mais *n'importe quelle essence conceptuelle*: chose, affaire, individu, etc. Tout peut avoir ainsi de *bons* et de *mauvais côtés* mais aussi, suivant le support, *des côtés aimables, plaisants, un côté rieur, un côté juste, un côté intéressant, favorable, discutable, trouble,* etc.

Quand il symbolise une situation typique, *côté* appartient à un ensemble de vocabulaire très précis. Il y fonctionne en relation avec une série de termes auxquels est dévolu le rôle de symboliser les différents systèmes de configuration de l'espace, que celui-ci ait deux ou trois dimensions. En ancien français il ne peut être séparé des déictiques *ci, là, jus, sus,* des prépositions à valeur directive et de substantifs tels que *figure, face, part, environs,* etc.

Pour une situation atypique, il fonctionne dans un autre ensemble. Les termes qui le configurent (*air(s), apparence(s), trait(s), partie(s), caractère(s)*) se hiérarchisent, semble-t-il, d'après le degré de superficialité ou de profondeur des propriétés reconnues à un être ou à une chose.

> *Quand, sur une personne on prétend se régler*
> *C'est par les beaux côtés qu'il lui faut ressembler.*

Est-ce trop s'avancer que de tenir *côté* pour le terme le plus conceptuel, le plus abstrait et le plus neutre de cette série?

Je m'en suis volontairement tenu jusqu'ici à une rapide analyse sémantique dans le cadre de la synchronie du français contemporain. Celle-ci demande, évidemment, à être étayée sur une étude historique. On aimerait savoir en particulier quand et surtout dans quels contextes *côté* en est venu à symboliser une situation atypique. Il est à peu près sûr que cela ne s'est pas produit avant la fin de ce qu'on appelle le moyen français, mais les circonstances m'en demeurent encore obscures et elles le demeureront tant qu'on n'aura pas méthodiquement étudié l'histoire des ensembles de vocabulaire relatifs à la configuration conceptuelle de l'espace, du temps et des volumes.

Mais il ne serait pas moins intéressant de considérer deux accidents qui sont intervenus au cours de la préhistoire de ces ensembles et qui ont eu des conséquences durables. À partir d'ici j'abandonnerai le ton didactique pour celui de l'interrogation, attendant des réponses et me gardant bien d'en suggérer, sinon par aventure et prudemment.

(1) Dès l'époque romane *costātum a dû entrer en conflit avec lātus. L'a. fr. lez montre que lātus n'a pas été sérieusement ébranlé. Il s'est maintenu dans des positions fortes, comme un seigneur indélogeable du castel et du donjon où il s'était retranché contre les assauts des vilains. Les dictionnaires attestent que le substantif lez et le substantif côté ont eu des emplois parallèles en ancien français.[6] Mais jusqu'à quand? Et jusqu'à quel point? Les énoncés narratifs ne masquent-ils pas une situation dans laquelle costé avait déjà établi sa prééminence sur lé? Lez, symbole de la proximité, n'a plus survécu que dans un morphème (-les-) dont la signification échappe aujourd'hui à la majorité des Français. La situation marginale du substantif lé n'est pas récente. Dès l'époque classique ce mot n'appartenait plus au vocabulaire du français commun.

(2) Plus grave, à coup sûr, a été l'intervention de flanc dans la nomenclature des parties du corps. Les valeurs de ce mot sont assez différentes de celles de côté. Les deux termes ont bien en commun le sème/latéral/ mais chacun implique des traits qui le diversifient. Le francique *hlanca désignait la hanche, nous enseignent les dictionnaires étymologiques, c'est-à-dire les points fixes autour desquels pivotent les côtés. Mais en français où hanche s'était déjà inséré, les flancs en sont venus à dénoter les surfaces (et non les lignes) qui limitent un réceptacle et en particulier le lieu supposé du développement de l'embryon.[7] Flanc, qui prolonge, flancum, forme latinisée au neutre de *hlanca, s'est appliqué tout de suite aux côtés des êtres humains comme des animaux. C'est entre eux que femmes et femelles portent leur progéniture, Les

---

[6] Cf. Altrfanz. Wörterbuch, articles costé et lez. Exemples s'esteit Paris li beaus armez, l'eaume lacié, l'espee al lez.—L'espee trait qu'il ot al lez.—Prendre par les lez.—Al diestre et al senestre lés; et concurremment: s'espee a sun costed.—Au costé l'espee li çaint.—Fendre, trancher le costé. L'ancien français ne confond jamais, semble-t-il, lé symbole de la notion de largeur et lez <lātus. Il est vraisemblable que ces deux mots ont souffert de l'homophonie consécutive à l'affaiblissement de l'articulation consonantique de lez.

[7] Il y a discordance entre le dictionnaire étymologique de Bloch-Wartburg (3e éd.) qui indique, à tort me semble-t-il, pour premier référend de *hlanka la hanche et la notice du f.e.w. sur ce mot (t.XVI, 212) où seule est posée la notion de /côté/. Si l'acception 'ventre de la mère' y est datée de 1250, c'est probablement dû au petit nombre de textes anciens dont nous disposons. L'équivalence costé—lez—flanc ressort des exemples fournis par l'Altfranz. Wörterbuch, III, 1907, dans l'article Flanc, acception Weiche.

dictionnaires attestent que dans cette valeur côtés s'employait aussi,[8] mais les deux termes n'étaient pas pour autant du même degré. Me trompé-je si je conjecture que leur concurrence a été l'indice d'un léger désarroi lexical? *Flanc* s'était imposé dès le haut moyen âge dans le vocabulaire des spécialistes (anatomistes, médecins) et il s'était taillé une place dans le vocabulaire commun. Pour les techniciens comme pour les gens du vulgaire, point de distinction entre femmes et femelles. La Vierge Marie elle-même avait porté l'enfant Jésus dans ses flancs. Toutefois quelques écrivains ont dû réagir contre une assimilation qui neutralisait une différence, clairement ressentie par les hommes (et à plus forte raison par des chrétiens) entre les espèces animales et la leur. Ces écrivains scrupuleux recoururent à l'emploi de *côtés* parce que ce mot leur semblait moins désobligeant que *flancs*.

Au sème/latéral/, à celui de/surface latérale d'un réceptacle/ s'associèrent deux traits secondaires sans lesquels certains des emplois actuels de *flanc* seraient inexplicables.

Le premier est celui de/léger renflement/. Les flancs d'un quadrupède mâle ne sont pas aussi bombés que ceux d'une femelle, mais ils ne sont pas rectilignes. Aussi bien *flancs* en vint-il très tôt à désigner les côtés du mâle (homme compris). Dès le XIIème siècle, ce mot (à mettre en relation avec *ventre* lui-même associé à *cuer*) s'applique aux pans (*destre* ou *senestre*) du corps masculin. L'épée pend au flanc d'un guerrier. Si celui-ci tombe au combat, c'est sur la face (*adenz*), sur le dos (*ados*) ou sur le flanc. De là, par extension, ce terme mordit sur les emplois de *côtés* pour évoquer les surfaces latérales d'un bâtiment, celles aussi d'un ensemble humain stationnaire ou en mouvement. On parla ainsi des flancs d'une *route* (puis d'une *troupe*), d'un *corps de bataille* ou d'une *armée*. Fut-ce au XVIème siècle que le mot s'inséra dans la nomenclature militaire? Avant de l'affirmer il faudrait avoir passé au peigne le vocabulaire des chroniqueurs du siècle précédent comme celui de l'auteur du *Jouvencel*. Mais sa valeur originelle a survécu dans toutes les collocations où *flancs* symbolise les surfaces extérieures d'un réceptacle creux et bombé. Exemples, les flancs d'une amphore, d'un

---

[8] Cf. *Altfranz. Wörterbuch*, III, 1907, acception *Mutterschoss*, et II, 934, article *costé*, acception *Leib* (*Mutterleib*). Je ne me dissimule pas que les exemples fournis par ce dictionnaire vont contre l'hypothèse d'une distinction de niveau entre *flans* et *costés*. Ils ne représentent toutefois qu'un rapide échantillonnage. Leur concurrence devrait être suivie de plus près.

vase (mais non d'une bouteille),⁹ d'un esquif, d'un navire, etc. Est-ce
parce que les montagnes passaient pour abriter dans leurs cavernes un
peuple de nains, de géants, d'êtres faés qu'on a dit *leurs flancs* (ex. *à
flanc de montagne ~ coteau*) pour leurs versants?¹⁰

Le second trait est relatif à la/mollesse/et à la/moindre résistance/des
parois de chaque flanc. Cette notion est familière aux chasseurs et aux
guerriers. Mais elle a servi aussi aux anatomistes puisque ceux-ci ont
associé à *ventre* l'adjectif *mou* (on parle encore du *ventre mou de la Chine*
par métaphore). Les flancs, avec quelques autres lieux du corps, étaient
naturellement exposés aux lésions des armes telles que flèches, dards,
lances et javelots. De tout temps les tacticiens avisés ont protégé les
flancs de leurs armées. Tout cela continue à être symbolisé en français
par la locution *prêter le flanc à . . .* qui n'a jamais été concurrencée par
**prêter le côté à*.

Le francique *hlanca* avait été aussi latinisé sous une forme *flanca* que
prolonge l'a. fr. *flanche*.¹¹ Le dérivé *flanquer*, formé sur *flanc*, est relative-
ment tardif (XVIᵉᵐᵉ siècle) et, dans sa valeur technique, demeure
cantonné aux confins de vocabulaires marginaux. *Flenchir*, au contraire,
est ancien. Il a pour sème/flexion, rotation/et *flanc* en est étymologique-
ment la base dans la mesure où les versions du thorax s'opèrent par les
flancs au-dessus du point d'appui fixe que constituent les hanches.¹² On

⁹ A moins que celle-ci ne soit pansue comme une fiasque. En revanche maints
poètes ont célébré les liqueurs qu'un *flacon* recèle entre ses *flancs*. L'allitération
y est sans doute pour quelque chose.

¹⁰ Cf. *Altfranz. Wörterbuch*, III, 1908, *Al flan d'une montegne lor est uns fluns
parus*, R. Alix, 66, 20.

¹¹ Tobler—Lommatzsch n'en fournissent pas d'exemple, sinon dans une glose,
pour la période de l'ancien français que couvre leur dictionnaire. Pour ses emplois
en moyen français cf. Godefroy, IV, 23.

¹² Les exemples de *flenchir—flechir* allégués par Godefroy et Tobler-Lommatzsch s'expliquent par le sème/tourner/; aucun ne requiert nettement d'être
traduit par 'céder' ou 'faire céder'. Sans doute est-il aisé de reconstituer idéalement
un passage de 'tourner le dos' (en parlant de troupes) à 'céder du terrain'. Mais on
aimerait étayer cette hypothèse sur des témoignages nets issus de texte. Or on
n'est pas jusqu'ici en mesure de le faire. Au reste, la situation réciproque des
verbes *flechir* et *flenchir* est confuse. L'étymon du premier est sans aucun doute
**flecticare* (F.E.W., III, 618). On postule un **hlankjan* pour le second (ibid., XVI,
213). Sous le couvert d'une ressemblance, les signifiés de ces deux mots ont dû
sinon se confondre, du moins s'apparenter. Si **hlankjan* n'est pas un fantôme, il
y a du **hlanka* derrière. *Flenchir* a pu dénoter, à l'origine, la rotation du thorax.
L'a. fr. *flenché* (=souple) atteste que ces verbes ont passé précocement de la conjugaison inchoative à la première. Mais à quel moment, dans quels contextes,
fléchir et *flancher* (rattaché, lui, manifestement à *flanc*) se sont-ils séparés? Autant

aimerait pouvoir suivre le passage de *flenchir* à *flancher* et connaître les premiers contextes dans lesquels ce terme a été pris comme synonyme de *céder*, *faiblir*. Même s'il s'est opéré anciennement une association entre *flache* (mou) et *flenchir*, les Français n'en ont actuellement plus conscience. Une enquête conduite auprès d'une centaine d'entre eux, représentant plusieurs niveaux de culture, m'a convaincu que quatre-vingt-dix sur cent le rattachent à *flanc*, c'est-à-dire à *être sur le flanc*. En ce qui concerne les dérivations, *côte* et *flanc* ont été productifs. *Côte*, avec *coster*, *costeier* et le parasynthétique *accoster* est au centre de toute une famille dont le F.E.W. démêle bien la structure. Dans la conscience populaire, *costal* est relié à *côte*. *Côté*, lui, a fait son chemin presqu'en solitaire. Sans doute l'associe-t-on encore spontanément à *côte*. Mais la relation qu'il entretient avec cette base étymologique n'est plus sentie, dans son originalité, que par des lexicologues ou des usagers pénétrants.

Ce signe, j'oserais presque dire qu'il a une valeur platonicienne dans la mesure où il sublimise en quelque sorte tous les concepts abstraits, tous les rapports, toutes les idées pures que l'esprit a pu concevoir, élaborer, à partir des représentations concrètes évoquées par *côte* et par *flanc*. On voit en lui, à travers les emplois auxquels il se prête, le produit d'une remarquable activité intellectuelle. Cette valeur apparaîtra mieux quand les romanistes, les médiévistes auront débrouillé de plus près que n'ont pu le faire Godefroy, Tobler puis Lommatzsch et Huguet son histoire ancienne ainsi que les collocations précises de *côte*, *flanc* et *côté*.

---

de questions qui attendent encore des réponses. *Flancher*, au sens de 'céder' n'est pas attesté, dit-on, avant le XIXeme siècle. Mais cette acception peut être plus ancienne. Elle implique, comme 'prêter le flanc', le sème de/mollesse, vulnérabilité/. Est-il imprudent de suggérer que ce néologisme s'est formé dans le jargon des soldats?

Comment on Three Passages from the Text of the Oxford *Roland*

†FREDERICK WHITEHEAD

University of Manchester

509 E Guenes l'ad pris par la main destre ad deiz.

The context makes it clear that it is not Ganelon who takes Blancandrin by the hand but Blancandrin who takes Ganelon. Hence all editors, myself included, have re-written the first hemistich as *Guenelun prist*. But V⁴, like O, has the perfect tense (*Si a preso Gay. et per brace et per manne*), and this points to the existence of the form *ad pris* in the original poem. Hence the reading that the Digby scribe had before him must have been either *E Guenelun ad pris* (the first hemistich of an alexandrine) or *E Guenes ad pris*, with one of those confusions between the cases of an imparisyllabic noun that are so frequent in the work.[1] If we assume the latter reading, O's alteration can be regarded as the result of a very natural mistake with regard to the grammatical function of the word *Guenes* and the consequential addition of *l'*.

> 1420 Franceis i perdent lor meillors guarnemenz,
> Ne reverrunt lor peres ne lor parenz
> Ne Carlemagne ki as porz les atent.

The transition from 1420 to 1421 is very abrupt. What possible connection can there be between the French losing 'their best equipment' and the fact that they will never see *lor peres ne lor parenz* again?

To avoid the difficulty, Foulet in his glossary to Bédier's edition supposes that *guarnemenz* in 1420 means 'defenders', which would

---

[1] The case-form being regulated by the position of the word in relation to the verb and not by its grammatical function: cf. ll. 222 (*ço . . . mandet li reis Marsiliun*), 766 (. . . *dist Rollant le barun*), 1471 (*Plus fel . . . n'out en sa cumpagnie*), 2437 (*Ne n'i adeist esquier ne garçun*) &c.

†The editors record with sorrow the death of Dr. Frederick Whitehead, which occurred while the present volume was being printed.

make it possible for us to take it as the subject of the following line. But the meaning that Foulet ascribes to the word is here an impossible one. The two lines cannot mean that the French people lose their best defenders (i.e. those now fighting at Roncesvaux), since *Franceis* here, as in 1416 and everywhere else in these battle scenes, refers to the forces now actually engaged in combat; that is to say, to the rearguard itself. Nor can they mean that the rearguard loses its best warriors, since up to this point there has been no slaughter among the Peers: it is in fact they who have done the killing.

It should be noted that 1412–37 form the second of two *laisses similaires*, 1396–1411 forming the first. It is instructive to compare the opening of the two:

1396:

La bataille est aduree endementres,
Franc e paien merveilus colps i rendent,
Fierent li un, li altre se defendent.

Tant[e] hanste i ad e fraite e sanglente,
Tant gunfanun rumpu e tant' enseigne.
Tant bon Franceis i perdent lor juvente!
Ne reverrunt lor meres ne lor femmes,
Ne cels de France ki as porz les atendent.

1412:

La bataille est merveilluse e pesant;
Mult ben i fiert Oliver e Rollant,
Li arcevesques plus de mil colps i rent,
Li .xii. per ne s'en targent nient,
E li Franceis i fierent comunement.
Moerent paien a millers e a cent.
Ki ne s'en fuit, de mort n'i ad guarent,
Voillet o nun, tut i laisset sun tens.
Franceis i perdent lor meillors guarnemenz,

Ne reverrunt lor peres ne lor parenz,
Ne Carlemagne ki as porz les atent.

The development in the first of these laisses is clear enough: the battle is hotly contested . . . weapons are shattered . . . many of the French fall. The second laisse starts in the same way as does the first; then follows a long amplification, in which the disaster to the Saracens is emphasized, next comes the ambiguous line 1420, followed, à *propos de rien*, by the assertion that the combatants will never see France again. The abruptness with which this last theme is introduced becomes all the more evident by the insistence on the success of the French earlier in the laisse.

What has happened seems clear enough. The Digby scribe has accidentally omitted a passage corresponding to 1399–1401 of the first laisse. When a passage of this sort is inserted, the ambiguities in 1420 are cleared up and an almost exact parallelism of thought as well as of expression established between the two *laisses*.

This train of reasoning is supported by the evidence of the collateral versions. C, for example, has the following:

> 2425 Franzois i perdent meint riche garniment:
> Tant bon espi noelé a argent,
> De lor espées sunt tot li brant sanglent.
> E si i perdent meint chevalier vaillent . . .
> Mais ne veront ni amis ni parent.

There is no need to assume that these lines (or the similar passage in the other versions) reproduce the *ipsissima verba* of the original. They do however help to prove the existence of a lacuna and justify the meaning 'gear' for *guarnemenz*.

The second hemistich of 1421 is hypermetric. A regular line can be obtained by reading *lur pers ne lor parenz*. The emendation offers no difficulty from the palaeographical point of view: *pers*, in full or abbreviated, could easily by mistaken for the more common word.

Jenkins and Bertoni both read *pers* but give the word the meaning 'spouse', obviously seeing in the line a reminiscence of 1402. But against this, it is sufficient to observe that the word *per*, although sometimes used for 'wife', is *not* the equivalent of *moillier* but has the primary meaning 'fellow, companion' and can only be used for a feminine companion when restricted and specialized in this sense by the context.[2]

The emendation is thus an attempt, at the cost of doing violence to the meaning of *per*, to reduce a hypermetric line to the normal length while at the same time bringing its meaning into close agreement with that of 1402. To my mind, the case for *pers* rests on quite different grounds. It could be argued that 1421–2 repeat the theme in 1402–3 not exactly, but with a significant variation. Both passages of course centre around the theme of loss, but whereas 1402–3 are concerned with domestic affections—wife and mother, friends and home—the emphasis in the second passage is placed upon feudal relationships: it is now their fellow-barons, their *parenz* (with all the military and juridical force of

[2] This is probably what Bédier meant by his remark (*Romania*, LXIV (1938), p. 511): 'Mais Jenkins et Bertoni n'ont pas observé que le mot ne se rencontre que déterminé par un autre mot qui en fait apparaître le genre. Dans le vers qu'ils imputent au poète, on ne sait que par leurs traductions qu'il s'agit de femmes et non pas d'hommes; le poète se serait-il permis de laisser ses lecteurs dans l'incertitude?' This is to cast doubt not merely on the rendering 'spouse' but on the admissibility of the word in this passage at all. The point is surely that there is no possibility of confusion: the meaning 'peers, fellow barons' is imposed by the context.

the word in O.F.) and Charlemagne, their supreme overlord, that the men of the rearguard will never see again.

For a long time, I placed great weight on this argument and in my two editions of the text, I adopted the Jenkins-Bertoni reading, without however overlooking the fact that there was a good deal to be said on the other side. I question now whether the arguments for retaining the Digby reading are not as convincing as those for its rejection.

The question really is: how serious is the need for making the line conform to the conventional metrical pattern? For critics who maintain that the author never under any circumstances wrote a line which was not a regular decasyllable, there is of course no difficulty. But those who believe that irregular lines abound in the original poem ought to have the courage of their convictions and refuse to consider a hypermetric line as *prima facie* evidence of corruption. This posited, the next question is how far the formula *pers ne parenz* is a usual one in early Old French. *Amis ne parenz* (which is in fact the CV⁷ reading here) is of course found from an early period onwards, but I have not so far been able to find another example of *pers ne parenz*. Further, we have to take into account the fact that there is a very close parallelism between *lor meres ne lor femmes* and *lor peres ne lor parenz*, a parallelism which looks intentional and which any alteration of the first word would disturb. Finally, we may question whether the intention to specialize the first passage in the direction of domestic associations and the second in that of feudal loyalties really formed part of the poet's design. What, to my mind, is against this is the fact that if *pers . . . parenz . . . Charlemagne* form a sequence linked by the same fundamental idea, the series *meres . . . femmes . . . cels de France* does not. *Cels de France qui as porz les atendent* obviously cannot mean the friends and acquaintances of the rearguard but only the main army that has already crossed the passes. The two lines are obviously a reminiscence of 818-24:

> Puis que il venent a la tere majur,
> Virent Guascuigne, la tere lur seignur.
> Dunc lur remembret des fius e des honurs
> E des pulceles e des gentilz oixurs :
> Cel nen i ad ki de pitet ne plurt.
> Sur tuz les altres est Carles anguissus :
> As porz d'Espaigne ad lesset sun nevold,

with the two ideas of the return home and the isolation of the rearguard treated from the point of view of the latter and not that of the main army. It thus seems that the right scheme for 1402–3 and 1421–2 is not this:

$$1402\text{–}03: \text{Meres} \rightarrow \text{femmes} \rightarrow \text{cels de France}$$

$$1421\text{–}2: \quad \text{Pers} \rightarrow \text{parenz} \rightarrow \text{Charlemagne,}$$

but this:

Lor meres ne lor femmes (1402)
$$= \text{Lor peres ne lor parenz (1421)}$$

Cels de France ki . . . atendent (1403)
$$= \text{Carlemagne ki . . . atent (1422).}$$

In other words, what 1421–2 does is to repeat the idea in 1402–3 with a variation in the formulation, while keeping intact the distinction between the waiting families on the one hand and the waiting army on the other.

> 1443 Il est escrit en la Geste Francor
> Que vassals est li nostre empereür.

'Ce texte', writes Bédier, 'n'est pas tout à fait absurde, à condition qu'on traduise, en y mettant beaucoup de complaisance: "C'est à bon droit que les Annales de France qualifient de preux notre empereur".'[3] Even so, the phrase is devoid of real meaning and Bédier is inclined to treat it as a *locus desperatus*.

The other versions however afford considerable assistance. The following are the relevant readings:

> V^4: Che bon vassal oit nostro imperaor.
> C: Qe proz vasal ont l'enperaor.
> PT: Que vassaux soient avec l'empereur.
> L: Que vassal soient avec l'emperaor.

These readings all seem to go back to a reading in α: *Que bons vassals ad nostre empereür*. The wrong case in α (*empereür* instead of *emperere*), tolerated by V^4, provoked later modifications; C's desperate *ont l'emperaor* and PTL's more reasonable *soient avec l'empereur*.

There is no doubt that α's *Que bons vassals ad nostre empereür* is better than Digby's *Que vassals est li nostre empereur*. The remark is singularly

---

pointless in Digby, and, what is more serious, the context contains nothing at all that would lead us to expect this eulogy of Charlemagne. On the other hand, admiration for Charles's barons is certainly in keeping here: with α's reading replacing O's, 1443–4 could be regarded as a very characteristic amplification of 1441–2,[4] which, in their turn, are a comment provoked by the valour of the French as described in ll. 1438–40.[5]

Nevertheless, if we accept α's reading, there is no reason to suppose that *bons* in the first hemistich is authentic. By supposing that the original Roland poet had *Que vassals ad li nostre empereür*, we can in fact explain the variant readings of α and O. In the original, the word *vassals* would have the meaning 'good vassal, doughty fighter'. Elsewhere in the poem, the author only seems to give the word this sense when it is used predicatively.[6] In order to clarify the meaning, α could therefore have inserted the adjective *bon*, while the Digby scribe, thinking that *vassals* must refer to Charlemagne, could have changed the verb from *ad* to *est*.

The reference to the *Geste Francor* remains, and with it the objection that Bédier brought against the whole passage: why cite any authority to substantiate so trite a remark?

The answer no doubt is that the line was intended by the poet to be mere *remplissage*. What it lacks in meaningful content, however, it fully makes up in grandiloquence. The case is in fact on a par with other cases where the poet, thinking more of sound than of sense, has recourse to some high-flown epic formula.

Whether this be the explanation of l. 1443 or not, we obviously have no right to reject it as spurious simply because we cannot make sense of it. The agreement of V^4CV^7PLO shows that the line *must* have been in the original poem.

Two of these suggestions imply that there was a 'wrong' case in the common source of all the versions; the third implies that there was a hypermetric line there. This may seem far too bold—like playing the game while violating all the rules. But the point surely is that we know nothing, except by conjecture, of the linguistic form of the original *Roland*, and we must leave all the possibilities open.

---

[4] . . . *nostre hume sunt mult proz./Suz ciel n'ad home, plus en ait de meillors.*

[5] *Franceis i unt ferut de coer e de vigur,/Paien sunt morz a millers e a fuls.*

[6] Cf. l. 3343: *Icist reis est vassals.*

Publications of T. B. W. Reid

Abbreviations: *A.L.* Archivum Linguisticum. *F.S.* French Studies. *M.Æ.* Medium Ævum. *M.L.R.* Modern Language Review.

1933 'Old French *giens*, Provençal *ges*, Catalan *gens*', *M.Æ.* II (1933) 64–67.
      'An Unrecognised Idiom in Middle French,' *M.L.R.* XXVIII (1933) 240–42.
1938 'A Note on the Origins of French *on*,' *M.Æ.* VII (1938) 199–203.
1939 'Notes on French Syntax [I *Du tout*, II *Non que*],' *M.L.R.* XXXIV (1939) 541–9.
      '*Non, nen* and *ne* with Finite Verbs in French,' *Studies . . . presented to M. K. Pope* (Manchester, 1939), pp. 305–13.
1940 Review of T. Franzén, *Étude sur la syntaxe des pronoms personnels sujets en ancien français*, *M.L.R.* XXXV (1940) 95–6.
1942 Chrestien de Troyes, *Yvain (Le Chevalier au Lion)*: The Critical Text of Wendelin Foerster, with Introduction, Notes and Glossary (French Classics), Manchester, 1942.
1944 Review of Anna Granville Hatcher, *Reflexive Verbs: Latin, Old French, Modern French*, *M.L.R.* XXXIX (1944) 300–01.
1948 'Worm's-Eye View' [a philologist's opinion on the purpose of modern language teaching in schools], *Modern Languages* XXIX (1948) 57–9.
      Review of W. von Wartburg and P. Zumthor, *Précis de syntaxe du français contemporain*, *M.L.R.* XLIII (1948) 271–2.
1949 'Grammar, Grimoire, Gomerel,' *Studies . . . presented to R. L. Graeme Ritchie* (Cambridge, 1949), pp. 181–8.
1951 Review of T. Fotitch, *The Narrative Tenses in Chrétien de Troyes*, *M.L.R.* XLVI (1951) 99–100.
      Review of A. Blinkenberg, *Le Problème de l'accord en français moderne*, *F.S.* V (1951) 273–5.
1952 Review of K. Togeby, *Structure immanente de la langue française*, *A.L.* 4, (1952) 87–9.

1953   'University Courses in Modern Languages,' *Modern Languages* XXXV (1953), 12–17.
       '*L'Heure du berger*,' *Studies . . . presented to John Orr* (Manchester, 1953), 245–51.
       Review of C. H. Livingston, *Le Jongleur Gautier le Leu: Étude sur les fabliaux*, *M.L.R.* XLVIII (1953) 209–12.
       Review of John Orr, *Words and Sounds in English and French*, and R. A. Sayce, *Style in French Prose* in the *Manchester Guardian*, 18 Aug. 1953.

1954   'Old French Formulas of Asseveration and Adjuration in Comparative Form,' *F.S.* VIII (1954) 193–206.
       Review of M. Cornu, *Les formes surcomposées en français*, and H. Weber, *Das Tempussystem des Deutschen und des Französischen*, *A.L.* 6 (1954) 150–53.

1955   'On the Analysis of the Tense-System of French,' *Revue de Linguistique romane* XIX (1955) 23–38.
       'The She-wolf's Mate,' *M.Æ.* XXIV (1955) 16–19.
       Review of L. C. Harmer, *The French Language Today*, *Modern Languages* XXXVI (1955) 79–80.

1956   'Linguistics, Structuralism and Philology,' *A.L.* 8 (1956) 28–37.
       Review of C. de Boer, *Syntaxe du français moderne*, 2e éd., *M.L.R.* LI (1956) 110–11.
       Review of Charles Bruneau, *Petite histoire de la langue française*, t. I, *F.S.* X (1956) 373–4.
       Review of E. Zellmer, *Altfranzösisch ço—neufranzösisch ça: eine syntaktische Betrachtung*, *F.S.* X (1956) 376.
       Obituary of Professor M. K. Pope, *Manchester Guardian*, 18 Sept. 1956.

1957   'A Note on *Cinament*,' *Bulletin of the Ulster Place-Name Society* V (1957) 12.
       Review of F. Kahn, *Le Système des temps de l'indicatif chez un Parisien et chez une Bâloise*, *A.L.* 8 (dated 1956, publ. 1957) 167–9.

1958   *Twelve Fabliaux from MS. F.fr.* 19152 *of the Bibliothèque Nationale* (French Classics), Manchester, 1958.
       Review of A. Jaeggi, *Le rôle de la préposition et de la locution prépositive dans les rapports abstraits en français moderne*, *M.L.R.* LIII (1958)256.
       Short Notice of A. Burger, *Lexique de la langue de Villon*, *M.L.R.* LIII (1958) 481–2.

Review of *Fabliaux*, edited by R. C. Johnston and D. D. R. Owen, *M.Æ.* XXVII (1958) 122–6.

1959 Short Notice of A. Ewert, *Of the Precellence of the French Tongue*, *M.L.R.* LIV (1959) 456.

1960 *Historical Philology and Linguistic Science* (Inaugural Lecture) (Oxford, 1960).
Review of S. Potter, *Language in the Modern World;* W. D. Elcock, *The Romance Languages;* H. and C. Laird, *The Tree of Language;* and M. Boulton, *Zamenhof: Creater of Esperanto*, *Times Literary Supplement*, no. 3059 (1960) p. 664.

1961 'On the Text of the *Jeu de Saint Nicolas*,' *Studies . . . presented to Alfred Ewert*, (Oxford, 1961), pp. 96–120.
'Glossarial Notes on the *Jeu de Saint Nicolas*,' *F.S.* XV (1961) 299–313.
Review of W. D. Elcock, *The Romance Languages*, *F.S.* XV (1961) 194–5.
Obituary of Professor W. D. Elcock, *Bulletin of Hispanic Studies*, April 1961.

1962 Review of A. Blinkenberg, *Le problème de la transitivité en français moderne: essai syntacto-sémantique*, *F.S.* XVI (1962) 164–6.
Review of A. Henry, *Etudes de syntaxe expressive. Ancien français et français moderne*, *F.S.* XVI (1962) 266–7.
Review of A. François, *Histoire de la langue française cultivée des origines à nos jours*, *M.L.R.* LVII (1962) 257–8.
Review of L. Kukenheim, *Esquisse historique de la linguistique française et de ses rapports avec la linguistique générale*, *F.S.* XVI (1962) 390–92.

1964 *The Romance of Horn* by Thomas, edited by Mildred K. Pope: Vol. II, revised and completed by T.B.W.R. (Anglo-Norman Text Society), Oxford, 1964.
'On the interpretation of Béroul, *Tristran* 4223–5', *Romania* 85 (1964) 366–7.
'Chaucer's *ferthing of grece*,' *Notes and Queries*, N.S. 11 (1964) 373–4.
Review of *Le 'Jeu de saint Nicolas' de Jehan Bodel*, edited by A. Henry, *F.S.* XVIII (1964) 38–40.
Review of John Orr, *Old French and Modern English Idiom; Three Studies on Homonymics; Essais d'étymologie et de philologie françaises*, *F.S.* XVIII (1964) 83–5.
Review of S. Andersson, *Nouvelles Etudes sur la syntaxe et la sémantique du mot français 'tout,'* *M.L.R.* LIX (1964) 139–40.

Review of A. Klum, *Verbe et adverbe* . . ., *A.L.* 15 (dated 1963, publ. 1964) 247–50.

1965   'Old French *acroire sor s'ame*, etc.', *Australian Journal of French Studies* II (1965) 1–8.

'On the text of the *Tristran* of Béroul', *Medieval Miscellany presented to Eugène Vinaver* (Manchester, 1965), pp. 263–88.

'The *Tristran* of Béroul: one author or two?,' *M.L.R.* LX (1965) 352–8.

Review of R. A. Hall, Jr., *Idealism in Romance Linguistics*, *F.S.* XIX (1965) 93–4.

1966   Review of *Dictionnaire des Lettres Françaises: Le Moyen Age*, *Romance Philology* XIX (1966) 499–502.

Review of B. Woledge and H. P. Clive, *Répertoire des plus anciens textes en prose française* . . ., *M.Æ.* XXXV (1966) 63–4.

1967   'The Dirty End of the Stick,' *Revue de Linguistique romane* XXXI (*Hommage à la mémoire de John Orr*) (1967) 55–63.

Review of *Les Congés d'Arras*, edited by P. Ruelle, *M.L.R.* 62 (1967) 329–31.

Review of *Le 'Jeu de saint Nicolas' de Jehan Bodel*, edited by A. Henry, 2e éd. revue, *F.S.* XXI (1967) 140–41.

Obituary of Professor John Orr, *M.L.R.* 62 (1967) 191–2.

1968   Review of K. Heger, *Die Bezeichnung temporal-diektischer Kategorien im französischen und spanischen Konjugationssystem*, *A.L.* 17 (dated 1965, publ. 1968) 63–6.

Review of W. Foerster—H. Breuer, *Worterbuch zu Kristian von Troyes' sämtlichen Werken*, 3.A., *A.L.* 17 (dated 1965, publ. 1968) 62–3.

1969   'A Further Note on the Language of Béroul,' *Romania* 90 (1969) 382–90.

1970   'Verbal Aspect in Modern French,' *The French Language: Studies presented to L. C. Harmer* (London, 1970), pp. 146–71.

1971   Review of *The Romance of Tristran by Béroul*, edited by Alfred Ewert, Vol. II, *F.S.* XXV (1971) 53–5.

Also some brief reviews, letters to the press, etc.

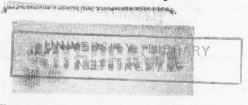

LIST OF SUBSCRIBERS

Prof. L. J. Austin
Prof. Kurt Baldinger
F. J. Barnett
Dr. Alexander Bell
Miss Madeleine Blaess
Mrs. M. B. Booth
G. N. Bromiley
Prof. Philip Butler
Prof. J. P. Collas
Mrs. Joan Crow
Prof. Ruth J. Dean
Miss Sybil de Souza
Prof. A. H. Diverres
Prof. Jean Frappier
Dr. K. O. Gore
Prof. Albert Henry
Prof. T. E. Hope
Tony Hunt
Mrs. Janice Johnson
Dr. C. A. Jones
Dr. Elspeth Kennedy
R. G. Lascelles
Prof. Dominica Legge
C. Legrand
Dr. Faith Lyons
Prof. W. H. Lyons
Prof. I. D. McFarlane
Miss M. M. MacLennan

Prof. Yakov Malkiel
Dr. J. H. Marshall
Hideichi Matsubara
Prof. I. D. Michael
Mrs. M. R. Morgan
Miss M. A. Muir
Prof. Robert Niklaus
Prof. F. P. Pickering
Prof. Glanville Price
Prof. H. Ramsden
Dr. Elizabeth Ratcliff
Prof. J. W. Rees
Dr. P. Rickard
Prof. William Roach
C. A. Robson
Prof. P. E. Russell
Miss E. M. Rutson
F. W. Saunders
Prof. J. Seznec
Dr. K. V. Sinclair
Prof. Norman B. Spector
Dr. Merlin Thomas
Prof. R. L. Wagner
Dr. Frederick Whitehead
Prof. Alan Wilshere
M. J. Winterburn
Prof. B. Woledge